Mathematical Accounting Principles

Guoping Jie

Mathematical Accounting Principles

First Edition

ISBN: 0995820309XXXX

ISBN-13: 978-0995820364 (Guoping Jie)

WWW.mathaccounting.com

Acknowledgements

I wish to take this opportunity to sincerely thank OSAP system (Canada) which gave me a chance to study.

Guoping Jie

After graduating from the Beijing University of Aeronautics and Astronautics, I immediately went to The National University of Defense Technology in Changsha, China. Three years later, I got my master degree and went to Shanghai XinLi Machinery Factory where I designed and developed motors as an engineer. In 2005, I immigrated to Canada with my child after having worked for many years. In 2007, I entered the Centennial College, Toronto, Canada to study accounting. During two years, I had had some thinking about accounting and its software. I went to the York University, Toronto, Canada in 2009 and graduated with the Honors BAS four years later. After having taken many years to research and develop mathematical accounting model and its MathAccounting software, I opened the Foreverr MathAccounting Software Company Ltd. in February, 2015.

For relaxation, I enjoy reading, driving, and music.

ABSTRACT

It should be time to study and apply a mathematical accounting model which is easy to understand and audit, and is accurate and reliable. The paper distinctly describes three accounting's concepts or models (physical accounting model, double-entry system model, and mathematical accounting model) and their relationships. The physical accounting model naturally exists since business emerging and is the basis of all other accounting models. The physical accounting model is actually consisted of every transaction which is based on a principle: exchange of equal values. The double-entry system model, which is still used all over the world, uses a logical method to keep recording transactions accurate. Its main characters are the T account with debit and credit, chart of accounts, two classes of permanent and temporary accounts, and trial balance. The mathematical accounting model is based on a basic expanding accounting equation and has developed following main characters: mathematica axiom principle, dynamic accounting equation, sub-equation of the dynamic accounting equation, five classes of permanent accounts, multi-subaccount name, structures of financial statements, and account flow statement. The same parts of the double-entry system and mathematical accounting models are to satisfy the basic accounting equation at the beginning of a fiscal year and the ending of a fiscal year, but the difference of them is that they take the different ways to reach the ending of the fiscal year. The book also introduces a concept of the great accounting which is based on the MathAccounting software and the wealth conservation law. The great accounting means two aspects. In the great data time, centered management of accounting is an inexorable trend. Every business company can login in a government's centered database by using of its business number. And every department in an organization can do part work of the accounting about itself duty. All works of the organization's departments will be made up of the financial statements. On the other hand, the two concepts of digital currency and internet of things are developed. The great accounting has many advantages, such as being difficult to draw up false accounts and to evade a tax.

Keywords: physical accounting model, double-entry system accounting model, mathematical accounting model, MathAccounting software, great accounting, digital currency, and internet of things

Contents

Chapter1

Introduction of Mathematical Accounting Model

It should be time to study and apply a mathematical accounting model which is easy to understand and audit, and is accurate and reliable. Moreover, mathematical accounting model has expended connotation of accounting. Mathematical accounting is responsible for not only the financial statements but also the internet of things which is based on digital currency and digital inventory. Meanwhile, accounting students should take a course of database at least, such as SQL Server or Oracle, to understand the mathematical accounting model clearly.

Three important accounting's concepts or models and their relationships can be identified clearly. They are the physical accounting model, the double-entry system model, and the mathematical accounting model.

1.1 Physical accounting model

First, what is the physical accounting model? Since business emerging, the physical accounting model naturally exists. The physical accounting model is the basis of all other accounting's models. It is consisted of every transaction. These transactions are naturally based on a principle: exchange of equal values. By using of mathematical language, each transaction based on this principle means each sub-equation, which actually implies a basic accounting equation:

Assets = Liabilities + Owne's Equity.

1.2 Double-entry system model

For knowing and understanding business performance, people has tried to build many accounting models to record and summarize the economic events in fact, such as an owner of a corner grocery store who might use a very simple accounting model to record his or her transactions. Just like a saying that all roads lead to Rome.

Without effective computing tools, the double-entry system model actually uses a logical method to keep recording transactions accurate, so this double-entry system accounting model has gradually become popular in the world and is still used all over the world now.

1.3 Mathematical accounting model

Last concept is the mathematical accounting model. In the mathematical accounting model, it is very important that the basic accounting equation must be an expanding form:

Assets = Liabilities + Equity + Incomes − Expenses

Based on this equation, the mathematical accounting model has been developed following main characters:

- Mathematical axiom principle.
- Dynamic accounting equation.
- Sub-equation of dynamic accounting equation. Every transaction is a sub-equation which is also called general equation.
- Five classes of the accounts. All accounts are divided into five classes of the accounts which are all the permanent accounts and have same position in the dynamic accounting equation. This concept is very important for developing the mathematical accounting model. The Assets are the first class of accounts, the Liabilities are the second class of accounts, the Equities are the third class of accounts, the Incomes are the fourth class of accounts, and the Expenses are the fifth class of accounts.

- Multi-subaccount name. Its form is the "A3<A2<A1". The A1, the A2, and the A3 are one-level subaccount, two-level subaccount, and three-level subaccount names of a parent account respectively. The three-level subaccount A3 must be unique if a parent account has any three-level subaccount. Obviously, if a parent account has only any two-level subaccount or any one-level subaccount, then the two-level subaccount A2 or the one-level subaccount A1 must be unique too.
- Structures of financial statements.
- Concept of account flows statement.

The mathematical accounting model is based on following mathematical axiom.

If $a + b = c + d$,

       $e + f = g + h$,

Then $a + b + e + f = c + d + g + h$

The mathematical axiom is the nucleus and framework of the mathematical accounting model, and is through all process of accounting. Meanwhile, the mathematical axiom also guarantees the recording accounting information correct and accurate.

In the mathematical accounting model, it is a great advantage that the increasing of an account's balance is the "+" and the decreasing of an account's balance is the "-" for all accounts of the assets, liabilities, equities, incomes, and expenses, which is the same as personal habit.

The basic accounting equation is rewritten and categorized, and I get the following dynamic accounting equation.

Assets (1) = Liabilities (2) + Equity (3) + Incomes (4) – Expenses (5)

In the above equation, each class account has many parent accounts, so the dynamic accounting equation can be again rewritten as an expanding dynamic accounting equation.

Assets (1) (Cash + Inventory + …) = Liabilities (2) (Account Payable + Notes Payable + …) + Equity (3) (Share capital + Retained earnings + …) + Incomes (4) (Sales + Other Revenues + …) – Expenses (5) (Cost of Sales Sold + Interest Expenses + …)

In fact, every transaction is a sub-equation of the dynamic accounting equation. If adding a sub-equation to the previous dynamic accounting equation, then I get a new dynamic accounting equation at a special time point. If you image that the accounting is a straight railway system, then every transaction is a railway sleeper and the train is a dynamic accounting equation and goes ahead. Each account does not need be closed. The financial statements are only the results of the moving and uniting the some terms in the dynamic accounting equation at a special time point.

What is relationship between the double-entry system model and the mathematical accounting model? The Figure 1-1 can clearly show the answer and explain the question.

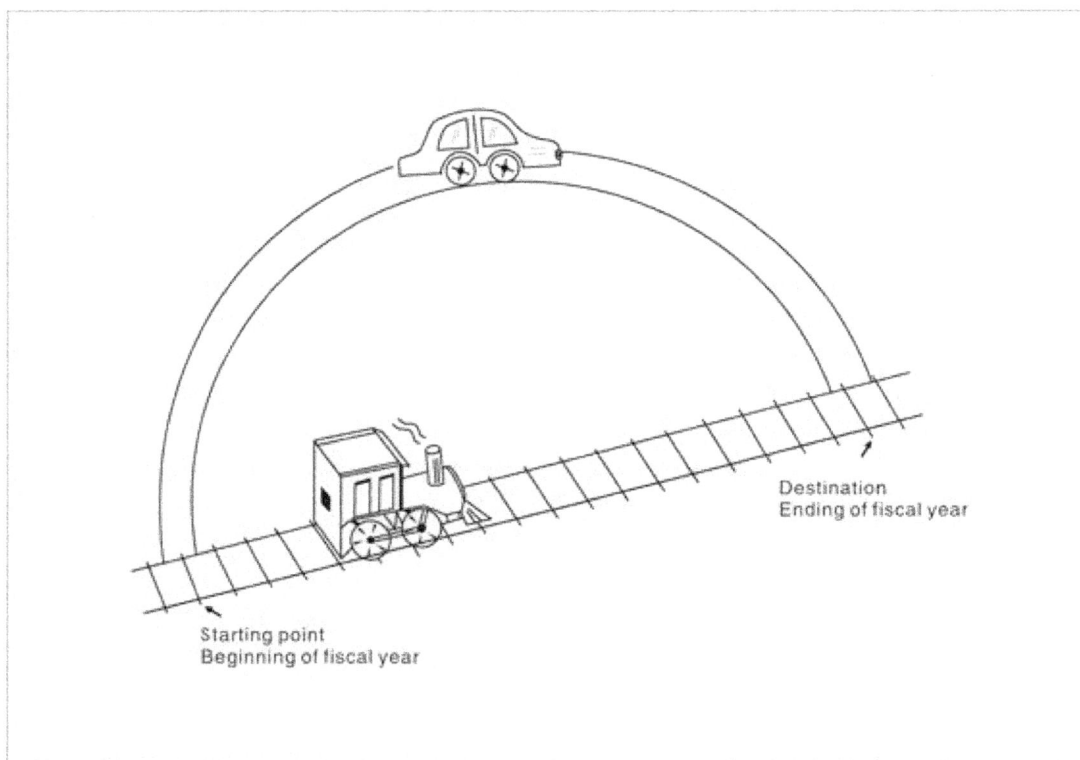

Figure 1-1 Same Parts and Difference of two Accounting Models

If you think that the time of a fiscal year is a stretch of rail, then the starting point of the rail is regarded as the beginning of the fiscal year and the destination of the rail is regarded as the ending of the fiscal year. The same parts of the two accounting models are that the two accounting models satisfy the basic accounting equation at the starting point of the rail (the beginning of the fiscal year) and the destination of the rail (the ending of the fiscal year). However, the two accounting models take the different ways to reach the destination from the starting point.

The mathematical accounting model drives on the rail track all the time until reaching the destination. The train is the dynamic accounting equation. Every railway sleeper is a sub-equation which is also called as a general equation in the MathAccounting software. The train is driving on the railway, which means that every sub-equation is being added to the previous dynamic accounting equation. When the train reaches the destination of the rail, the last dynamic accounting equation is finally gotten at the ending of the fiscal year. The double-entry system model leaves the rail track at the starting point after all ledger accounts being checked to satisfy the basic accounting equation, and takes the other road to reach the destination. The road is consisted of all T accounts with debit and credit, general journalizing transactions, and chart of accounts which is the framework of this model. The car is consisted of posting to ledger accounts and calculating trial balance. After reaching the destination, all ledger accounts must be checked again to satisfy the basic accounting equation.

In the mathematical accounting model, the following five transactions can be written by using five sub-equations.

- Investment by owners. On January 2, 2021, Ping Wang, Hua Li and Mike Newsome decide to open a RF trade business, so Ping Wang invests $40,000 cash in business, and Hua Li and Mike Newsome each invest $30,000 cash in business. The sub-equation can be written as following:

Cash (1): 100000 = Share capital (3): 40000 + Share capital (3): 30000

+ Share capital (3): 30000

This sub-equation is also the dynamic accounting equation on January 2, 2021 (in other word, the first dynamic accounting equation is the "0 = 0" for a new company). It can be rewritten as following:

Cash (1): 100000= Share capital (3): 100000

- Purchase of the Office supplies by cash. On January 3, 2021, the RR Company purchases some Office supplies by $193 cash from AA Company. Then the sub-equation is:

Cash (1): -193 + Office supplies (1): 193 = 0

Adding this sub-equation to the previous dynamic accounting equation, I get a new dynamic accounting equation on January 3, 2021. It is:

Cash (1): 99807 + Office supplies (1): 193 = Share capital (3): 100000

- Cash payments for Hua Li's taxi fee expenses (Administrative expenses). On the same day, Hua Li takes taxi to carry on the Office supplies by $47 cash. Then the sub-equation is:

Cash (1): -47 = - Administration expenses (5): 47

On the same day, the new dynamic accounting equation after adding this transaction sub-equation is:

Cash (1): 99760 + Office supplies (1): 193 = Share capital (3): 100000 - Administrative expenses (5): 47

- Purchase of inventory by some cash and other on credit. On January 5, 2021, the RR Company purchases $3,670 inventory by cash -$670 and other on credit from A1 Company (phone number: 987654321). Then the sub-equation is:

  Cash (1): -670 + Inventory (1): 3670 = Account payable (2): 3000

  On January 5, 2021, the new dynamic accounting equation after adding this transaction is:

  Cash (1): 99090 + Office supplies (1): 193 + Inventory (1): 3670 = Account payable (2): 3000 + Share capital (3): 100000 - Taxi expenses (5): 47

- Sales for some cash and other on credit. On January 5, 2021, the RR Company (Xiao Zhou) sells $1,900 inventory to B1 Company (phone number: 123456789) for sales of $2,530, and receives cash 300. Then the sub-equation is:

  Cash (1): 300 +Inventory (1): -1900 + Account receivable (1): 2230 = Sales (4): 2530 - Cost of sales (5): 1900

  On the same day, the new dynamic accounting equation after adding this transaction sub-equation is:

  Cash (1): 99390 + Office supplies (1): 193 + Inventory (1): 1770 + Account receivable (1): 2230 = Account payable (2): 3000 + Share capital (3): 100000 + Sales (4): 2530 – Administrative expenses (5): 47 – Cost of Sales (5): 1900

In a word, the sub-equation of the first transaction is also the dynamic accounting equation on January 2, 2021. Adding the second transaction's sub-equation to this dynamic accounting equation, I get a new dynamic accounting equation on January 3, 2021. Finally, I get a new dynamic accounting equation on January 5, 2021. It is:

Cash (1): 99390 + Office supplies (1): 193 + Inventory (1): 1770 + Account receivable (1): 2230 = Account payable (2): 3000 + Share capital (3): 100000 + Sales (4): 2530 − Administrative expenses (5): 47 − Cost of Sales (5): 1900

The total assets are $103,583, and the sum of the liabilities, equity, incomes, and expenses are $103,583 too. By moving and uniting the terms in the dynamic accounting equation at a time point, I can easily get income statements, balance sheet, cash flows statement, and so on.

Real business is more complicate than this example. Moreover, many accounts have multi-level subaccounts, such as the account of the "Administrative Expenses". It may have three-level subaccounts (different persons, different departments, and taxi fees). In fact, there is obviously an account which has the one-level subaccounts in this example. Do you find it? It is the account of the "Share capital" that is consisted of the three one-level subaccounts of the "Capital-Ping Wang", the "Capital-Hua Li", and the "Capital-Mike Newsome".

For dealing with complicate business, an effective computing tool of the SQL Database or the Oracle Database must be used. For meeting the requirement of the SQL Database or the Oracle Database, the above basic dynamitic accounting equation must be rewritten by using of mathematical language. It is:

$$X1 = X2 + X3 + X4 - X5$$

Here the X1 is the Assets, the X2 is the Liabilities, the X3 is the Equity, the X4 is the Incomes, and the X5 is the Expenses.

The expanding dynamic accounting equation is:

$$(X11 + X12 + X13 + ...) = (X21 + X22 + X23 + ...) + (X31 + X32 + X33 + ...)$$
$$+ (X41 + X42 + X43 + ...) - (X51 + X52 + X53 + ...)$$

All terms in the above equation are called the parent accounts, and will appear on the financial statements.

If a parent account, such as the X12, has one-level subaccounts, then its one-level subaccounts are the X121, X122, X123, and so on.

If a parent account, such as the X41, has two-level subaccounts, then its one-level subaccounts are the X411, X412, X413, and so on. The one-level subaccounts may have their two-level subaccounts. For a one-level subaccount, such as the X 412, its two-level accounts are the X4121, X4122, X4123, and so on.

If a parent account, such as the X53, has three-level subaccounts, then its one-level subaccounts are the X531, X532, X533, and so on. For a one-level subaccount, such as the X533, its two-level accounts are the X5331, X5332, X5333, and so on. For a two-level subaccount, such as the X5331, its three-level subaccounts are the X53311, X53312, X53313, and so on. From theory, an account can have the infinite-level subaccounts.

Therefore, the expanding dynamic equation is very huge and very complicate for a company with many three-level subaccounts. You do not worry about that. The computer can do difficult calculation and categorizing work behind the screen in the digital time. You must only understand a basic principle. When a sub-equation, which is the lowest-level sub-equation and is checked to be correct, is added to the previous dynamic accounting equation, all terms of this sub-equation will be added to its relevant parent accounts and upper subaccounts.

There is a problem which must be technically solved. If a parent account X11 has more than 10 one-level subaccounts, such as 22 one-level subaccounts, then its twelfth one-level subaccount X1112 may be confused with a two-level subaccount X1112, whose one-level subaccount and parent account are the X111 and the X11 respectively, by the computer. For resolving the problem, every parent account and its multi-level subaccount are represented by using of two digital numbers if the maximum numbers of them are less than 100.

The expanding dynamic accounting equation is rewritten as:

$$(X101 + X102 + X103 + ... + X199) = (X201 + X202 + X203 + ... + X299) + (X301 + X302 + X303 + ... + X399) + (X401 + X402 + X403 + ... + X499) - (X501 + X502 + X503 + ... + X599)$$

If the parent account X197 has the 99 one-level subaccounts, then its 6th one-level subaccount is the X19706 and the 99th one-level subaccount is the X19799.

In the above example, the twelfth one-level subaccount with the parent account X101 should be the X10112. The second two-level subaccount with the parent account X101 and the one-level subaccount X10101 should be the X1010102.

The parent accounts will appear on the balance sheet and the income statements, so I design the structures of the balance sheet and income statements, as the Figure 1-2 on the next page.

To design own balance sheet and income statement, a user can enter subtotal name into the big box at the left of the Figure 1-2 and its row number into the right box; the user needs also enter parent account name into the small box at the left of the Figure 1-2 and the account's row number into the right box. Obviously, the two row numbers cannot be same. The two row numbers must not be sequence, but they must be in a scope, such as a scope of 201 to 301. Because each scope is enough for all possible parent accounts, I recommend that the row number of a new subtotal name will be odd number and a new parent account's row number will be even number. If a company has any income that must not pay tax or any expense that cannot be deducted, the user can put them under the parent account of the "Income taxes expenses". Their row numbers should be between 600 and 650.

The subtotal names and the parent account names will appear in the income statements and the balance sheet by the order of the numbers that the user entered.

ASSETS   101

Total assets   xxxxx

LIBILITIES   201

Total liabilities   xxxxx

SHAREHOLDERS' EQUITY   301

Total shareholders' equity   xxxxx
Total liabilities and shareholders' equity   xxxxx

                                              401

Total

Total   xxxxx

Gross Margin   451

Total

Total   xxxxx

                                              xxxxx

Earnings Before Income Taxes   551

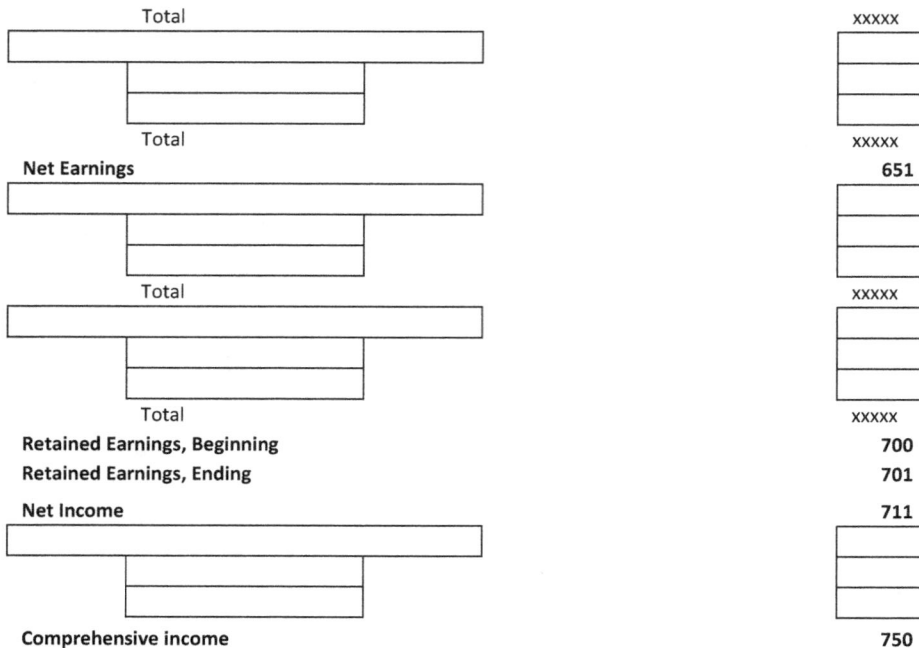

Figure 1-2   Structures of Balance Sheet and Income Statements

For the above first transaction, a user can enter a subtotal name of the "Current assets" into the big box at the left of the Figure 1-2 and the number "103" or other appropriate number you like into the right box; the user needs also enter the parent account of the "Cash" into the small box at the left of the Figure 1-2 and its row number "104" or other appropriate number you like into the right box. Then the user can enter a subtotal name of the "Owners' capital" into the big box at the left of the Figure 1-2 and the number "303" or other appropriate number you like into the right box; the user needs also enter the parent account of the "Share capital" into the small box at the left of the Figure 1-2 and the number "304" or other appropriate number you like into the right box.

I can use the tool of the subaccount concept to build cash flows statement. The Figure 1-3, seeing the next page, shows the structure of the cash flows statement.

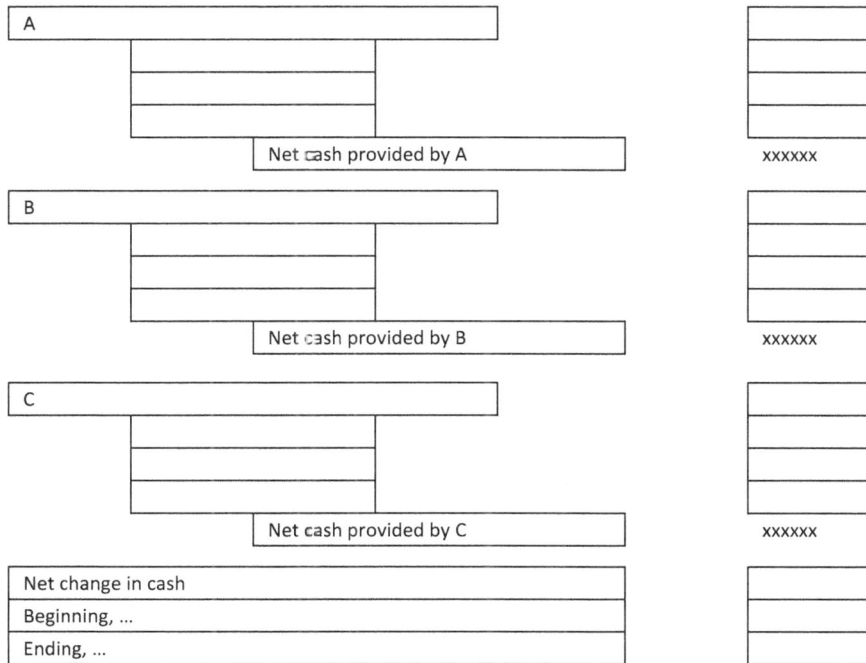

Figure 1-3   Structure of Cash Flow Statement

The cash account has the three one-level subaccounts: operating activities, investing activities, and financing activities. Of course, every one-level subaccount can have the unlimited two-level subaccounts. The contents of the big boxes at the left of the Figure 1-3 are the names of the one-level subaccounts, and the contents of the small boxes at the left of the Figure 1-3 are the names of the two-level subaccounts; the contents of the right boxes are all one-level subaccounts and the two-level subaccounts' balances which can be gotten from the tables which I will create below.

If cash is paid to a supplier for inventory, then its one-level subaccount name is the "Operating activities" and its two-level subaccount name is the "Cash payments to suppliers". If cash is paid for a share or a bond, then its one-level subaccount name is the "Investing activities" and its two-level subaccount name is the "Cash payments of investment". The one-level subaccounts' names of the "Operating activities" and the "Investing activities" will appear in the A box and the B box respectively. The two-level subaccounts' names of the "Cash payments to suppliers" and the "Cash payments of investment" will appear in the small boxes under the A box and the B box respectively. So I can design my style of the cash flows statement by using of this structure. At the ending of every fiscal year, I can get the cash flows statement from the tables which I will create below. In fact, I can get the cash flows statement just clicking a box in the MathAccounting software. It is so easy.

From this idea, I can get a new concept of account flows statement if an account has the two-level subaccounts. If number of its one-level subaccounts is more than three, then the top three one-level subaccounts' names according to their balances will appear on the account flow statement.

For account receivable and account payable accounts, they only have different customers and different suppliers respectively. Because each customer or each supplier's telephone number is unique, I can use the tool of subaccount concept again to think that the customers' or suppliers' telephone numbers are the one-level subaccounts' names of the account receivable or the account payable.

So far, a new parent account has following items that a user must enter in a database at most:

- TransDate.
- General ID.
- Explanation.
- Class (1-5).
- MultiSubaccount name. Its form is the "A3<A2<A1". Every the lowest subaccount must be sole.
- Amount.
- Subtotal Name (including its row number). Its form is the "subtotal name, its row number".
- Reference (account row number, or account receivable or account payable's General ID).

For a new customer or supplier, the information of customer or supplier's name, address, E-mail, postal code, city, state, and country must also be entered too.

In the mathematical accounting model, designing of multi-subaccount name is a key factor. Reasonable and correct design of a multi-subaccount can get more useful information, such as digital currency and digital inventory.

A sample of original proof of a transaction is showed in the Figure 1-4 on the next page. In filling in an original proof, you must change the amounts of the fifth class accounts to the negative amounts.

Transaction Original Proof							
TransDate:						General ID	
Explanation:							
No.	Class	Account Name	Left Amount	Right Amount	Multi-subaccount Name	Subtotal Name	Reference
1							
2							
3							
4							
5							
6							
7							
8							
Total							
Customer or Supplier's Name		Address		E-mail		Postal Code	
City		State		Country			

Person Handling: Manager:

Date: Date:

Figure 1-4   Original Proof of Transaction

Now, I will show you the process of manually recording the accounting information by using of the mathematical accounting model.

For calculating the parent accounts' and the subaccounts' balances after a transaction, the following steps must be done.

First, a transaction sub-equation must be built after filling in an original proof. Then, the sub-equation must be changed to a mathematical sub-equation.

Second, all subaccounts in this transaction must be identified to build the multi-level sub-equations. All terms or items' amounts in the lowest-level sub-equation can be gotten from the transaction original proof directly.

Third, when the three-level sub-equation is added to the two-level sub-equation or when the two-level sub-equation is added to the one-level sub-equation, the lower level subaccounts' amounts are added to upper level subaccounts' amounts (them belonging to the same parent account). However, the amounts for two same terms in the different sub-equations must not be added together, which means that their amounts do not change. When the one-level sub-equation is add to the transaction sub-equation, all parent accounts' amounts can respectively be gotten from their related one-level subaccounts.

Finally, for getting the parent accounts' balances after the transaction, the transaction sub-equation must be added to a previous dynamic accounting equation.

For recording the transaction and getting the parent accounts and all related subaccounts' balances, I must design and fill in the related tables.

The Figure 1-5 shows the original proof of the first transaction, seeing the next page. First, the transaction sub-equation is:

Cash (1) = Share capital (3)

Because the "Cash" account is the first parent account of writing into 1 class accounts (X1) table and the "Share capital" account is also the first parent account of writing into 3 class accounts (X3) table, the transaction's mathematical sub-equation is:

X101 = X301

Second, the account of the X101 has a two-level subaccount and the account of the X301 has the three one-level subaccounts (seeing the Figure 1-5), so the one-level and the two-level expanding mathematical sub-equations are the following:

One-level sub-equation   X10101 = X30101 + X30102 + X30103

Two-level sub-equation   X1010101 = X30101 + X30102 + X30103

From the Figure 1-5, the X10101 is the "Financing activities" and the X1010101 is the "Cash receipts from owners"; the X30101, the X30102, and the X30103 are respectively the "Capital-Ping Wang", the "Capital-Hua Li", and the "Capital-Mike Newsome". In addition, the terms of the X1010101, the X30101, the X30102, and the X30103 in the above two-level sub-equation are the lowest subaccounts of their parent accounts in this transaction, so their amounts are $10,000, $4,000, $3,000, and $3,000 respectively.

Transaction Original Proof							
TransDate: 1/2/2021						General ID	1
Explanation: Ping Wang, Hua Li and Mike Newsome decide to open a RR trade business							
No.	Class	Account Name	Left Amount	Right Amount	MultiSubaccount Name	Subtotal Name	Ref
1	1	Cash	100000		Cash receipts from owners< Financing activities	Current assets,103	104
2	3	Share capital		40000	Capital-Ping Wang	Owners'capital,303	304
3	3	Share capital		30000	Capital-Hua Li		
4	3	Share capital		30000	Capital-Mike Newsome		
5							
6							
7							
8							
Total			100000	100000			
Customer or Supplier's Name			Address		E-mail		Postal Code
	City		State		Country		

Person Handling: Manager:
Date: Date:

Figure 1-5   Original Proof of First Transaction

Third, when the two-level sub-equation is added to the one-level sub-equation, the amount of the upper subaccount X10101 is $10,000 (= X1010101) and the amounts of the X30101, X30102, and X30103 do not change. When the one-level sub-equation is added to the transaction sub-equation, the amount of the parent account X101 is $10,000 (= X10101) and the amount of the parent account X301 is $10,000 (= X30101 + X30102 + X30103).

Finally, for getting the balances of all related parent accounts and their subaccounts, I should create some tables: General equation, Class accounts, Parent accounts, and subaccounts. Then, I fill in these tables with this transaction information and calculate their balances. The Table 1-1 shows the general equation. The Table 1-2 shows the class accounts of the assets accounts (X1) and the shareholders' equity accounts (X3). The Table 1-3 shows the parent accounts of the "Cash (X101)" and the "Share capital (X301)". The Table 1-4 shows the one-level subaccounts of the "Financing activities (X10101)", the "Capital-Ping Wang (X30101)", the "Capital-Hua Li (X30102)", and the "Capital-Mike Newsome (X30103)". The Table 1-5 shows the two-level subaccount of the "Cash receipts from owners (X1010101)".

Table 1-1 General equation

GeID	TransDate	General Equation	Left Amount	Right Amount	Explanation	Enter Date
1	2021-1-2	Cash(1): 100000 = Share capital(3): 40000 + Share capital(3): 30000 + Share capital(3): 30000	100000	100000	Ping Wang, Hua Li and Mike Newsome decide to open a RR trade business	2021-1-4
Total Amount			100000	100000		

Table 1-2 Class Accounts

Assets (X1)

ID	Account Name (Mathematical Name)	Subtotal	Ref (Row)	Balance
1	Cash (X101)	Current assets,103	104	100000

Shareholders' Equity (X3)

ID	Account Name (Mathematical Name)	Subtotal	Ref (Row)	Balance
1	Share capital (X301)	Owners' Capital,303	304	100000

Table 1-3 Parent Accounts

Cash (X101)

ID	MultiName	TransDate	Amount	Balance	GeID	SubFirst	SubSecond	SubThird	Unit
1	Cash receipts from owners<Financing activities	2021-1-2	100000	100000	1	Financing activities	Cash receipts from owners		1

Share capital (X301)

ID	MultiName	TransDate	Amount	Balance	GeID	SubFirst	SubSecond	SubThird	Unit
1	Capital-Ping Wang	2021-1-2	40000	40000	1	Capital-Ping Wang			1
2	Capital-Hua Li	2021-1-2	30000	70000	1	Capital-Hua L			1
3	Capital-Mike Newsome	2021-1-2	30000	100000	1	Capital-Mike Newsome			1

Table 1-4 One-level subaccounts

Financing activities (X10101) < Parent account: Cash (X101)

ID	MultiName	Amount	Ref	GeID	TransDate	Balance
1	Cash receipts from owners<Financing activities	100000		1	2021-1-2	100000

Capital-Ping Wang (X30101) < Parent account: Share capital (X301)

ID	MultiName	Amount	Unit	GeID	TransDate	Balance
1	Capital-Ping Wang	40000		1	2021-1-2	40000

Capital- Hua Li (X30102) < Parent account: Share capital (X301)

ID	MultiName	Amount	Unit	GeID	TransDate	Balance
1	Capital-Hua Li	30000		1	2021-1-2	30000

Capital-Mike Newsome (X30103) < Parent account: Share capital (X301)

ID	MultiName	Amount	Unit	GeID	TransDate	Balance
1	Capital- Mike Newsome	30000		1	2021-1-2	30000

Table 1-5 Two-level subaccount

Cash receipts from owners (X1010101) << Parent account: Cash (X101)

ID	MultiName	Amount	Unit	GeID	TransDate	Balance
1	Cash receipts from owners<Financing activities	100000		1	2021-1-2	100000

I write the lowest subaccounts' amounts into their tables respectively and calculate their balances. The table "Cash receipts from owners (X1010101)" in the Table 1-5 is the lowest subaccount (two-level subaccount) of the parent account "Cash (X101)", so I write the $10,000 into this table in the Table 1-5. The three tables of the "Capital-Ping Wang(X30101)", the "Capital-Hua Li(X30102)" , and the "Capital-Mike Newsome(X30103)" in the Table 1-4 are the lowest subaccounts (one-level subaccounts) of the parent account "Share capital (X301)", so I respectively write the $4,000, $3,000, and $3,000 into the three tables in the Table 1-4.

Another table "Financing activities (X10101)" in the Table 1-4 can be gotten from the table "Cash receipts from owners (X1010101)" in the Table 1-5. The accounts of the "Cash(X101)" and the "Share capital(X301)" parent accounts in the Table 1-3 can be respectively gotten from the table of the "Financing activities (X10101)" and the tables of the "Capital-Ping Wang (X30101)", the "Capital- Hua Li (X30102)", and the "Capital-Mike Newsome (X30103)" in the Table 1-4.

The two tables' balances in the Table 1-2 can be gotten from the two tables of the "Cash (X101)" and the "Share capital (X301) in the Table 1-3 respectively.

In fact, database can do the work easily by using of the MathAccounting software. After entering the transaction, the database has created two tables of the "Cash (X101)" and the

"Share capital (X301)" parent accounts, and calculated their balances. Meanwhile, the tables of all subaccounts (including one-level subaccounts of the "Financing activities (X10101)", the "Capital-Ping Wang (X30101)", the "Capital-Hua Li (X30102)", and the "Capital-Mike Newsome (X30103)" and the two-level subaccount of the "Cash receipts from owners (X1010101)"), and their balances can be gotten by using of the database query. The Figure 1-6 shows the original proof of the second transaction.

Transaction Original Proof							
TransDate: 1/3/2021						General ID	2
Explanation: Purchase of Office supplies							
No.	Class	Account Name	Left Amount	Right Amount	MultiSubaccount Name	Subtotal Name	Ref
1	1	Cash	-193		Cash payments for operating expenses< Operating activities		
2	1	Office supplies	193		N	Current assets,103	106
3							
4							
5							
6							
7							
8							
Total			0	0			
Customer or Supplier's Name			Address		E-mail		Postal Code
City			State		Country		

Person Handling: Manager:

Date: Date:

Figure 1-6   Original Proof of Second Transaction

If the harmonized sales tax (HST, 13%) is not considered in the second transaction for the simplity, the transaction sub-equation is:

Cash (1) + Office supplies (1) = 0

Because the "Office supplies" is the second parent account of writing into 1 class accounts (X1) table, the transaction's mathematical sub-equation is:

X101 + X102 = 0

The account of the X101 has a different two-level subaccount (whose one-level subaccount is also different from the first transaction) and the account of the X102 has not any subaccount (seeing the Figure 1-6), so the one-level and the two-level expanding mathematical sub-equations are the following:

One-level sub-equation   X10102 + X102 = 0
Two-level sub-equation   X1010201 + X102 = 0

From the Figure 1-6, the X10102 is the "Operating activities" and the X1010201 is the "Cash payments for operating expenses". The amounts of the X1010201 and the X102 in the two-level sub-equation are respectively -$193 and $193.

When the two-level sub-equation is added to the one-level sub-equation, the amount of the upper subaccount X10102 is -$193 (= X1010201) and the amount of the parent account X102 does not change. When the one-level sub-equation is added to the transaction sub-equation, the amount of the parent account X101 is -$193 (= X10102) and the amount of the parent account X102 is $193 (= X102).

For recording the transaction, I should create three tables of the parent account "Office supplies (X102)", one-level subaccount "Operating activities (X10102)", and the two-level subaccount "Cash payments for operating expenses (X1010201)". Then, I calculate their balances. The two tables of the general equation and the parent account "Cash (X101)" have existed, so I should only update their information.

The Table 1-6 shows the general equation. The Table 1-7 shows the class accounts of the assets accounts (X1). The Table 1-8 shows the parent accounts of the "Cash (X101)" and "Office supplies (X102)", The Table 1-9 shows the one-level subaccount "Operating activities (X10102. The Table 1-10 shows the two-level subaccount "Cash payments for operating expenses (X1010201)".

Table 1-6 General equation

GeID	TransDate	General Equation	Left Amount	Right Amount	Explanation	Enter Date
1	2021-1-2	Cash(1): 100000 = Share capital(3): 40000 + Capital(3): 30000 + Capital(3): 30000	100000	100000	Ping Wang, Hua Li and M ke Newsome decide to open a RR trade business	2021-1-4
2	2021-1-3	Cash(1): -193 + Office supplies(1): 193 = 0	0	0	Purchase of Office supplies	2021-1-4
Total Amount			**100000**	**100000**		

Table 1-7 Class Accounts

Assets (X1)

ID	Account Name (Mathematical Name)	Subtotal	Ref (Row)	Balance
1	Cash (X101)	Current assets,103	104	99807
2	Office supplies (X102)	Current assets,103	106	193

Table 1-8 Parent accounts

Cash (X101)

ID	MultiName	TransDate	Amount	Balance	GeID	SubFirst	SubSecond	SubThird	Unit
1	Cash receipts from owners<Financing activities	2021-1-2	100000	100000	1	Financing activities	Cash receipts from owners		1
2	Cash payments for operating expenses<Operating activities	2021-1-3	-193	99807	2	Operating activities	Cash payments for operating expenses		1

Office supplies (X102)

ID	MultiName	TransDate	Amount	Balance	GeID	SubFirst	SubSecond	SubThird	Unit
1	n	2021-1-3	193	193	2				1

Table 1-9 One-level subaccount

Operating activities (X10102) < Parent account: Cash (X101)

ID	MultiName	Amount	Ref	GeID	TransDate	Balance
1	Cash payments for operating expenses<Operating activities	-193		2	2021-1-3	-193

Table 1-10 Two-level subaccount

Cash payments for operating expenses (X1010201) << Parent account: Cash (X101)

ID	MultiName	Amount	Ref	GeID	TransDate	Balance
1	Cash payments for operating expenses<Operating activities	-193		2	2021-1-3	-193

I write the lowest subaccounts' amounts into their tables respectively and calculate their balances. The table "Cash payments for operating expenses (X1010201)" in the Table 1-10 is the lowest subaccount (two-level subaccount) of the parent account "Cash (X101)", so I write the -$193 into this table in the Table 1-10. Because the parent account "Office supplies (X102)" has not any subaccount, I write the $193 into the parent account table "Office supplies (X102)" in the Table 1-8.

The table "Operating activities (X10102)" in the Table 1-9 can be gotten from the table "Cash payments for operating expenses(X1010201)" in the Table 1-10.

The parent account of the "Cash (X101)" in the Table 1-8 can be gotten from the table of the "Operating activities(X10102)" in the Table 1-9.

The balances of the table "Assets (X1)" in the Table 1-7 can be gotten from the tables of the "Cash (X101)" and the "Office supplies (X102)" in the Table 1-8.

For the third transaction, the Taxi expenses account is recorded as a parent account in the book "A Mathematical Accounting Model and its MathAccounting Software". In this book, I record the taxi expenses as a one-level subaccount of the parent account "Administrative expenses".

Problem: If the Office supplies includes the pens (one box of pencil, two boxes of expensive pens and three boxes of cheap pens) and books (three different sizes of the books), then what are the forms of the multi-subaccounts for the parent account Office suppliers?

Solution: Because there are the six lowest subaccounts, there are six forms of the multi-subaccount for the parent account Office suppliers. They respectively are:

Pencil 1<Pens

Expensive pens<Pen1<Pens

Cheap pens<Pen1<Fens

Small book1<Book1

Medium book1<Bock1

Large book1<Book1

The Figure 1-7 on the next page shows the original proof of the third transaction. From the Figure 1-7, the Administrative expenses has a three-level subaccount. The transaction sub-equation is:

Cash (1) = Administrative expenses (5)

Because the "Administrative expenses" is the first parent account of writing into 5 class accounts (X5) table, the transaction's mathematical sub-equation is:

X101 = X501

The account X101 has a two-level subaccount. The account X501 has a three-level subaccounts (seeing the Figure 1-7), so the one-level, the two-level, and the three-level expanding mathematical sub-equations are the following:

One-level sub-equation   X10102 = X50101

Two-level sub-equation   X1010201 = X5010101

Three-level sub-equation   X1010201 = X501010101

From the Figure 1-7, the X10102 is the "Operating activities" and X1010201 is the "Cash payments for operating expenses"; the X50101 is the "Taxi expenses", X5010101 is the "Purchase department-taxi", and X501010101 is the "Hua Li-taxi".

Transaction Original Proof							
TransDate: 1/3/2021						General ID	3
Explanation: Cash payment for Hua Li's taxi fee expense							
No.	Class	Account Name	Left Amount	Right Amount	MultiSubaccount Name	Subtotal Name	Ref
1	1	Cash	-47		Cash payments for operating expenses< Operating activities		
2	5	Administrative expenses		-47	Hua Li-taxi< Purchase department-taxi< Taxi expenses	Operating and administrative expenses,453	454
3							
4							
5							
6							
7							
8							
Total			-47	-47			
Customer or Supplier's Name			Address		E-mail	Postal Code	
City			State		Country		

Person Handling: Manager:

Date: Date:

Figure 1-7   Original Proof of Third Transaction

The same method can be used to calculate the amounts of the parent accounts and their subaccounts.

For recording the transaction, I should create the three tables of the parent account

"Administrative expenses (X501)", the one-level subaccount "Taxi expenses (X50101)", and the two-level subaccount "Purchase department-taxi (X5010101)", and the Three-level subaccount "Hua Li-taxi (X501010101)". Then I calculate their balances. The tables of the parent account "Cash (X101)", the one-level subaccount "Operating activities (X10102)", and the two-level subaccount "Cash payments for operating expenses (X10102001)" have existed, so I should only update their information.

The Table 1-11 shows the general equation. The Table 1-12 shows the class accounts of the assets accounts (X1) and the expenses accounts (X5). The Table 1-13 shows the parent accounts of the "Cash (X101)" and "Administrative expenses (X501)". The Table 1-14 shows the one-level subaccounts of the "Operating activities (X10102)" and the "Taxi expenses (X50101)". The Table 1-15 shows the two-level subaccounts of the "Cash payments for operating expenses (X1010201)" and the "Purchase department-taxi (X5010101)". The Table 1-16 shows the three-level subaccount of the "Hua Li-taxi (X501010101)".

Table 1-11 General equation

GeID	TransDate	General Equation	Left Amount	Right Amount	Explanation	Enter Date
1	2021-1-2	Cash(1): 100000 = Share capital(3): 4000 + Capital(3): 30000 + Capital(3): 30000	100000	100000	Ping Wang, Hua Li and Mike Newsome decide to open a RR trade business	2021-1-4
2	2021-1-3	Cash(1): -193 + Office supplies(1): 193 = 0	0	0	Purchase of Office supplies	2021-1-4
3	2021-1-3	Cash(1): -47 = Administrative expenses (5): -47	-47	-47	Cash payments for Hua Li's taxi fee expense	2021-1-4
Total Amount			99953	99953		

Table 1-12 Class accounts

Assets (X1)

ID	Account Name (Mathematical Name)	Subtotal	Ref (Row)	Balance
1	Cash (X101)	Current assets,103	104	99760
2	Office supplies (X102)	Current assets,103	106	193

Expenses (X5)

ID	Account Name (Mathematical Name)	Subtotal	Ref (Row)	Balance
1	Administrative expenses (X501)	Operating and administrative expenses,453	454	-47

Table 1-13 Parent accounts

Cash (X101)

ID	MultiName	TransDate	Amount	Balance	GeID	SubFirst	SubSecond	SubThird	Unit
1	Cash receipts from owners<Financing activities	2021-1-2	10000	100000	1	Financing activities	Cash receipts from owners		1
2	Cash payments for operating expenses<Operating activities	2021-1-3	-193	99807	2	Operating activities	Cash payments for operating expenses		1
3	Cash payments for operating expenses<Operating activities	2021-1-3	-47	99760	3	Operating activities	Cash payments for operating expenses		1

Administrative expenses (X501)

ID	MultiName	TransDate	Amount	Balance	GeID	SubFirst	SubSecond	SubThird	Unit
1	Hua Li-taxi< Purchase department-taxi<Taxi expenses	2021-1-3		-47	3	Purchase Department-taxi	Hua Li-taxi		1

Table 1-14 One-level subaccounts

Operating activities (X10102) < Parent account: Cash (X101)

ID	MultiName	Amount	Ref	GeID	TransDate	Balance
1	Cash payments for operating expenses<Operating activities	-193		2	2021-1-3	-193
2	Cash payments for operating expenses<Operating activities	-47		3	2021-1-3	-240

Taxi expenses (X50101) < Parent account: Administrative expenses (X501)

ID	MultiName	Amount	Unit	GeID	TransDate	Balance
1	Hua Li-taxi< Purchase department-taxi<Taxi expenses	-47	1	3	2021-1-5	-47

Table 1-15 Two-level subaccounts

Cash payments for operating expenses (X1010201) << Parent account: Cash (X101)

ID	MultiName	Amount	Ref	GeID	TransDate	Balance
1	Cash payments for operating expenses<Operating activities	-193	1	2	2021-1-3	-193
2	Cash payments for operating expenses<Operating activities	-47	1	3	2021-1-3	-240

Purchase department-taxi (X5010101) << Parent account: Administrative expenses (X501)

ID	MultiName	Amount	Unit	GeID	TransDate	Balance
1	Hua Li-taxi< Purchase department-taxi<Taxi expenses	-47		3	2021-1-3	-47

Table 1-16 Three-level subaccounts

Hua Li-taxi (X501010101) <<< Parent account: Administrative expenses (X501)

ID	MultiName	Amount	Unit	GeID	TransDate	Balance
1	Hua Li-taxi< Purchase department-taxi<Taxi expenses	-47	1	3	2021-1-3	-47

I write the lowest subaccounts' amounts into their tables respectively and calculate their balances. The "Cash payments for operating expenses (X1010201)" table in the Table 1-15 and the "Hua Li-taxi (X501010101)" table in the Table 1-16 are the lowest subaccounts (two-level subaccounts) of the parent accounts of the "Cash(X101)" and "Administrative expenses (X501)" respectively, so I write the -$47 into the two tables respectively.

The "Purchase department-taxi (X5010101)" table in the Table 1-14 can be gotten from the "Hua Li-taxi (X501010101)" table in the Table 1-15.

The two tables of the "Operating activities (X10102)" and "Taxi expenses (X50101)" in the Table 1-14 can be gotten from the two table of the "Cash payments for operating expenses (X1010201)" and the "Purchase department-taxi (X5010101)" in the Table 1-16 respectively.

The two tables of the parent accounts of the "Cash (X101)" and the "Administrative expenses (X501)" in the Table 1-13 can be gotten from the two tables of the "Operating activities (X10102)" and the "Taxi expenses (X50101)" in the Table 1-14 respectively.

The balance of the "Cash (X101)" in the "Assets (X1)" table and the balance of the "Administrative expenses (X501)" in the "Expenses (X5)" table (seeing the Table 1-12) can be updated from the two tables of the "Cash (X101)" and the "Administrative expenses (X501)" in the Table 1-13 respectively.

The Figure 1-8 on the next page shows the original proof of the fourth transaction. The transaction sub-equation is:

Cash (1) + Inventory (1) = Account payable (2)

Because the "Inventory" is the third parent account of writing into 1 class accounts (X1) table and the "Account payable" is the first parent account of writing into 2 class accounts (X2) table, the transaction's mathematical sub-equation is:

X101 + X103 = X201

The account of the X101 has a different two-level subaccount (seeing the Figure 1-8), the account of the X103 has the three-level subaccounts, and the account of the X201 has a one-level subaccount, so the one-level, the two-level, and the three-level expanding mathematical sub-equations are the following:

One-level sub-equation   X10102 + X10301 = X20101
Two-level sub-equation   X1010202 + X1030101 + X1030102 + X1030103 = X20101
Three-level sub-equation   X1010202 + X103010101 + X103010102 + X103010201 +
                           X103010202 + X1030103 = X20101

Transaction Original Proof

TransDate: 1/5/2021 | General ID | 4

Explanation: RR purchases $3,670 inventory by $670 cash and other on credit from A1 company (phone number: 987654321)

No.	Class	Account Name	Left Amount	Right Amount	MultiSubaccount Name	Subtotal Name	Ref
1	1	Cash	-670		Cash payments to suppliers< Operating activities		
2	1	Inventory	1C*165		Inven111<Inven11<Inven1	Current assets,103	108
3	1	Inventory	4*225		Inven112<Inven11<Inven1		
4	1	Inventory	0.8*650		Inven121<Inven12<Inven1		
5	1	Inventory	5*66		Inven122<Inven12<Inven1		
6	1	Inventory	30*9		Inven13<Inven1		
7	2	Account payable		3000	987654321	Current liabilities,203	204
8							
Total			3000	3000			

Customer or Supplier's Name	Address	E-mail	Postal Code
A1	A2	A3	A4
City	State	Country	
A5	A6	A7	

Person Handling: Manager:

Date: Date:

Figure 1-8   Original Proof of Fourth Transaction

From the Figure 1-8, the X10102 is the "Operating activities" and the X1010202 is the "Cash payments to suppliers"; the X10301, the X1030101, the X1030102, the X1030103, the X103010101, the X103010102, the X103010201, and the X103010202 are respectively the "Inven1", the "Inven11", the "Inven12", the "Inven13", the "Inven111", the "Inven112", the "Inven121", and the "Inven122"; the X20101 is the "987654321".

The same method can be used to calculate the amounts of the parent accounts and their subaccounts.

For recording the transaction, I should create two tables of the parent accounts of the "Inventory (X103)" and "Account payable (X201)", and calculated their balances. Meanwhile, I should also create the tables of one-level subaccounts (including the "Inven1", the "Inven2", the "Inven3", and the "987654321"), two-level subaccounts (including the "Cash payments to suppliers", the "Inven11", the "Inven12", and the "Inven13"), and three-level subaccounts (including the "Inven111", the "Inven112", the "Inven121", and the "Inven122"). The table of the parent account "Cash (X101)" has existed, so I should only update its information, including its subaccounts' information.

The Table 1-17 shows the general equation. The Table 1-18 shows the class accounts of the assets accounts (X1) and the liabilities accounts (X2). The Table 1-19 shows the three parent accounts of the "Cash (X101)", the "Inventory (X103)", and the "Account payable (X201)". The Table 1-20 shows the three one-level subaccounts of the "Operating activities", the"Inven1", and the "987654321". The Table 1-21 shows the four two-level subaccounts of the "Cash payments to suppliers", the "Inven11", the "Inven12", and the "Inven13". The Table 1-22 shows the four three-level subaccounts of the "Inven111", the "Inven112", the "Inven121", and the "Inven122", seeing the following tables.

In addition, I should also create a table to record the suppliers' information, seeing the Table 1-23 which is below the Table 1-22.

Table 1-17 General equation

GeID	TransDate	General Equation	Left Amount	Right Amount	Explanation	Recording Date
1	2021-1-2	Cash(1): 10000 = Share capital(3): 4000 + Capital(3): 3000 + Capital(3): 3000	10000	10000	Ping Wang, Hua Li and Mike Newsome decide to open a RR trade business	2021-1-4
2	2021-1-3	Cash(1): -193 + Office supplies(1): 193 = 0	0	0	Purchase of Office supplies	2021-1-4
3	2021-1-3	Cash(1): -47 = Administrative expenses (5): -47	-47	-47	Cash payments for Hua Li's taxi fee expense	2021-1-4
4	2021-1-5	Cash(1): -670 + Inventory(1): 3670 = Account payable(2): 3000	3000	3000	RR purchases $3,670 inventory by $670 cash and other on credit from A1 company (phone number: 987654321)	2021-1-6
Total Amount			12953	12953		

Table 1-18 Class accounts

Assets (X1)

ID	Account Name (Mathematical Name)	Subtotal	Ref (Row)	Balance
1	Cash (X101)	Current assets,103	104	9090
2	Office supplies (X102)	Current assets,103	106	193
3	Inventory (X103)	Current assets,103	108	3670

Liabilities (X2)

ID	Account Name (Mathematical Name)	Subtotal	Ref (Row)	Balance
1	Account payable (X201)	Current liabilities,203	204	3000

Table 1-19 Parent accounts

Cash (X101)

ID	MultiName	TransDate	Amount	Balance	GeID	SubFirst	SubSecond	SubThird	Unit
1	Cash receipts from owners<Financing activities	2021-1-2	10000	10000	1	Financing activities	Cash receipts from owners		1
2	Cash payments for operating expenses<Operating activities	2021-1-2	-193	9807	2	Operating activities	Cash payments for operating expenses		1
3	Cash payments for operating expenses<Operating activities	2021-1-3	-47	9760	3	Operating activities	Cash payments for operating expenses		1
4	Cash payments to suppliers< Operating activities	2021-1-5	-670	9090	4	Operating activities	Cash payments to suppliers		1

Inventory (X103)

ID	MultiName	TransDate	Amount	Balance	GeID	SubFirst	SubSecond	SubThird	Unit
1	Inven111<Inven11<Inven1	2021-1-5	10*165	1650	4	Inven1	Inven11	Inven111	165
2	Inven112<Inven11<Inven1	2021-1-5	4*225	2550	4	Inven1	Inven11	Inven112	225
3	Inven121<Inven12<Inven1	2021-1-5	0.3*650	3070	4	Inven1	Inven12	Inven121	650
4	Inven122<Inven12<Inven1	2021-1-5	5*66	3400	4	Inven1	Inven12	Inven122	66
5	Inven13<Inven1	2021-1-5	30*9	3670	4	Inven1	Inven13		9

Account payable (X201)

ID	MultiName	TransDate	Amount	Balance	GeID	SubFirst	SubSecond	SubThird	Unit
1	987654321	2021-1-5	3000	3000	4	987654321			1

Table 1-20 One-level subaccounts

Operating activities (X10102) < Parent account: Cash (X101)

ID	MultiName	Amount	Ref	GeID	TransDate	Balance
1	Cash payments for operating expenses<Operating activities	-193		2	2021-1-3	-193
2	Cash payments for operating expenses<Operating activities	-47		3	2021-1-3	-240
3	Cash payments to suppliers< Operating activities	-670		4	2021-1-5	-910

Inven1 (X10301) < Parent account: Inventory (X103)

ID	MultiName	Amount	Unit	GeID	TransDate	Balance
1	Inven111<Inven11<Inven1	10*165	165	4	2021-1-5	1650
2	Inven112<Inven11<Inven1	4*225	225	4	2021-1-5	2550
3	Inven121<Inven12<Inven1	0.8*650	650	4	2021-1-5	3070
4	Inven122<Inven12<Inven1	5*66	66	4	2021-1-5	3400
5	Inven13<Inven1	30*9	9	4	2021-1-5	3670

987654321 (X20101) < Parent account: Account payable (X201)

ID	MultiName	Amount	Ref	GeID	TransDate	Balance
1	987654321	3000		4	2021-1-5	3000

Table 1-21 Two-level subaccounts

Cash payments to suppliers (X1010202) << Parent account: Cash (X101)

ID	MultiName	Amount	Ref	GeID	TransDate	Balance
1	Cash payments to suppliers< Operating activities	-670		4	2021-1-5	-670

Inven11 (X1030101) << Parent account: Inventory (X103)

ID	MultiName	Amount	Unit	GeID	TransDate	Balance
1	Inven111<Inven11<Inven1	10*165	165	4	2021-1-5	1650
2	Inven112<Inven11<Inven1	4*225	225	4	2021-1-5	2550

Inven12 (X1030102) << Parent account: Inventory (X103)

ID	MultiName	Amount	Unit	GeID	TransDate	Balance
1	Inven121<Inven12<Inven1	0.8*650	650	4	2021-1-5	520
2	Inven122<Inven12<Inven1	5*66	66	4	2021-1-5	850

Inven13 (X1030103) << Parent account: Inventory (X103)

ID	MultiName	Amount	Unit	GeID	TransDate	Balance
1	Inven13<Inven1	30*9	9	4	2021-1-5	270

Table 1-22 Three-level subaccounts

Inven111 (X103010101) <<< Parent account: Inventory (X103)

ID	MultiName	Amount	Unit	GeID	TransDate	Balance
1	Inven111<Inven11<Inven1	10*165	165	4	2021-1-5	1650

Inven112 (X103010102) <<< Parent account: Inventory (X103)

ID	MultiName	Amount	Unit	GeID	TransDate	Balance
1	Inven112<Inven11<Inven1	4*225	225	4	2021-1-5	900

Inven121 (X103010201) <<< Parent account: Inventory (X103)

ID	MultiName	Amount	Unit	GeID	TransDate	Balance
1	Inven121<Inven12<Inven1	0.8*650	650	4	2021-1-5	520

Inven122 (X103010202) <<< Parent account: Inventory (X103)

ID	MultiName	Amount	Unit	GeID	TransDate	Balance
1	Inven122<Inven12<Inven1	5*66	66	4	2021-1-5	330

Table 1-23 Suppliers information

Suppliers

ID	Supplier Phone	Supplier Name	Address	E-mail	Postal Code	City	State	Country
1	987654321	A1	A2	A3	A4	A5	A6	A7

Supplier A1- Account payable (X201)

ID	MultiName	Amount	Reference	General ID	TransDate
1	987654321	3000		4	2021-1-6

In fact, this table of the "Supplier A1- Account payable (X201)" is the same as the one-level subaccount table of the "987654321 (X20101) < Parent account: Account payable (X201)" in the Table 1-20. Writing this table again is just for convenience to get the detail information of every supplier.

I write the lowest subaccounts' amounts into their tables respectively and calculate their balances. The four tables of the "Inven111 (X103010101)", the "Inven112 (X103010102)", the "Inven121 (X103010201)", and the "Inven122 (X103010202)" in the Table 1-22 are the lowest subaccounts (three-level subaccounts) of the parent account of the "Inventory (X103)" respectively, so I write the $10*165, $4*225, $0.8*650, and $5*66 into the four tables in the Table 1-22 respectively. The two tables of the "Cash payments to suppliers (X1010202)" and the "Inven13 (X1030103)" in the Table 1-21 are the lowest subaccounts (two-level subaccounts) of the parent accounts of the "Cash (X101)" and the "Inventory (X103)" respectively, so I write -$670 and $30*9 into the two tables in Table 1-20 respectively. The table of the "987654321 (X20101)" in the Table 1-20 is the lowest subaccount (one-level subaccount) of the parent account "Account payable (X201)", so I write $3,000 into this table in the Table 1-20. In addition, I also write the supplier's information into the Table 1-23 which is below the Table 1-22.

The two tables of the "Inven11 (X1030101)" and the "Inven12 (X1030102)" in the Table 1-21 can be gotten from the four tables of the "Inven111 (X103010101)", the "Inven112

(X103010102)", the "Inven121 (X103010201)", and the "Inven122 (X103010202)" in the Table 1-22 respectively.

The two tables of the "Operating activities (X10102)" and the "Inven1 (X10301)" in the Table 1-20 can be gotten from the four tables of the "Cash payments to suppliers (X1010202)", the "Inven11 (X1030101)", the "Inven12 (X1030102)", and the "Inven13 (X1030103)" in the Table 1-21 respectively.

The three tables of the parent accounts of the "Cash(X101)", the "Inventory (X103)", and the "Account payable (X201)" in the Table 1-19 can be gotten from the three tables of the one-level subaccounts of the "Operating activities (X10102)", the "Inven1 (X10301)", and the "987654321 (X20101)" in the Table 1-20 respectively.

The balances of the tables of the "Assets (X1)" and the "Liabilities (X2)" in the Table 1-18 can be updated from the three tables of the "Cash (X101)", the "Inventory (X103)", and the "Account payable (X201)" in the Table 1-19 respectively.

Problem: What is the transaction sub-equation if harmonized sales tax (HST, 13%) is used in the fourth transaction? What is the form of the multi-subaccount for the parent account HST recoverable?

Solution: There are two situations. If the Inventory data includes the HST, the transaction sub-equation is:

Cash (1) -670 + Inventory (1) 3247.79 + HST recoverable (1) 422.21 = Account payable (2) 3000

If the Inventory data does not include the HST, the transaction sub-equation is:

Cash (1) -670 + Inventory (1) 3670 + HST recoverable (1) 477.10 = Account payable (2) 3477.10

In these situations, the HST recoverable account should have the one-level multi-subaccount which is the supplier's identity or the telephone number. In this book, the HST recoverable account does not have any multi-subaccount. The HST recoverable account should be included in the subtotal of the "Current assets" and its reference (row) number is the "109". The second situation is used in this book, so the new tables should be created and the related tables should be updated, seeing the followings.

Table 1-17 General equation

GeID	TransDate	General Equation	Left Amount	Right Amount	Explanation	Enter Date
1	2021-1-2	Cash(1): 100000 = Share capital(3): 4000 + Capital(3): 3000 + Capital(3): 3000	100000	100000	Ping Wang, Hua Li and Mike Newsome decide to open a RR trade business	2021-1-4
2	2021-1-3	Cash(1): -193 + Office supplies(1): 193 = 0	0	0	Purchase of Office supplies	2021-1-4
3	2021-1-3	Cash(1): -47 = Administrative expenses (5): -47	-47	-47	Cash payments for Hua Li's taxi fee expense	2021-1-4
4	2021-1-5	Cash(1): -670 + Inventory(1): 3670 + HST recoverable (1) 477.10 = Account payable(2): 3477.10	3477.10	3477.10	RR purchases $3,670 inventory by $670 cash and other on credit from A1 company (phone number: 987654321)	2021-1-6
Total Amount			103430.1	103430.1		

Table 1-18 Class accounts

Assets (X1)

ID	Account Name (Mathematical Name)	Subtotal	Ref (Row)	Balance
1	Cash (X101)	Current assets,103	104	99090
2	Office supplies (X102)	Current assets,103	106	193
3	Inventory (X103)	Current assets,103	108	3670
4	HST recoverable (X104)	Current assets,103	109	477.10

Liabilities (X2)

ID	Account Name (Mathematical Name)	Subtotal	Ref (Row)	Balance
1	Account payable (X201)	Current liabilities,203	204	3477.10

Table 1-19 Parent accounts

HST recoverable (X104)

ID	MultiName	TransDate	Amount	Balance	GeID	SubFirst	SubSecond	SubThird	Unit
1	N	477.10		477.10	4				1

Account payable (X201)

ID	MultiName	TransDate	Amount	Balance	GeID	SubFirst	SubSecond	SubThird	Ref
1	987654321	2021-1-5	3477.10	3477.10	4	987654321			

Table 1-20 One-level subaccounts

987654321 (X20101) < Parent account: Account payable (X201)

ID	MultiName	Amount	Ref	GeID	TransDate	Balance
1	987654321	3477.10		4	2021-1-5	3477.10

Table 1-23 Suppliers information

Supplier A1: Account payable (X201)

ID	MultiName	Amount	Reference	General ID	TransDate
1	987654321	3477.10		4	2021-1-6

The Figure 1-9 on the next page shows the original proof of the fifth transaction. Based on the fact that the Inventory data does not include the HST recoverable, there are two situations. If the Sale data includes the HST payable, the transaction sub-equation is:

Cash (1) 300 + Inventory (1) 1900 + Account receivable (1) 2230 = HST payable (2) 291.06 + Sales (4) 2238.94 + Cost of sales (5) 1900

Transaction Original Proof

TransDate: 1/5/2021						General ID	5

Explanation: RR (Xiao Zhou) sells $1,900 inventory to B1 Company (phone number: 123456789) for sales of $2,530 and receives $300 cash

No.	Class	Account Name	Left Amount	Right Amount	MultiSubaccount Name	Subtotal Name	Ref
1	1	Cash	300		Cash receipts from customers<Operating activities		
2	1	Inventory	-10*91		Inven111<Inven11<Inven1		
3	1	Inventory	-4*130		Inven112<Inven11<Inven1		
4	1	Inventory	-0.8*375		Inven121<Inven12<Inven1		
5	1	Inventory	-5*34		Inven122<Inven12<Inven1		
6	1	Account receivable	2558.90		123456789	Current assets,103	110
7	2	HST payable		328.90	N	Current liabilities,203	205
8	4	Sales		2530	Xiao Zhou-sales	Revenues,403	404
9	5	Cost of sales		-1900	N	Cost,431	432
Total			958.9	958.9			

Customer or Supplier's Name	Address	E-mail		Postal Code	
B1	B2	B3		B4	
City	State	Country			
B5	B6	B7			

Person Handling: Manager:

Date: Date:

Figure 1-9   Original Proof of Fifth Transaction

If the Inventory data does not include the HST payable, the transaction sub-equation is:

Cash (1) 300 + Inventory (1) 1900 + Account receivable (1) 2558.90 = HST payable (2) 328.90 + Sales (4) 2530 + Cost of sales (5) 1900.

In these situations, the HST payable account should have the one-level multi-subaccount which is the customer's identity or the telephone number. In this book, the form of this multi-subaccount is the "N". The HST payable account should be included in the subtotal of the "Current liabilities" and its reference (row) number is the "205". By the way, when digital currency and digital inventory are introduced in the later chapters, the supplier ID or customer ID will be embedded the two accounts of the HST recoverable and the HST payable automatically. Therefore, the forms of the two accounts' multi-subaccounts should all be the "N". The second situation is used in this book.

Because the "Account receivable" is the fourth parent account of writing into 1 class accounts (X1) table, the "HST payable" is the second parent account of writing into 2 class accounts (X4) table, the "Sales" is the first parent account of writing into 4 class accounts (X4) table, and the "Cost of sales" is the second parent account of writing into 5 class accounts (X5) table, so the transaction's mathematical sub-equation is:

$$X101 + X103 + X104 = X202 + X401 + X502$$

The account of the X101 has a different two-level subaccount, the account of the X103 has the three-level subaccounts, the accounts of the X104 and X401 have the one-level subaccounts, and the accounts of the X202 and the X502 have not any subaccount (seeing the Figure 9), so the one-level, the two-level and three-level expanding mathematical sub-equations are the following:

One-level sub-equation $X10102 + X10301 + X10401 = X202 + X40101 + X502$

Two-level sub-equation $X1010203 + X1030101 + X1030102 + X10401 = X202 +$
                                      $X40101 + X502$

Three-level sub-equation $X1010203 + X103010101 + X103010102 + X103010201 +$
                                      $X103010202 + X10401 = X202 + X40101 + X502$

From the Figure 1-9, the X10102 is the "Operating activities" and the X1010203 is the "Cash receipts from customers"; the X10301, the X1030101, the X1030102, the X103010101, the X103010102, the X103010201, and the X103010202 are respectively the "Inven1", the "Inven11", the "Inven12", the "Inven111", the "Inven112", the "Inven121", and the "Inven122"; the X10401 is the "123456789"; the X40101 is the "Xiao Zhou-sales".

The same method can be used to calculate the amounts of the parent accounts and their subaccounts.

For recording the transaction, I should create four tables of the parent accounts of the "Account receivable", the "HST payable", the "Sales", and the "Cost of sales", and calculate their balances. Meanwhile, I should also create two tables for the one-level subaccounts of the "987654321" and the "Xiao Zhou-sales. The tables of the parent accounts of the "Cash" and the "Inventory" have existed, so I should only update their information, including their subaccounts' information.

The Table 1-24 shows the general equation. The Table 1-25 shows the class accounts of the assets accounts (X1), the liabilities (X2), the revenues accounts (X4), and the expenses accounts (X5). The Table 1-26 shows the parent accounts of the "Cash", the "Account receivable", the "HST payable", the "Sales", and the "Cost of sales". The Table 1-27 shows the one-level subaccounts (including the "Operating activities", the "Inven1", the "123456789", and the "Xiao Zhou-sales), the Table 1-28 shows the two-level subaccounts (including the "Cash receipts from customers", the "Inven11", the "Inven12", and the "Inven13"), and the Table 1-29 shows the three-level subaccounts (including the "Inven111", the "Inven112", the "Inven121", and the "Inven122"), seeing the following tables.

In addition, I should also create a table to record the customers' information, seeing the Table 1-30 which is below the Table 1-29.

Table 1-24 General equation

GeID	TransDate	General Equation	Left Amount	Right Amount	Explanation	Enter Date
1	2021-1-2	Cash(1): 100000 = Share capital(3): 40000 + Capital(3): 30000 + Capital(3): 30000	100000	100000	Ping Wang, Hua Li and Mike Newsome decide to open a RR trade business	2021-1-4
2	2021-1-3	Cash(1): -193 + Office supplies(1): 193 = 0	0	0	Purchase of Office supplies	2021-1-4
3	2021-1-3	Cash(1): -47 = Administrative expenses (5): -47	-47	-47	Cash payments for Hua Li's taxi fee expense	2021-1-4
4	2021-1-5	Cash(1): -670 + Inventory(1): 3670 + HST recoverable (1) 477.10 = Account payable(2): 3477.10	3477.10	3477.10	RR purchases $3,670 inventory by $670 cash and other on credit from A1 company (phone number: 987654321)	2021-1-6

5	2021-1-5	Cash(1): 300 + Inventory(1): -1900 + Account receivable(1): 2558.90 = HST payable(2 : 328.90 + Sales(4): 2530 + Cost of sales (5): -1900	958.90	958.90	RR sells $1,900 inventory to B1 Company (phone number: 123456789) for sales of $2,530 and receives $300 cash	2021-1-6
Total Amount			104389	104389		

Table 1-25 Class accounts

Assets (X1)

ID	Account Name (Mathematical Name)	Subtotal	Ref (Row)	Balance
1	Cash (X101)	Current assets,103	104	99390
2	Office supplies (X102)	Current assets,103	106	193
3	Inventory (X103)	Current assets,103	108	1770
4	HST recoverable (X104)	Current assets,103	109	477.10
5	Account receivable (X105)	Current assets,103	110	2558.90

Liabilities (X2)

ID	Account Name (Mathematical Name)	Subtotal	Ref (Row)	Balance
1	Account payable (X201)	Current liabilities,203	204	3000
2	HST payable (X202)	Current liabilities,203	205	328.90

Revenues (X4)

ID	Account Name (Mathematical Name)	Subtotal	Ref (Row)	Balance
1	Sales (X401)	Revenues,403	404	2530

Expenses (X5)

ID	Account Name (Mathematical Name)	Subtotal	Ref (Row)	Balance
1	Taxi expenses (X501)	Operating and administrative expenses,453	454	-47
2	Cost of sales (X502)	Cost,431	432	-1900

Table 1-26 Parent accounts

Cash (X101)

ID	MultiName	TransDate	Amount	Balance	GeID	SubFirst	SubSecond	SubThird
1	Cash receipts from owners<Financing activities	2021-1-2	100000	100000	1	Financing activities	Cash receipts from owners	
2	Cash payments for operating expenses<Operating activities	2021-1-3	-193	99807	2	Operating activities	Cash payments for operating expenses	
3	Cash payments for operating expenses<Operating activities	2021-1-3	-47	99760	3	Operating activities	Cash payments for operating expenses	
4	Cash payments to suppliers< Operating activities	2021-1-5	-670	99090	4	Operating activities	Cash payments to suppliers	
5	Cash receipts from customers< Operating activities	2021-1-5	300	99390	5	Operating activities	Cash receipts from customers	

Inventory (X103)

ID	MultiName	TransDate	Amount	Balance	GeID	SubFirst	SubSecond	SubThird	Unit
1	Inven111<Inven11<Inven1	2021-1-5	10*165	1650	4	Inven1	Inven11	Inven111	165
2	Inven112<Inven11<Inven1	2021-1-5	4*225	2550	4	Inven1	Inven11	Inven112	225
3	Inven121<Inven12<Inven1	2021-1-5	0.8*650	3070	4	Inven1	Inven12	Inven121	650
4	Inven122<Inven12<Inven1	2021-1-5	5*66	3400	4	Inven1	Inven12	Inven122	66
5	Inven13<Inven1	2021-1-5	30*9	3670	4	Inven1	Inven13		9
6	Inven111<Inven11<Inven1	2021-1-5	-10*91	2760	5	Inven1	Inven11	Inven111	-91
7	Inven112<Inven11<Inven1	2021-1-5	-4*130	2240	5	Inven1	Inven11	Inven112	-130
8	Inven121<Inven12<Inven1	2021-1-5	-0.8*375	1940	5	Inven1	Inven12	Inven121	-375
9	Inven122<Inven12<Inven1	2021-1-5	-5*34	1770	5	Inven1	Inven12	Inven122	-34

Account receivable (X105)

ID	MultiName	TransDate	Amount	Balance	GeID	SubFirst	SubSecond	SubThird	Ref
1	123456789	2021-1-5	2558.90	2558.90	5	123456789			

HST payable (X202)

ID	MultiName	TransDate	Amount	Balance	GeID	SubFirst	SubSecond	SubThird	Unit
1	N	2021-1-5	328.90	328.90	5				1

Sales (X401)

ID	MultiName	TransDate	Amount	Balance	GeID	SubFirst	SubSecond	SubThird	Unit
1	Xiao Zhou-sales	2021-1-5	2530	328.90	5	Xiao Zhou-sales			1

Cost of sales (X502)

ID	MultiName	TransDate	Amount	Balance	GeID	SubFirst	SubSecond	SubThird	Unit
1	n	2021-1-5	-1900	-1900	5				1

Table 1-27 One-level subaccounts

Operating activities (X10102) < Parent account: Cash (X101)

ID	MultiName	Amount	Ref	GeID	TransDate	Balance
1	Cash payments for operating expenses<Operating activities	-193		2	2021-1-3	-193
2	Cash payments for operating expenses<Operating activities	-47		3	2021-1-3	-240
3	Cash payments to suppliers< Operating activities	-670		4	2021-1-5	-910
4	Cash receipts from customers< Operating activities	300		5	2021-1-5	-610

Inven1 (X10301) < Parent account: Inventory (X103)

ID	MultiName	Amount	Unit	GeID	TransDate	Balance
1	Inven111<Inven11<Inven1	10*165	165	4	2021-1-5	1650
2	Inven112<Inven11<Inven1	4*225	225	4	2021-1-5	2550
3	Inven121<Inven12<Inven1	0.8*650	650	4	2021-1-5	3070
4	Inven122<Inven12<Inven1	5*66	66	4	2021-1-5	3400
5	Inven13<Inven1	30*9	9	4	2021-1-5	3670
6	Inven111<Inven11<Inven1	-10*91	91	5	2021-1-5	2760
7	Inven112<Inven11<Inven1	-4*130	130	5	2021-1-5	2240
8	Inven121<Inven12<Inven1	-0.8*375	375	5	2021-1-5	1940
9	Inven122<Inven12<Inven1	-5*34	34	5	2021-1-5	1770

123456789 (X10401) < Parent account: Account receivable (X104)

ID	MultiName	Amount	Ref	GeID	TransDate	Balance
1	123456789	2230		5	2021-1-5	2230

Xiao Zhou-sales (X40101) < Parent account: Sales (X401)

ID	MultiName	Amount	Unit	GeID	TransDate	Balance
1	Xiao Zhou-sales	2530	1	5	2021-1-5	2530

Table 1-28 Two-level subaccounts

Cash receipts from customers (X1010203) << Parent account: Cash (X101)

ID	MultiName	Amount	Ref	GeID	TransDate	Balance
1	Cash receipts from customers< Operating activities	300		5	2021-1-5	300

Inven11 (X1030101) << Parent account: Inventory (X103)

ID	MultiName	Amount	Unit	GeID	TransDate	Balance
1	Inven111<Inven11<Inven1	10*165	165	4	2021-1-5	1650
2	Inven112<Inven11<Inven1	4*225	225	4	2021-1-5	2550
3	Inven111<Inven11<Inven1	-10*91	91	5	2021-1-5	1640
4	Inven112<Inven11<Inven1	-4*130	130	5	2021-1-5	1120

Inven12 (X1030102) << Parent account: Inventory (X103)

ID	MultiName	Amount	Unit	GeID	TransDate	Balance
1	Inven121<Inven12<Inven1	0.8*650	650	4	2021-1-5	520
2	Inven122<Inven12<Inven1	5*66	66	4	2021-1-5	850
3	Inven121<Inven12<Inven1	-0.8*375	375	5	2021-1-5	550
4	Inven122<Inven12<Inven1	-5*34	34	5	2021-1-5	380

Table 1-29 Three-level subaccount

Inven111 (X103010101) <<< Parent account: Inventory (X103)

ID	MultiName	Amount	Unit	GeID	TransDate	Balance
1	Inven111<Inven11<Inven1	10*165	165	4	2021-1-5	1650
2	Inven111<Inven11<Inven1	-10*91	91	5	2021-1-5	740

Inven112 (X103010102) <<< Parent account: Inventory (X103)

ID	MultiName	Amount	Unit	GeID	TransDate	Balance
1	Inven112<Inven11<Inven1	4*225	225	4	2021-1-5	900
2	Inven112<Inven11<Inven1	-4*130	130	5	2021-1-5	380

Inven121 (X103010201) <<< Parent account: Inventory (X103)

ID	MultiName	Amount	Unit	GeID	TransDate	Balance
1	Inven121<Inven12<Inven1	0.8*650	650	4	2021-1-5	520
2	Inven121<Inven12<Inven1	-0.8*375	375	5	2021-1-5	220

Inven122 (X103010202) <<< Parent account: Inventory (X103)

ID	MultiName	Amount	Unit	GeID	TransDate	Balance
1	Inven122<Inven12<Inven1	5*66	66	4	2021-1-5	330
2	Inven122<Inven12<Inven1	-5*34	34	5	2021-1-5	160

Table 1-30 Customers information

Customers

ID	Customer Phone	Customer Name	Address	E-mail	Postal Code	City	State	Country
1	123456789	B1	B2	B3	B4	B5	B6	B7

Customer B1: Account receivable (X105)

ID	MultiName	Amount	Reference	General ID	TransDate
1	123456789	2553.90		5	2021-1-6

I write the lowest subaccounts' amounts into their tables respectively and calculate their balances. The four tables of the "Inven111 (X103010101)", the "Inven112 (X103010102)", the "Inven121 (X103010201)", and the "Inven122 (X103010202)" in the Table 1-29 are the lowest subaccounts (three-level subaccounts) of the parent account of the "Inventory (X103)" respectively, so I write the -$10*91, -$4*130, -$0.8*375, and -$5*34 into the four tables in the Table 1-29 respectively. The table of the "Cash receipts from customers (X1010203)" in the Table 1-28 are the lowest subaccount (two-level subaccount) of the parent account of the "Cash (X101)", so I write the $300 into the Table 1-28. The two tables of the "123456789 (X10401)" and the "Xiao Zhou-sales (X40101)" in the Table 1-27 are the lowest subaccounts (one-level subaccounts) of the parent accounts of the "Account receivable (X104)" and the "Sales (X401)" respectively, so I write the $2230 and the $2530 into the two tables in the Table 1-27 respectively. The parent account of the "Cost of sales (X502)" has not any subaccount, so I write -$1,900 into the table of the "Cost of sales (X502)" in the Table 1-26. In addition, I also write the customer's information into the Table 1-30 which is below the Table 1-29.

The two tables of the "Inven11 (X1030101)" and the "Inven12 (X1030102)" in the Table 1-28 can be gotten from the four tables of the "Inven111 (X103010101)", the "Inven112 (X103010102)", the "Inven121 (X103010201)", and the "Inven122 (X103010202)" in the Table 1-29 respectively.

The two tables of the "Operating activities (X10102)" and "Inven1 (X10301)" in the Table 1-27 can be gotten from the three tables of the "Cash receipts from customers (X1010203)", the "Inven11 (X1030101)", and the "Inven12 (X1030102)" in the Table 1-28 respectively.

The four tables of the parent accounts of the "Cash (X101)", the "Inventory (X103)", the "Account receivable (X104)", and the "Sales (X401)" in the Table 1-26 can be gotten from the four tables of the one-level subaccounts of the "Operating activities(X10102)", the "Inven1 (X10301)", the "123456789 (X10401)", and the "Xiao Zhou-sales (X40101)" in the Table 1-27 respectively.

The balances of the three tables of the "Assets (X1)", the "Revenues (X4)", and the "Expenses (X5)" in the Table 1-25 can be updated from the five tables of the parent accounts of the "Cash (X101)", the "Inventory (X103)", "Account receivable (X104)", the "Sales (X401)", and the "Cost of sales (X502)" in the Table 1-26 respectively.

On January 7, 2021, the RR Company receives $1,500 cash from B1 Company (phone number: 123456789) with the General ID 5.

The following Figure 1-10 shows the original proof of sixth transaction.

Transaction Original Proof							
TransDate: 1/7/2021						General ID	6
Explanation: RR Company receives $1,500 cash from B1 Company (phone number: 123456789) with the General ID 5							
No.	Class	Account Name	Left Amount	Right Amount	MultiSubaccount Name	Subtotal Name	Ref
1	1	Cash	1500		Cash receipts from customers< Operating activities		
2	1	Account receivable	-1500		123456789		5
3							
4							
5							
6							
7							
8							
Total			0	0			
Customer or Supplier's Name			Address		E-mail		Postal Code
City			State		Country		

Person Handling: Manager:

Date: Date

Figure 1-10   Original Proof of Sixth Transaction

Here, you must pay attention for the sixth transaction. In fact, when I receive the $1,500 cash, I know that B1 Company pays the cash with a General ID of the related transaction. Therefore, I borrow the Reference box to write the General ID of the related transaction into. This General ID can be gotten from the previous transaction original proofs and is the "5".

Maybe you ask why I do not use the customer's phone number as a judging standard.

Because RR Company may sale the inventory to this customer for several times and the General ID of a transaction is sole, I must choose the General ID as a judging standard.

From the Figure 1-10, the Reference box in the row with the account name of the "Account Receivable" is written into the relevant General ID of the "5" which is bold. The transaction sub-equation and the transaction mathematical sub-equation respectively are:

Cash (1) + Account receivable (1) = 0

X101+ X104 = 0

Because the account of the X101 has the two-level subaccount and the account of the X104 has the one-level subaccount (seeing the Figure 1-10), the one-level and the two-level expanding mathematical sub-equations are the following:

One-level sub-equation   X10102 + X10401 =0
Two-level sub-equation   X1010203 + X10401 = 0

From the Figure 1-10, the X10102 is the "Operating activities" and the X1010203 is the "Cash receipts from customers"; the X10401 is the "123456789".

The same method can be used to calculate the amounts of the parent accounts and their subaccounts.

For recording the transaction, I just update the related parent accounts and their subaccounts information.

The Table 1-31 shows the general equation, the Table 1-32 shows the class accounts of the assets accounts (X1), the Table 1-33 shows the parent accounts of the "Cash" and the "Account receivable", the Table 1-34 shows the one-level subaccounts of the "Operating activities" and the "123456789", and the Table 1-35 shows the two-level subaccount "Cash receipts from customers", seeing the following tables.

Table 1-31 General equation

GeID	TransDate	General Equation	Left Amount	Right Amount	Explanation	Enter Date
1	2021-1-2	Cash(1): 100000 = Share capital(3): 40000 + Capital(3): 30000 + Capital(3): 30000	100000	100000	Ping Wang, Hua Li and Mike Newsome decide to open a RR trade business	2021-1-4
2	2021-1-3	Cash(1): -193 + Office supplies(1): 193 = 0	0	0	Purchase of Office supplies	2021-1-4
3	2021-1-3	Cash(1): -47 = Administrative expenses (5): -47	-47	-47	Cash payments for Hua Li's taxi fee expense	2021-1-4
4	2021-1-5	Cash(1): -670 + Inventory(1): 3670 + HST recoverable (1) 477.10 = Account payable(2): 3477.10	3477.10	3477.10	RR purchases $3,670 inventory by $670 cash and other on credit from A1 company (phone number: 9876543217)	2021-1-6
5	2021-1-5	Cash(1): 300 + Inventory(1): -1900 + Account receivable(1): 2558.90 = HST payable(2): 328.90 – Sales(4): 2530 + Cost of sales (5): -1900	958.90	958.90	RR sells $1,900 inventory to B1 Company (phone number: 123456789) for sales of $2,530 and receives $300 cash	2021-1-6
6	2021-1-7	Cash(1): 1500 + Account receivable(1): -1500 = 0	0	0	RR Company receives $1,500 cash from B1 Company (phone number: 123456789) with the General ID 5	2021-1-8
Total Amount			104389	104389		

Table 1-32 Class accounts

Assets (X1)

ID	Account Name (Mathematical Name)	Subtotal	Ref (Row)	Balance
1	Cash (X101)	Current assets,103	104	100890
2	Office supplies (X102)	Current assets,103	106	193
3	Inventory (X103)	Current assets,103	108	1770
4	HST recoverable (X104)	Current assets,103	109	477.10
5	Account receivable (X105)	Current assets,103	110	1058.90

Table 1-33 Parent accounts

Cash (X101)

ID	MultiName	TransDate	Amount	Balance	GeID	SubFirst	SubSecond	SubThird
1	Cash receipts from owners<Financing activities	2021-1-2	100000	100000	1	Financing activities	Cash receipts from owners	
2	Cash payments for operating expenses<Operating activities	2021-1-3	-193	99807	2	Operating activities	Cash payments for operating expenses	
3	Cash payments for operating	2021-1-3	-47	99760	3	Operating activities	Cash payments for	

	expenses<Operating activities							operating expenses	
4	Cash payments to suppliers< Operating activities	2021-1-5	-670	99090	4	Operating activities	Cash payments to suppliers	
5	Cash receipts from customers< Operating activities	2021-1-5	300	99390	5	Operating activities	Cash receipts from customers	
6	Cash receipts from customers< Operating activities	2021-1-7	1500	100890	6	Operating activities	Cash receipts from customers	

Account receivable (X105)

ID	MultiName	TransDate	Amount	Balance	GeID	SubFirst	SubSecond	SubThird	Ref
1	123456789	2021-1-5	2558.90	2558.90	5	123456789			
2	123456789	2021-1-7	-1500	1058.90	6	123456789			5

Table 1-34 One-level subaccounts

Operating activities (X10102) < Parent account: Cash (X101)

ID	MultiName	Amount	Ref	GeID	TransDate	Balance
1	Cash payments for operating expenses<Operating activities	-193		2	2021-1-3	-193
2	Cash payments for operating expenses<Operating activities	-47		3	2021-1-3	-240
3	Cash payments to suppliers< Operating activities	-670		4	2021-1-5	-910
4	Cash receipts from customers< Operating activities	300		5	2021-1-5	-610
5	Cash receipts from customers< Operating activities	1500	5	6	2021-1-7	890

123456789 (X10401) < Parent account: Account receivable (X105)

ID	MultiName	Amount	Ref	GeID	TransDate	Balance
1	123456789	2558.90		5	2021-1-5	2558.90
2	123456789	-1500	5	6	2021-1-7	1058.90

Table 1-35 Two-level subaccount

Cash receipts from customers (X1010203) << Parent account: Cash (X101)

ID	MultiName	Amount	Ref	GeID	TransDate	Balance

1	Cash receipts from customers< Operating activities	300		5	2021-1-5	300
2	Cash receipts from customers< Operating activities	1500	5	6	2021-1-7	1800

I write the lowest subaccounts' amounts into their tables respectively and calculate their balances. The table of the "Cash receipts from customers (X1010203)" in the Table 1-35 is the lowest subaccount (two-level subaccount) of the parent account of the "Cash (X101)", so I write $1,500 into the table of the "Cash receipts from customers (X1010203)" in the Table 1-35. The table of the "123456789 (X10401)" is the lowest subaccount (one-level subaccount) of the parent account of the "Account receivable (X104)" in the Table 1-34, so I write -$1,500 and the related GeID "5" into the table of the "123456789 (X10401)" in the Table 1-34.

The table of the "Operating activities (X10102)" in the Table 1-34 can be gotten from the table of the "Cash receipts from customers (X1010203)" in the Table 1-35.

The two tables of the parent accounts of the "Cash (X101)" and the "Account receivable (X104)" in the Table 1-33 can be gotten from the two tables of the "Operating activities (X10102)" and the "123456789 (X10401)" in the Table 1-34 respectively.

The balances of the table of the "Assets (X1)" in the Table 1-32 can be gotten from the two tables of the "Cash (X101)" and the "Account receivable (X104)" in the Table 1-33 respectively.

In addition, for getting the financial statements and checking information easily, I also create the Table 1-36 (by the order of the row number), the Table 1-37, and the Table 1-38 after recording the sixth transaction, seeing the following tables.

Table 1-36 Reference

ID	Account Name (Subtotal Name)	Row	GeID	Balance
1	**Current assets**	**103**	**1**	**104389**
2	Cash	104	1	100890
3	Office supplies	106	2	193
4	Inventory	108	4	1770

5	HST recoverable	109	4	477.10
6	Account receivable	110	5	1058.90
7	**Current liabilities**	**203**	**4**	**3806**
8	Account payable	204	4	3477.10
9	HST payable	205	5	328.90
10	**Owners' capital**	**303**	**1**	**100000**
11	Share capital	304	1	100000
12	**Revenues**	**403**	**5**	**2530**
13	Sales	404	5	2530
14	**Cost**	**431**	**5**	**-1900**
15	Cost of sales	432	5	-1900
16	**Operating and administrative expenses**	**453**	**3**	**-47**
17	Administrative expenses	454	3	-47

Table 1-37 Subtotal Name

ID	Subtotal Name	Row	GeID	Class
1	Current assets,103	103	1	1
2	Current liabilities,203	203	4	2
3	Owners' capital,303	303	1	3
4	Revenues,403	403	5	4
5	Cost,431	431	5	5
6	Operating and administrative expenses,453	453	3	5

Table 1-38 Multi-subaccounts

ID	Multi-subaccount Name	Parent Account	GeID	Class
1	Cash receipts from owners<Financing activities	Cash	1	1
2	Capital-Ping Wang	Share capital	1	3
3	Capital-Hua Li	Share capital	1	3
4	Capital-Mike Newsome	Share capital	1	3
5	Cash payments for operating expenses<Operating activities	Cash	2	1
6	N	Office supplies	2	1
7	Hua Li-taxi<Purchase department-taxi<Taxi expenses	Administrative expenses	3	5
8	Cash payments to suppliers<Operating activities	Cash	4	1
9	Inven111<Inven11<Inven1	Inventory	4	1
10	Inven112<Inven11<Inven1	Inventory	4	1
11	Inven121<Inven12<Inven1	Inventory	4	1
12	Inven122<Inven12<Inven1	Inventory	4	1

13	Inven13<Inven1	Inventory	4	1
14	987654321	Account payable	4	2
15	Cash receipts from customers<Operating activities	Cash	5	1
16	123456789	Account receivable	5	1
17	Xiao Zhou-sales	Sales	5	4
18	N	Cost of sales	5	5

There is a little problem in the Table 1-38. Would you look for it?

Table 1-39 Customers information

Customer B1: Account receivable (X105)

ID	MultiName	Amount	Reference	General ID	TransDate
1	123456789	2558.90		5	2021-1-6
2	123456789	-1500	5		2021-1-8

So far, I have recorded 6 transactions' data. For checking whether the recording data is reliable and correct, I will do the following three calculations which also ensure integrity of the recorded data.

- Check whether the cynamic accounting equation is equal.

  From the Table 1-31, when the 6 general equations are added together, I get the left amount $104,389 and the right amount $104,389 of the dynamic accounting equation on February 7, 2014. These two amounts are equal.

- Check whether the sum of all assets accounts' balances is equal to the sum of all liabilities accounts, all equity accounts, all incomes accounts, and all expenses accounts' balances.

  1. For all assets accounts

     From the Table 1-33, I get that the balance of the parent account "Cash" is $100,890 and the balance of the parent account "Account receivable" is $1,058.90.

From the Table 1-26, I get that the balance of the parent account "HST recoverable is $477.10 and the balance of the parent account "Inventory" is $1,770.

From the Table 8, I get that the balance of the parent account "Office supplies" is $193.

Therefore, the sum of the assets accounts' balances is $104,389 (= $100,890 + $1,058.90 + $477.10 + $1,770 + $193).

Of course, I can also get that the sum of the assets accounts' balances is $104,389 from the table "Assets (X1)" in the Table 1-32.

2. For all liabilities accounts

From the Table 1-18, I get that the balance of the parent account "Account payable" is $3,477.10. From the Table 1-26, I get that the balance of the parent account "HST payable" is $328.90.

Therefore, the total amount of the liabilities accounts' balances is $3806 (= $3,477.10 + $328.90).

Of course, I can also get that the sum of the liabilities accounts' balances is $3,328.90 from the table "Liabilities (X2)" in the Table 1-25.

3. For all shareholders' equity accounts

From the Table 1-3, I get that the balance of the parent account "Share capital" is $100,000.

Therefore, the sum of the shareholders' equity account's balance is $100,000.

Of course, I can also get that the sum of the shareholders' equity account's balance is $100,000 from the table "Shareholders' equity (X3)" in the Table 1-2.

4. For all revenues accounts

From the Table 1-26, I get that the balance of the parent account "Sales" is

$2,530.

Therefore, the sum of the revenues account's balance is $2,530.

Of course, I can also get that the sum of the revenues account's balance is $2,530 from the table "Revenues (X4)" in the Table 1-25.

5. For all expenses accounts

From the Table 1-26, I get that the balance of the parent account "Cost of sales" is -$1,900.

From the Table 1-13, I get that the balance of the parent account "Administrative expenses" is -$47.

Therefore, the sum of the expenses accounts' balances is -$1,947 (= -$1,900 -$47).

Of course, I can also get that the sum of the expenses accounts' balances is -$1,947 from the table "Expenses (X5)" in the Table 1-25.

The sum of all liabilities accounts, all shareholders' equity accounts, all revenues accounts, and all expenses accounts is $104,389 (= $3,806 + $100,000 + $2,530 - $1,947).

The sum of all assets accounts is also $104,389.

These two sum amounts are equal. They are $104,389.

- After the previous two steps are correct, I check whether the left (or right) amount of the dynamic accounting equation is equal to the sum of all assets accounts' balances (or the sum of all liabilities, all equity accounts, all incomes accounts, and all expenses accounts' balances).

Obviously, the requirement is satisfied.

The above three requirements are satisfied, so the mathematical accounting model is reliable and correct.

The above tables are mainly classified by the multi-subaccounts. In fact, there are another method to classify these tables. You can imagine that there are six big cabinets which put together against a wall, seeing the Figure 1-11.

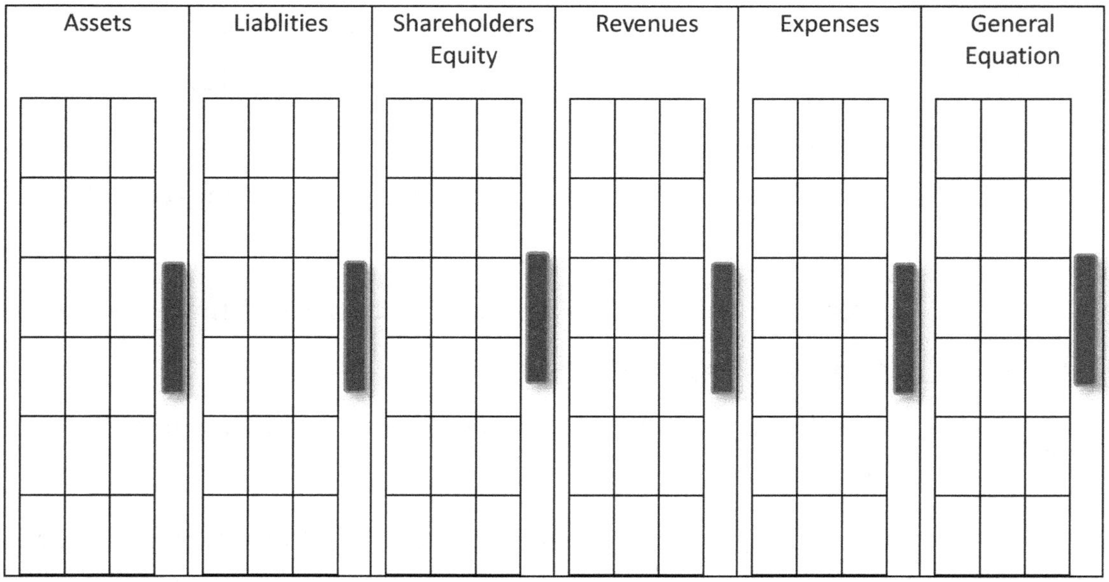

Assets	Liablities	Shareholders Equity	Revenues	Expenses	General Equation

Figure 1-11   Six Cabinets

For the sixth cabinet, there is a General equation table on the door. For the other five cabinets, there are respectively the Assets table, the Liabilities table, the Shareholders' Equity table, the Revenues table, and the Expenses table on their doors.

When I open the door of a cabinet with the General equation table, I see many drawers on which there are respectively the Reference label, the Multi-subaccounts label, the Subtotal Name label, the Customers Information table, Suppliers Information table, the Income Statement label, the Balance Sheet label, the Cash Flows label, the Comprehensive Income Statement label, and the Inventory Account Flows, seeing the Figure 1-12 on the next page.

When I respectively open these drawers, I see two different sizes of the cards in every drawers. The large cards are all the same date cards. Another small cards are all table cards, seeing the Figure 1-13 on the next page.

Reference	MultSubaccount Name	Subtotal Name
Suppliers Information	Customers Information	
Income Statement	Balance Sheet	Cash Flows
Comprehensive Income Statement	Account Flows	

Figure 1-12   Labels and Tables

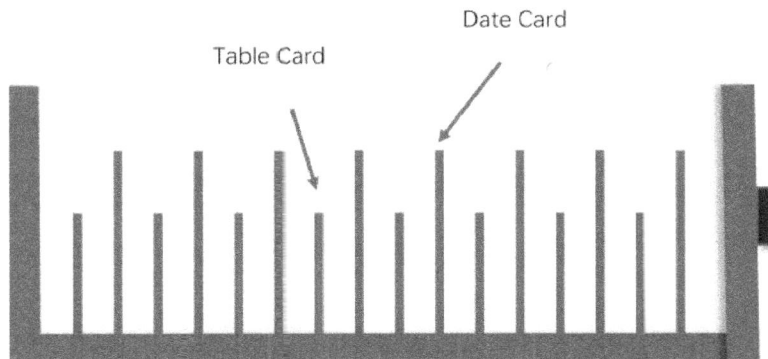

Figure 1-13   Date Cards and Table Cards

When I respectively open the other five cabinets, I see many drawers in every cabinet. On each drawer, there is a parent account table, seeing the Figure 1-14.

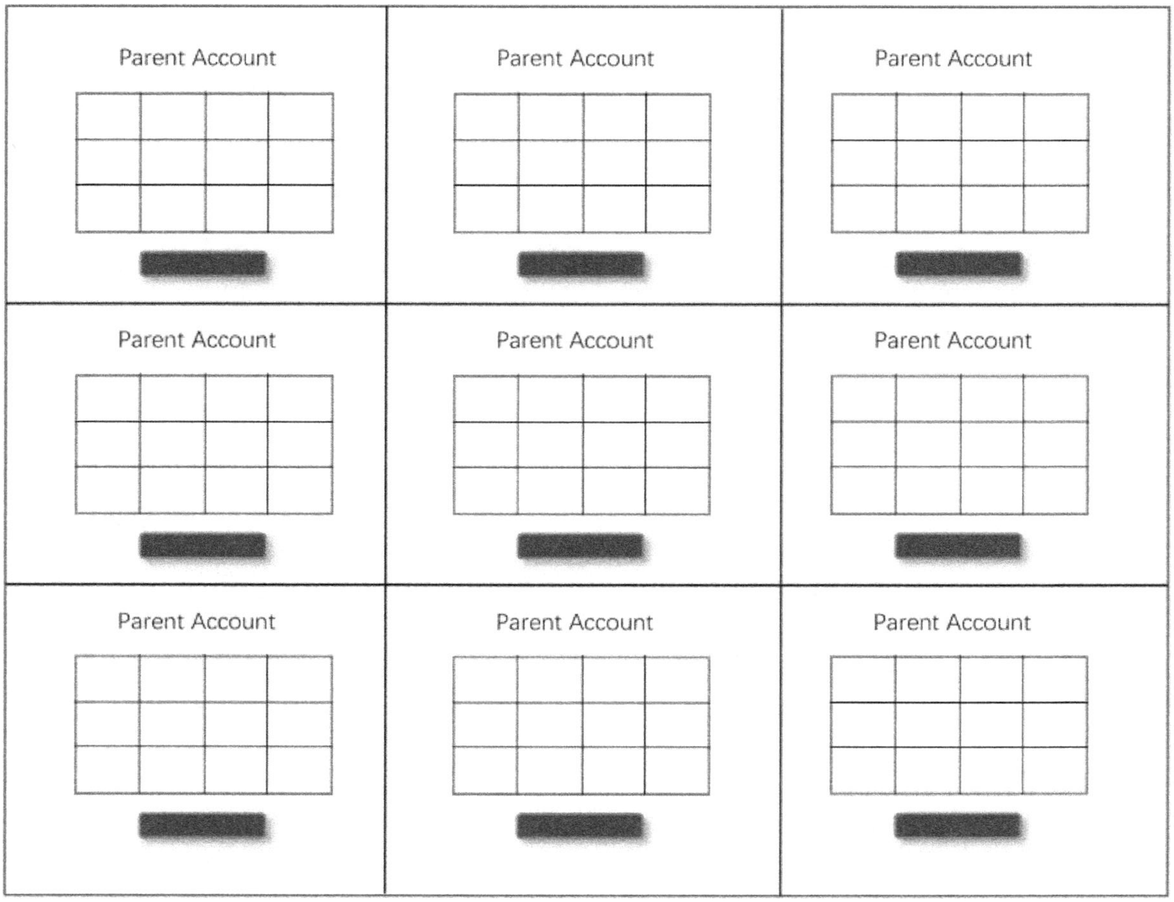

Figure 1-14   Parents Account Tables

When I open the all drawers, I see the three sizes of cards in each drawer. There are respectively the One-level subaccounts table, the Two-level subaccounts table, and the Three-level subaccounts table on the large cards, medium cards, and small cards, seeing the Figure 1-15 on the next page.

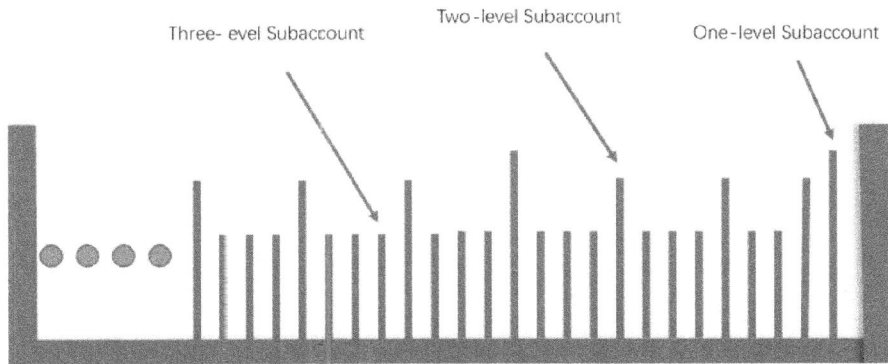

Figure 1-15   Multi-subaccount Cards

After I put the above tables into the different cabinets, I will continue to introduce the first fiscal year transactions by using of the new classified method.

Chapter 2

Sample of an accounting fiscal year

I will record more transactions to complete an accounting fiscal year. During recording these transactions, I will introduce some new contents. Finally, I will build the five tables: Income Statement, Balance Sheet, Cash Flows Statement, Comprehens ve Income Statement, and Account Flows Statement, and begin second fiscal year.

2.1 First fiscal year

RR Company has the following transactions in January 2021.

- RR Company raises funds of $500,000 cash with interest rate 8% (paying interest at the end of each year) and two years from TD bank on January 7, 2021.

  The following Figure 2-1 shows the original proof of this transaction.

Transaction Original Proof							
TransDate: 1/7/2021						General ID	7
Explanation: get funds of $500,000 cash from TD bank.							
No.	Class	Account Name	Left Amount	Right Amount	MultiSubaccount Name	Subtotal Name	Ref
1	1	Cash	500000		Cash receipts from banks< Financing activities		
2	2	Note payable		500000	n	Long term liabilities, 251	252
3							
4							
5							
6							
7							

8								
Total			500000	500000				
Customer or Supplier's Name		Address		E-mail			Postal Code	
City		State		Country				

Person Handling: Manager:

Date: Date:

Figure 2-1   Original Proof of Seventh Transaction

The transaction sub-equation is:

Cash (1): 500000 = Note payable (2): 500000

Because the Note payable account is the third account in the class 2 of accounts, the transaction mathematical sub-equation is:

X101: 500000 = X203: 500000

For the Cash account, the Multisubaccount name is the "Cash receipts from banks< Financing activities". For the new account of the Note payable, its Subtotal name and Multisubaccount name are the "Long term liabilities, 251" and the "n" respectively. Therefore, the one-level and the two-level expanding mathematical sub-equation are respectively:

One-level sub-equation   X10101 = X203
Two-level sub-equation   X1010102 = X203

For recording this transaction, I should create a table X203 for the parent account Note payable and a table X1010102 for the two-level subaccount of the "Cash receipts from banks". The related tables must be updated, seeing the following tables.

First, the General equation table on the sixth cabinet's door must be updated after entering this transaction, seeing the following table.

General equation

GeID	TransDate	General Equation	Left Amount	Right Amount	Explanation	Enter Date
1	2021-1-2	Cash(1): 100000 = Share capital(3): 40000 + Capital(3): 30000 + Capital(3): 30000	100000	100000	Ping Wang, Hua Li and Mike Newsome decide to open a RR trade business	2021-1-4
2	2021-1-3	Cash(1): -193 + Office supplies(1): 193 = 0	0	0	Purchase of Office supplies	2021-1-4
3	2021-1-3	Cash(1): -47 = Administrative expenses (5): -47	-47	-47	Cash payments for Hua Li's taxi fee expense	2021-1-4
4	2021-1-5	Cash(1): -670 + Inventory(1): 3670 + HST recoverable(1): 477.10 = Account payable(2): 3477.10	3477.10	3477.10	RR purchases $3,670 inventory by $670 cash and other on credit from A1 company (phone number: 987654321)	2021-1-6
5	2021-1-5	Cash(1): 300 + Inventory(1): -1900 + Account receivable(1): 2558.90 = HST payable(2): 328.90 + Sales(4): 2530 + Cost of sales (5): -1900	958.90	958.90	RR sells $1,900 inventory to B1 Company (phone number: 123456789) for sales of $2,530 and receives $300 cash	2021-1-6
6	2021-1-7	Cash(1): 1500 + Account receivable(1): -1500 = 0	0	0	RR Company receives $1,500 cash from B1 Company (phone number: 123456789) with the General ID 5	2021-1-8
7	2021-1-7	Cash (1): 500000 = Note payable (2): 500000	500000	500000	RR Company raises funds of $500,000 cash with interest rate 8% (paying interest at the end of each year) and two years from TD bank on January 7, 2014.	2021-1-8
Total Amount			**604389**	**604389**		

Second, the Class accounts must be updated. The "Cash" account and the "Note payable" account respectively belong to the "Assets" and "Liabilities", so the "Assets (X1)" table on the first cabinet's door and the "Liabilities (X2)" table on the second cabinet's door must be updated, seeing the following tables.

Assets (X1)

ID	Account Name (Mathematical Name)	Subtotal	Ref (Row)	Balance
1	Cash (X101)	Current assets,103	104	600890
2	Office supplies (X102)	Current assets,103	106	193

3	Inventory (X103)	Current assets,103	108	1770
4	HST recoverable (X104)	Current assets,103	109	477.10
5	Account receivable (X105)	Current assets,103	110	1058.90

Liabilities (X2)

ID	Account Name (Mathematical Name)	Subtotal	Ref (Row)	Balance
1	Account payable (X201)	Current liabilities,203	204	3477.10
2	HST payable (X202)	Current liabilities,203	205	328.90
3	Note payable (X203)	Long term liabilities, 251	253	500000

Third, the "Cash" account is an existed parent account and the one-level subaccount "Financing activities (X10101)" is an existed one-level subaccount, the "Cash (X101)" table on the Cash drawer in the first cabinet and its one-level subaccount "Financing activities (X10101)" table on the large card in the Cash drawer are only updated. The two-level subaccount of the "Cash receipts from banks (X1010102)" is a new two-level subaccount, so the "Cash receipts from banks (X1010102)" table must be created on the medium card in the Cash drawer, seeing the following tables.

Parent account

Cash (X101)

ID	MultiName	TransDate	Amount	Balance	GeID	SubFirst	SubSecond	SubThird
1	Cash receipts from owners<Financing activities	2021-1-2	100000	100000	1	Financing activities	Cash receipts from owners	
2	Cash payments for operating expenses<Operating activities	2021-1-3	-193	9807	2	Operating activities	Cash payments for operating expenses	
3	Cash payments for operating expenses<Operating activities	2021-1-3	-47	9760	3	Operating activities	Cash payments for operating expenses	
4	Cash payments to suppliers< Operating activities	2021-1-5	-670	9090	4	Operating activities	Cash payments to suppliers	
5	Cash receipts from customers< Operating activities	2021-1-5	300	9390	5	Operating activities	Cash receipts from customers	
6	Cash receipts from customers< Operating activities	2021-1-7	1500	10890	6	Operating activities	Cash receipts from customers	

| 7 | Cash receipts from banks< Financing activities | 2021-1-7 | 500000 | 600890 | 7 | Financing activities | Cash receipts from banks | |

One-level subaccount

Financing activities (X10101) < Parent account: Cash (X101)

ID	MultiName	Amount	Ref	GeID	TransDate	Balance
1	Cash receipts from owners<Financing activities	100000		1	2021-1-2	100000
2	Cash receipts from banks< Financing activities	500000		7	2021-1-7	510000

Two-level subaccount

Cash receipts from banks (X1010102) << Parent account: Cash (X101)

ID	MultiName	Amount	Ref	GeID	TransDate	Balance
1	Cash receipts from banks< Financing activities	500000		7	2021-1-7	500000

Last, the "Note payable" account is a new parent account without any Multisubaccount, so I created a table for the "Note payable" account on a drawer in the second cabinet, and create a table "Subtotal Name" on the small card in the drawer with the label "Subtotal Name" in the sixth cabinet. Of course, I also write the date on the large card in the same drawer, seeing the following tables.

Parent account

Note payable (X203)

ID	MultiName	TransDate	Amount	Balance	GeID	SubFirst	SubSecond	SubThird
1	n	2021-1-7	500000	500000	7			

Subtotal Name

ID	Subtotal Name	Row	GeID	Class
1	Current assets,103	103	1	1
2	Current liabilities,203	203	4	2
3	Long term liabilities,251	251	7	2

4	Owners' capital,303	303	1	3
5	Revenues,403	403	5	4
6	Cost,431	431	5	5
7	Operating and administrative expenses,453	453	3	5

- On same day, the RR Company purchases two lands (Land1, Downtown for $270,000; Land2, North York for $180,000) for $450,000 cash as available for sale.

  If the harmonized sales tax (HST, 13%) is not considered in this transaction, the transaction sub-equation is:

  Cash (1): -450000 + Land (1): 450000 = 0

  For the entry of the "Cash" account, the Multisubaccount name is the "Cash payments for investment<Investing activities".

  For the entry of the "Land" account with two one-level subaccounts, the Subtotal Name is the "Long term investments,141" and the Multisubaccount name are the "Land1, Downtown" and "Land2, North York".

  For recording this transaction, I create a table X106 for a parent account "Land", three tables (X10103, X106101, and X106102) for the one-level subaccounts (Investing activities, Land1, Downtown, and Land2, North York), and a table X1010301 for the "Cash payments for investment". The related tables are updated.

First, the General equation table on the sixth cabinet's door must be updated after entering this transaction, seeing the following table.

General equation

GeID	TransDate	General Equation	Left Amount	Right Amount	Explanation	Enter Date
1	2021-1-2	Cash(1): 100000 = Share capital(3): 40000 + Capital(3): 30000 + Capital(3): 30000	100000	100000	Ping Wang, Hua Li and Mike Newsome decide to open a RR trade business	2021-1-4
2	2021-1-3	Cash(1): -193 + Office supplies(1): 193 = 0	0	0	Purchase of Office supplies	2021-1-4

3	2021-1-3	Cash(1): -47 = Administrative expenses (5): -47	-47	-47	Cash payments for Hua Li's taxi fee expense	2021-1-4
4	2021-1-5	Cash(1): -670 + Inventory 1): 3670 + HST recoverable (1): 477.10 = Account payable(2): 3477.10	3477.10	3477.10	RR purchases $3,670 inventory by $670 cash and other on credit from A1 company (phone number: 987654321)	2021-1-6
5	2021-1-5	Cash(1): 300 – Inventory(1): -1900 + Account receivable(1): 2558.90 = HST payable(2): 328.90 + Sales(4): 2530 + Cost of sales (5): -1900	958.90	958.90	RR sells $1,900 inventory to B1 Company (phone number: 123456789) for sales of $2,530 and receives $300 cash	2021-1-6
6	2021-1-7	Cash(1): 1500 + Account receivable(1) -1500 = 0	0	0	RR Company receives $1,500 cash from B1 Company (phone number: 123456789) with the General ID 5	2021-1-8
7	2021-1-7	Cash (1): 500000 = Note payable (2): 500000	500000	500000	RR Company raises funds of $500,000 cash with interest rate 8% (paying interest at the end of each year) and two years from TD bank on January 7, 2014.	2021-1-8
8	2021-1-7	Cash (1): -450000 + Land (1): 450000 = 0	0	0	RR Company purchases two lands (Land1, Downtown for $270,000; Land2, North York for $180,000) for $450,000 cash as available for sale	2021-1-8
Total Amount			604389	604389		

Second, the Class accounts must be updated. The "Cash" account and the "Land" account all belong to the "Assets", so the "Assets (X1)" table on the first cabinet's door must be updated, seeing the following table.

Assets (X1)

ID	Account Name (Mathematical Name)	Subtotal	Ref (Row)	Balance
1	Cash (X101)	Current assets,103	104	140890
2	Office supplies (X102)	Current assets,103	106	193
3	Inventory (X103)	Current assets,103	108	1770
4	HST recoverable (X104)	Current assets,103	109	477.10
5	Account receivable (X105)	Current assets,103	110	1058.90
6	Land (X106)	Long term investments,141	143	450000

Third, the "Cash" account is an existed parent account, so the "Cash (X101)" table on the Cash drawer in the first cabinet is only updated. The one-level subaccount "Investing activities (X10103)" is a new one-level subaccount, so I create a table of the "Investing activities (X10103)" on the large card in the Cash drawer. The two-level subaccount of the "Cash payments for investment (X1010301)" is a new two-level subaccount, so the "Cash payments for investment (X1010301)" table must be created on the medium card in the Cash drawer, seeing the following tables.

Parent account

Cash (X101)

ID	MultiName	TransDate	Amount	Balance	GeID	SubFirst	SubSecond	SubThird
1	Cash receipts from owners<Financing activities	2021-1-2	100000	100000	1	Financing activities	Cash receipts from owners	
2	Cash payments for operating expenses<Operating activities	2021-1-3	-193	99807	2	Operating activities	Cash payments for operating expenses	
3	Cash payments for operating expenses<Operating activities	2021-1-3	-47	99760	3	Operating activities	Cash payments for operating expenses	
4	Cash payments to suppliers< Operating activities	2021-1-5	-670	99090	4	Operating activities	Cash payments to suppliers	
5	Cash receipts from customers< Operating activities	2021-1-5	300	99390	5	Operating activities	Cash receipts from customers	
6	Cash receipts from customers< Operating activities	2021-1-7	1500	100890	6	Operating activities	Cash receipts from customers	
7	Cash receipts from banks< Financing activities	2021-1-7	500000	600890	7	Investing activities	Cash payments for investment	
8	Cash payments for investment<Investing activities	2021-1-7	-450000	150890	8	Operating activities	Cash payments for machinery	

One-level subaccounts

Investing (X10103) < Parent account: Cash (X101)

ID	MultiName	Amount	Ref	GeID	TransDate	Balance
1	Cash payments for investment<Investing activities	450000		8	2021-1-7	450000

Two-level subaccount

Cash payments for investment (X1010301) << Parent account: Cash (X101)

ID	MultiName	Amount	Ref	GeID	TransDate	Balance
1	Cash payments for investment<Investing activities	450000		8	2021-1-7	450000

Last, the "Land" account is a new parent account with the two one-level subaccounts of the "Land1, Downtown (X10601)" and the "Land2, North York (X10602)", so I created a table "Land (X106)" on a drawer with the "Land (X106)" in the first cabinet. I respectively create the two tables of the "Land1, Downtown (X10601)" and the "Land2, North York (X10602)" on the two large cards in the Land drawer, Meanwhile, I also updated the table "Multisubaccount" on the drawer with the table "Multisubaccount" and create a table "Subtotal Name" on the small card in the drawer with the label "Subtotal Name" in the sixth cabinet, seeing the following tables.

Parent account

Land (X106)

ID	MultiName	TransDate	Amount	Balance	GeID	SubFirst	SubSecond	SubThird
1	Land1, Downtown	270000		270000	8	Land1, Downtown		
2	Land2, North York	180000		180000	8	Land2, North York		

One-level subaccounts

Land1, Downtown (X10601) < Parent account: Land (X106)

ID	MultiName	Amount	Unit	GeID	TransDate	Balance
1	Land1, Downtown	270000	1	8	2021-1-7	270000

Land2, North York (X10602) < Parent account: Land (X106)

ID	MultiName	Amount	Unit	GeID	TransDate	Balance
1	Land2, North York	180000	1	8	2021-1-7	180000

Multi-subaccounts

ID	Multi-subaccount Name	Parent Account	GeID	Class
1	Cash receipts from owners<Financing activities	Cash	1	1
2	Capital-Ping Wang	Share capital	1	3
3	Capital-Hua Li	Share capital	1	3
4	Capital-Mike Newsome	Share capital	1	3

5	Cash payments for operating expenses<Operating activities	Cash	2	1
6	N	Office supplies	2	1
7	Hua Li-taxi<Purchase department-taxi<Taxi expenses	Administrative expenses	3	5
8	Cash payments to suppliers<Operating activities	Cash	4	1
9	Inven111<Inven11<Inven1	Inventory	4	1
10	Inven112<Inven11<Inven1	Inventory	4	1
11	Inven121<Inven12<Inven1	Inventory	4	1
12	Inven122<Inven12<Inven1	Inventory	4	1
13	Inven13<Inven1	Inventory	4	1
14	987654321	Account payable	4	2
15	Cash receipts from customers<Operating activities	Cash	5	1
16	123456789	Account receivable	5	1
17	Xiao Zhou-sales	Sales	5	4
18	N	Cost of sales	5	5
19	Land1, Downtown	Land	8	1
20	Land2, North York	Land	8	1

Subtotal Name

ID	Subtotal Name	Row	GeID	Class
1	Current assets,103	103	1	1
2	Long term investments,141	141	8	1
3	Current liabilities,203	203	4	2
4	Long term liabilities,251	251	7	2
5	Owners' capital,303	303	1	3
6	Revenues,403	403	5	4
7	Cost,431	431	5	5
8	Operating and administrative expenses,453	453	3	5

- On January 8, 2021, the RR Company purchases a truck for $45,000 cash.

  For first entry of the "Cash" account, the Multisubaccount name is the "Cash payments for machinery<Operating activities". For second entry of the "Truck" account, the Multisubaccount name is the "Truck1" and the Subtotal Name is the "Equipment, 171". In fact, this transaction does not include the harmonized sales tax.

Problem 1: What is the original proof of this transaction? How many tables must be created for recording this transaction? What parent accounts or what multi-subaccounts are they for? What are the related tables which must be updated?

Problem 2: What is the transaction sub-equation f the harmonized sales tax (HST, 13%) is used in the transaction and the truck price $45,000 includes the HST?

Problem 3: What is the transaction sub-equation for the supplier if the truck price $45,000 includes the HST?

Problem 4: What is the "Subtotal Name" table?

- On the same day, the RR Company pays $367 cash to Ping Wang (Office department) for the opening company expenses.

  Here, I put the opening company expenses into the "Administrative expenses" account and its one-level subaccount is the "Other expenses". The Other expenses is divided by the different persons and the different departments.

  Because the one-level subaccount of the "Taxi expenses" is also divided by the different persons and the different departments, I must give a different multi-subaccount name to distinguish them. Its multi-subaccount form is the "Ping Wang-xxxxx<Office department-xxxxx<Other expenses". Of course, you can give your distinguishing signal. For the transaction, the multi-subaccount form is the "Ping Wang-open company<Office department-open company <Other expenses".

  For recording this transaction, I should create three tables (X50102, X5010201, and X501020101) for the one-level subaccount of the "Other expenses", the two-level subaccount of the "Office department-other", and the three-level subaccount of the "Ping Wang-other" respectively. The related tables must also be updated.

- On January 9, 2021, the RR Company purchases $25,000 inventory for $2,000 cash and $23,000 on credit from C1 Company (phone number: 987654322). The HST is 13% for the inventory.

The inventory's multi-subaccounts are:

"Inven221<Inven22<Inven2" for $10*320,

"Inven222<Inven22<Inven2" for $5*1000,

"PPUK parts <ASD parts<Inven2" for $4*1200,

"PPGH parts <ASD parts<Inven2" for $2*1900,

"Inven31<Inven3" for $10*530,

"Inven32<Inven3" for $5*580.

For recording this transaction, I should create ten tables for the subaccounts, seeing the following tables. The related tables must also be updated. The C1 Company's information need be recorded.

First, the General equation table on the sixth cabinet's door must be updated after entering this transaction, seeing the following table.

General equation

GeID	TransDate	General Equation	Left Amount	Right Amount	Explanation	Enter Date
1	2021-1-2	Cash(1): 100000 = Share capital(3): 40000 + Capital(3): 30000 + Capital(3): 30000	100000	100000	Ping Wang, Hua Li and Mike Newsome decide to open a RR trade business	2021-1-4
2	2021-1-3	Cash(1): -193 + Office supplies(1): 193 = 0	0	0	Purchase of Office supplies	2021-1-4
3	2021-1-3	Cash(1): -47 = Administrative expenses (5): -47	-47	-47	Cash payments for Hua Li's taxi fee expense	2021-1-4
4	2021-1-5	Cash(1): -670 + Inventory(1): 3670 + HST recoverable (1): 477.10 = Account payable(2): 3477.10	3477.10	3477.10	RR purchases $3,670 inventory by $670 cash and other on credit from A1 company (phone number: 987654321)	2021-1-6
5	2021-1-5	Cash(1): 300 + Inventory(1): -1900 + Account receivable(1): 2558.90 = HST payable(2): 328.90 + Sales(4): 2530 + Cost of sales (5): -1900	958.90	958.90	RR sells $1,900 inventory to B1 Company (phone number: 123456789) for sales of $2,530 and receives $300 cash	2021-1-6
6	2021-1-7	Cash(1): 1500 + Account receivable(1): -1500 = 0	0	0	RR Company receives $1,500 cash from B1 Company (phone number: 123456789) with the General ID 5	2021-1-8
7	2021-1-7	Cash (1): 500000 = Note payable (2): 500000	500000	500000	RR Company raises funds of $500,000 cash with interest rate 8% (paying interest at the end of each year) and two years from TD bank on January 7, 2014.	2021-1-8
8	2021-1-7	Cash (1): -450000 + Land (1): 450000 = 0	0	0	RR Company purchases two lands (Land1, Downtown for $270,000; Land2, North York	2021-1-8

					for $180,000) for $450,000 cash as available for sale	
9	2021-1-8	Cash (1): -45000 + Truck (1): 45000 = 0	0	0	RR Company purchases a truck for $45,000 cash	2021-1-9
10	2021-1-8	Cash (1): -367 = Administrative expenses (5): -367	-367	-367	RR Company pays $367 cash to Ping Wang (Office department) for opening company expenses	2021-1-9
11	2021-1-9	Cash(1): -2000 + Inventory(1): 25000 + HST recoverable (1) 3250 = Account payable(2): 26250	26250	26250	RR Company purchases $25,000 inventory for $2,000 cash and $23,000 on credit from C1 Company (phone number: 987654322).	2021-1-10
Total Amount			630272	630272		

Second, the Class accounts must be updated. The "Cash" account, "Inventory" account, and the "HST recoverable" account all belong to the "Assets", so the "Assets (X1)" table on the first cabinet's door must be updated. The "Account payable" account belongs to the "Liabilities", so the "Liabilities (X2)" table on the second cabinet's door must be updated, seeing the following tables.

Assets (X1)

ID	Account Name (Mathematical Name)	Subtotal	Ref (Row)	Balance
1	Cash (X101)	Current assets,103	104	138890
2	Office supplies (X102)	Current assets,103	106	193
3	Inventory (X103)	Current assets,103	108	26770
4	HST recoverable (X104)	Current assets,103	109	3727.10
5	Account receivable (X105)	Current assets,103	110	1058.90
6	Land (X106)	Long term investments,141	143	450000

Liabilities (X2)

ID	Account Name (Mathematical Name)	Subtotal	Ref (Row)	Balance
1	Account payable (X201)	Current liabilities,203	204	29727.10
2	HST payable (X202)	Current liabilities,203	205	328.90
3	Note payable (X203)	Long term liabilities, 251	253	500000

Third, the "Cash" account, the "Inventory" account, the "HST recoverable" account, and the "Account payable" account are the four existed parent accounts, so the "Cash (X101)" table on the Cash drawer in the first cabinet, the "Inventory (X103)" table on the Inventory drawer in the first cabinet, the "Account receivable (X105)" table on the Account receivable drawer in the first cabinet, and the "Account payable (X201)" table on the Account payable drawer in the second cabinet are only updated. The existed one-level subaccount and the two-level subaccount of the "Cash" parent account are also updated. The "Inven2 (X10302)" and the "Inven2 (X10303)" are two new one-level subaccounts, so I create a table of the "Inven2 (X10302)" on the large card in the Inventory drawer, and create another table of the "Inven2 (X10303)" on the another large card in the same drawer. Of course, the tables of their two-level subaccounts and of their three-level subaccounts are also created on the medium cards and the small cards following the above two large cards respectively, seeing the following tables.

Parent account

Cash (X101)

ID	MultiName	TransDate	Amount	Balance	GeID	SubFirst	SubSecond	SubThird
1	Cash receipts from owners<Financing activities	2021-1-2	100000	100000	1	Financing activities	Cash receipts from owners	
2	Cash payments for operating expenses<Operating activities	2021-1-3	-193	99807	2	Operating activities	Cash payments for operating expenses	
3	Cash payments for operating expenses<Operating activities	2021-1-3	-47	99760	3	Operating activities	Cash payments for operating expenses	
4	Cash payments to suppliers< Operating activities	2021-1-5	-670	99090	4	Operating activities	Cash payments to suppliers	
5	Cash receipts from customers< Operating activities	2021-1-5	300	99390	5	Operating activities	Cash receipts from customers	
6	Cash receipts from customers< Operating activities	2021-1-7	1500	100890	6	Operating activities	Cash receipts from customers	
7	Cash receipts from banks< Financing activities	2021-1-7	500000	600890	7	Financing activities	Cash receipts from banks	
8	Cash payments for investment<Investing activities	2021-1-7	-450000	150890	8	Investing activities	Cash payments for investment	
9	Cash payments for machinery<Operating activities	2021-1-8	-45000	105890	9	Operating activities	Cash payments for machinery	
10	Cash payments for operating	2021-1-8	-367	105523	10	Operating activities	Cash payments for	

ID	MultiName	TransDate	Amount	Ref	GeID			MultiName	
	expenses<Operating activities							operating expenses	
11	Cash payments to suppliers< Operating activities	2021-1-9	-2000	103523	11		Operating activities	Cash payments to suppliers	

One-level subaccounts

Operating activities (X10102) < Parent account: Cash (X101)

ID	MultiName	Amount	Ref	GeID	TransDate	Balance
1	Cash payments for operating expenses<Operating activities	-193		2	2021-1-3	-193
2	Cash payments for operating expenses<Operating activities	-47		3	2021-1-3	-240
3	Cash payments to suppliers< Operating activities	-670		4	2021-1-5	-910
4	Cash receipts from customers< Operating activities	300		5	2021-1-5	-610
5	Cash receipts from customers< Operating activities	1500	5	6	2021-1-7	890
10	Cash payments for operating expenses<Operating activities	-367		10	2021-1-8	523
11	Cash payments to suppliers< Operating activities	-2000		11	2021-1-9	-1477

Two-level subaccount

Cash payments to suppliers (X1010202) << Parent account: Cash (X101)

ID	MultiName	Amount	Ref	GeID	TransDate	Balance
1	Cash payments to suppliers< Operating activities	-670		4	2021-1-5	-670
11	Cash payments to suppliers< Operating activities	-2000			2021-1-9	-2670

Parent account

Inventory (X103)

ID	MultiName	TransDate	Amount	Balance	GeID	SubFirst	SubSecond	SubThird	Unit
1	Inven111<Inven11<Inven1	2021-1-5	10*165	1650	4	Inven1	Inven11	Inven111	165
2	Inven112<Inven11<Inven1	2021-1-5	4*225	2550	4	Inven1	Inven11	Inven112	225
3	Inven121<Inven12<Inven1	2021-1-5	0.8*650	3070	4	Inven1	Inven12	Inven121	650
4	Inven122<Inven12<Inven1	2021-1-5	5*56	3400	4	Inven1	Inven12	Inven122	66
5	Inven13<Inven1	2021-1-5	30*9	3670	4	Inven1	Inven13		9

6	Inven111<Inven11<Inven1	2021-1-5	-10*91	2760	5	Inven1	Inven11	Inven111		-91
7	Inven112<Inven11<Inven1	2021-1-5	-4*130	2240	5	Inven1	Inven11	Inven112		-130
8	Inven121<Inven12<Inven1	2021-1-5	-0.8*375	1940	5	Inven1	Inven12	Inven121		-375
9	Inven122<Inven12<Inven1	2021-1-5	-5*34	1770	5	Inven1	Inven12	Inven122		-34
10	Inven221<Inven22<Inven2	2021-1-9	10*320	4970	11	Inven2	Inven22	Inven221		320
11	Inven222<Inven22<Inven2	2021-1-9	5*1000	9970	11	Inven2	Inven22	Inven222		1000
12	PPUK parts <ASD parts< Inven2	2021-1-9	4*1200	14770	11	Inven2	ASD parts	PPUK parts		1200
13	PPGH parts <ASD parts< Inven2	2021-1-9	2*1900	18570	11	Inven2	ASD parts	PPGH parts		1900
14	Inven31<Inven3	2021-1-9	10*530	23870	11	Inven3	Inven31			530
15	Inven32<Inven3	2021-1-9	$5*580	26770	11	Inven3	Inven32			580

One-level subaccounts

Inven2 (X10302) < Parent account: Inventory (X103)

ID	MultiName	Amount	Unit	GeID	TransDate	Balance
1	Inven221<Inven22<Inven2	10*320	320	11	2021-1-9	3200
2	Inven222<Inven22< Inven2	5*1000	1000	11	2021-1-9	8200
3	PPUK parts <ASD parts<Inven2	4*1200	1200	11	2021-1-9	13000
4	PPGH parts <ASD parts<Inven2	2*1900	1900	11	2021-1-9	16800

Inven3 (X10303) < Parent account: Inventory (X103)

ID	MultiName	Amount	Unit	GeID	TransDate	Balance
1	Inven31<Inven3	10*530	530	11	2021-1-9	5300
2	Inven32<Inven3	5*580	580	11	2021-1-9	8200

Two-level subaccount

Inven22 (X1030201) << Parent account: Inventory (X103)

ID	MultiName	Amount	Unit	GeID	TransDate	Balance
1	Inven221<Inven22<Inven2	10*320	320	11	2021-1-9	3200
2	Inven222<Inven22<Inven2	5*1000	1000	11	2021-1-9	8200

ASD parts (X1030202) << Parent account: nventory (X103)

ID	MultiName	Amount	Unit	GeID	TransDate	Balance
1	PPUK parts<ASD parts<Inven2	4*1200	1200	11	2021-1-9	4800
2	PPGH parts<ASD parts<Inven2	2*1900	1900	11	2021-1-9	8600

Inven31 (X1030301) << Parent account: Inventory (X103)

ID	MultiName	Amount	Unit	GeID	TransDate	Balance
1	Inven31<Inven3	10*530	530	11	2021-1-9	5300

Inven32 (X1030302) << Parent account: Inventory (X103)

ID	MultiName	Amount	Unit	GeID	TransDate	Balance
1	Inven31<Inven3	5*580	580	11	2021-1-9	2900

Three-level subaccount

Inven221 (X103020101) <<< Parent account: Inventory (X103)

ID	MultiName	Amount	Unit	GeID	TransDate	Balance
1	Inven221<Inven22<Inven2	10*320	320	11	2021-1-9	3200

Inven222 (X103020102) <<< Parent account: Inventory (X103)

ID	MultiName	Amount	Unit	GeID	TransDate	Balance
1	Inven222<Inven22<Inven2	5*1000	1000	11	2021-1-9	5000

Inven222 (X103020201) <<< Parent account: Inventory (X103)

ID	MultiName	Amount	Unit	GeID	TransDate	Balance
1	PPUK parts<ASD parts<Inven2	4*1200	1200	11	2021-1-9	4800

Inven22 (X103020202) <<< Parent account: Inventory (X103)

ID	MultiName	Amount	Unit	GeID	TransDate	Balance
1	PPGH parts<ASD parts<Inven2	2*1900	1900	11	2021-1-9	3800

Parent account

HST recoverable (X104)

ID	MultiName	TransDate	Amount	Balance	GeID	SubFirst	SubSecond	SubThird
1	N	2021-1-5	477.10	477.10	4			
2	N	2021-1-9	3250	3727.1	11			

Parent account

Account payable (X201)

ID	MultiName	TransDate	Amount	Balance	GeID	SubFirst	SubSecond	SubThird	Ref
1	987654321	2021-1-5	3477.10	3477.10	4	987654321			
2	987654322	2021-1-9	26250	29727.10	11	987654322			

One-level subaccounts

987654321 (X20102) < Parent account: Account payable (X201)

ID	MultiName	Amount	Ref	GeID	TransDate	Balance
1	987654322	26250		11	2021-1-9	26250

Last, the suppliers' information must be updated. The "Suppliers" table on the drawer in the sixth cabinet is updated. Meanwhile, the table "Supplier C1 Company" is created on the small card in the drawer and the date is also written on the large card in the same drawer. In addition, the "Multi-subaccounts" on the drawer in the sixth cabinet is created, seeing the following tables.

Later, I only create these two tables of the "MultiSubaccount Name" and the "Subtotal Name" at the end of every month for simplification in this book.

Suppliers information

Suppliers

ID	Supplier Phone	Supplier Name	Address	E-mail	Postal Code	City	State	Country
1	987654321	A1	A2	A3	A4	A5	A6	A7
2	987654322	C1	C2	C3	C4	C5	C6	C7

Supplier C1 Company

ID	MultiName	Amount	Reference	General ID	TransDate
1	987654322	26250		11	2021-1-9

Multi-subaccounts

ID	Multi-subaccount Name	Parent Account	GeID	Class
1	Cash receipts from owners<Financing activities	Cash	1	1
2	Capital-Ping Wang	Share capital	1	3
3	Capital-Hua Li	Share capital	1	3
4	Capital-Mike Newsome	Share capital	1	3
5	Cash payments for operating expenses<Operating activities	Cash	2	1
6	N	Office supplies	2	1
7	Hua Li-taxi<Purchase department-taxi<Taxi expenses	Administrative expenses	3	5
8	Cash payments to suppliers<Operating activities	Cash	4	1
9	Inven111<Inven11<Inven1	Inventory	4	1
10	Inven112<Inven11<Inven1	Inventory	4	1
11	Inven121<Inven12<Inven1	Inventory	4	1
12	Inven122<Inven12<Inven1	Inventory	4	1
13	Inven13<Inven1	Inventory	4	1
14	987654321	Account payable	4	2
15	Cash receipts from customers<Operating activities	Cash	5	1
16	123456789	Account receivable	5	1
17	Xiao Zhou-sales	Sales	5	4
18	N	Cost of sales	5	5
19	Land1, Downtown	Land	8	1
20	Land2, North York	Land	8	1
21	Inven221<Inven22<Inven2	Inventory	11	1
22	Inven222<Inven22<Inven2	Inventory	11	1
23	PPUK parts<ASD parts<Inven2	Inventory	11	1
24	PPGH parts <ASD parts<Inven2	Inventory	11	1

25	Inven31<Inven3	Inventory	11	1
26	Inven32<Inven3	Inventory	11	1

- On same day, the RR Company purchases $12,000 inventory on credit from D1 Company (phone number: 987654323).

The inventory's multi-subaccounts are:

"Inven331<Inven33<Inven3" for $2*1350,

"Inven332<Inven33< Inven3" for $5*620,

"HGFCVB parts<QASXC parts<Inven3" for $10*490,

"PPGHUP parts<ASDUP parts<Inven3" for $10*130.

For recording this transaction, I should create seven tables for the two-level and the three-level subaccounts, seeing the following tables. The related tables must also be updated. The D1 Company's information need be recorded.

The following seven tables are the two-level and the three-level subaccounts of the parent account "Inventory (X103)".

Two-level subaccount

Inven33 (X1030303) << Parent account: Inventory (X103)

ID	MultiName	Amount	Unit	GeID	TransDate	Balance
1	Inven331<Inven33<Inven3	2*1350	1350	12	2021-1-9	2700
2	Inven332<Inven33<Inven3	5*620	620	12	2021-1-9	5800

QASXC parts (X1030304) << Parent account: Inventory (X103)

ID	MultiName	Amount	Unit	GeID	TransDate	Balance
1	HGFCVB parts<QASXC parts<Inven3	10*490	490	12	2021-1-9	4900

ASDUP parts (X1030305) << Parent account: Inventory (X103)

ID	MultiName	Amount	Unit	GeID	TransDate	Balance
1	PPGHUP parts<ASDUP parts<Inven3	10*130	130	12	2021-1-9	1300

Three-level subaccount

Inven331 (X103030301) <<< Parent account: Inventory (X103)

ID	MultiName	Amount	Unit	GeID	TransDate	Balance
1	Inven331<Inven33<Inven3	2*1350	1350	12	2021-1-9	2700

Inven332 (X103030302) <<< Parent account: Inventory (X103)

ID	MultiName	Amount	Unit	GeID	TransDate	Balance
1	Inven332<Inven33<Inven3	5*620	620	12	2021-1-9	3100

HGFCVB parts (X103030401) <<< Parent account: Inventory (X103)

ID	MultiName	Amount	Unit	GeID	TransDate	Balance
1	HGFCVB parts<QASXC parts<Inven3	10*490	490	12	2021-1-9	4900

PPGHUP parts (X103030402) <<< Parent account: Inventory (X103)

ID	MultiName	Amount	Unit	GeID	TransDate	Balance
1	PPGHUP parts<ASDUP parts<Inven3	2*130	130	12	2021-1-9	1300

- On January 11, 2021, Xiao Zhou sales $17,700 inventory for $3,500 cash and $26,000 on credit to E1 Company (phone number: 123456788).

  The inventory's multi-subaccounts are:

  "Inven221<Inven22<Inven2" of cost $-10*290,

  "Inven222<Inven22<Inven2" of cost $-5*940,

  "PPUK parts<ASD parts< Inven2" of cost $-4*650,

  "Inven32<Inven3" of cost $-5*380,

"HGFCVB parts<QASXC parts<Inven3" of cost $-10*480,

"PPGHUP parts<ASDUP parts<Inven3" of cost $-10*80.

The transaction sub-equation is:

Cash (1): 3500 + Account receivable (1): 29385 + Inventory (1): -17700

= HST payable (2): 3835 + Sales (4): 29500 + Cost of sales (5): -17700

For recording this transaction, I need only update the related tables. The E1 Company's information need be recorded.

- On January 15, 2021, ZhenDao Yuan sales $13,200 inventory for $21,700 on credit to F1 Company (phone number: 123456787).

  The inventory's multi-subaccounts are:

  "PPGH parts<ASD parts<Inven2" of cost $-2*1550,

  "Inven31<Inven3" of cost $-10*500,

  "Inven331<Inven33<Inven3" of cost $-2*1100,

  "Inven332<Inven33< Inven3" of cost $-5*580.

  For recording this transaction, I need only update the related tables. The F1 Company's information need be recorded.

- On January 17, 2021, the RR Company purchases $12,500 inventory on credit from G1 Company (phone number: 987654324).

  The inventory's multi-subaccounts are:

  "Inven411<Inven41<Inven4" for $5*1020,

  "Inven412<Inven41<Inven4" for $2*1850,

  "TTTCU parts<TTT parts<Inven4" for $2*1150,

  "RRRHJK parts< Inven4" for $2*700.

- On the same day, the RR Company receives $21,000 cash from E1 Company (phone number: 123456788) with the General ID 13.

When I receive the $21,000 cash, I know that E1 Company pays the cash.

I use the General ID as the judging signal because a company may sale the inventory to this customer for a few of times and the General ID of a transaction is sole. Later, I will use the information to build up a table of the Account receivable age.

Problem: What is the original proof of this transaction? How many tables must be created or updated for recording this transaction?

- On January 21, 2021, the RR Company pays $14,000 cash to C1 Company (phone number: 987654322) with the General ID 11.

  The same thing is for the supplier.

- On same day, the RR Company pays $6,000 cash to D1 Company (phone number: 987654323) with the General ID 12.

- On January 22, 2021, the RR Company purchases $21,500 inventory on credit from C1 Company (phone number: 987654322).

  The inventory's multi-subaccounts are:

  "PPUK parts<ASD parts<Inven2" for $4*1625,

  "PPGH parts<ASD parts<Inven2" for $2*3000,

  "Inven31<Inven3" for$10*530,

  "Inven32<Inven3" for $5*740.

- On January 23, 2021, Yi Liu sales $12,000 inventory for $19,900 on credit to F1 Company (phone number: 123456787).

  The inventory's multi-subaccounts are:

  "PPUK parts<ASD parts<Inven2" of cost $-4*825,

  "PPGH parts<ASD parts<Inven2" of cost $-2*1950,

  "Inven31<Inven3" of cost $-10*250,

  "Inven32<Inven3" of cost $-5*460.

- On January 25, 2021, ZhenDao Yuan sales $7,500 inventory for $13,700 on credit to

H1 Company (phone number: 123456786).

The inventory's multi-subaccounts are:

"PPUK parts<ASD parts<Inven2" of cost $-4*750,

"PPGH parts<ASD parts<Inven2" of cost $-2*900,

"Inven31<Inven3" of cost $-10*270.

- On January 28, 2021, the RR Company purchases $5,600 computers equipment for $5,600 cash.

    The computer account has three one-level subaccounts of the computer1 ($1,600), the computer server ($1,800), and the POS system ($2,200). It belongs to the Subtotal of the "Equipment, 171".

- On January 29, 2021, Jun Wang sales $3,500 inventory for $6,200 on credit to B1 Company (phone number: 123456789).

The inventory's multi-subaccounts are:

"PPUK parts<ASD parts<Inven2" of cost $-4*550,

"Inven32<Inven3" of cost $-5*260.

- On January 30, 2021, the RR Company receives $2558.90 cash from B1 Company (phone number: 123456789) with the General ID 5 ($828.9) and General ID 23 ($1730).

    Problem: What is the original proof of this transaction? How many tables must be updated for recording this transaction?

- On the same day, the RR Company receives $15,000 cash from F1 Company (phone number: 123456787) with the General ID 14.

- On the same day, the RR Company receives $8,475 cash from H1 Company (phone number: 123456786) with the General ID 21.

- On the same day, the RR Company pays $7,500 cash to C1 Company (phone number: 987654322) with the General ID 11.

- On the same day, the RR Company pays $232.76 cash to Dan Zhu (Purchase department) for the taxi expenses $178 and the mobile expenses $54.76.

  Here, I put the mobile expenses into the "Administrative expenses" account and its one-level subaccount is the"Mobile expenses". The Mobile expenses is divided by the different persons and the different departments. Its multi-subaccount form is "Dan Zhu-mobile < Purchase department-mobile < Mobile expenses".

- On the same day, the RR Company pays $221.30 cash to Hua Li (Purchase department) for the taxi expenses $135.12 and the other expenses $86.18.

- On the same day, the RR Company pays $339.52 cash to Xiao Zhou (Sales department) for the taxi expenses $243 and the other expenses $96.52.

- On the same day, the RR Company pays $132.26 cash to Jun Wang (Sales department) for the other expenses.

- On the same day, the RR Company pays $82.33 cash to Zhendao Yuan (Sales department) for the other expenses.

- On January 31, 2021, the RR Company receives $13,000 cash from F1Company (phone number: 123456787) with the General ID 23.

- On the same day, the RR Company pays $8,000 cash to G1Company (phone number: 987654324) with the General ID 16.

- On the same day, the RR Company pays $419.55 cash to Yi Liu (Sales department) for the taxi expenses $347.7 and the other expenses $71.85.

- On the same day, the RR Company records the Office supplies expenses $88.

  The Office supplies expenses is recorded as the one-level subaccount of the parent account "Administrative expenses". The related tables must be updated.

- On the same day, the RR Company pays $18,756 cash for all salary of January, 2014.

  Here, I just consider the total salary and have no the detail information of the payments. The human resource function will be introduced in the other book.

  The Salary expenses is as a parent account.

- On the same day, the RR Company records the truck's amortization expenses $750 one month (5 years, straight line, and full first month).

  The "Amortization expenses" account is a parent account which will appear in the income statement. It has a one-level subaccount "Truck-amortization" now.

  The "Accumulated amortization" is a contra account of the "Truck" account, so I should reverse the amount of the contra account while putting the contra account into the class 1 accounts. The reversing amount means that increasing amount is the "-" and decreasing amount is the "+". The "Accumulated amortization" should be under the "Truck" parent account whose row number is the "172", so its row number should be the "173". Because the contra account "Accumulated amortization: truck" will also appear in the financial statements, it seems a parent account and has a one-level subaccount "Truck-accumulated amortization" now.

  There are other contra accounts too, such as the "Allowance for doubtful account" for the "Account receivable" account and the "Discount on bonds payable" for the "Bonds payable" account. The same method can be used for them.

- On the same day, the RR Company records the computers' amortization expenses $101.39.

  The "Amortization expenses" account has two one-level subaccounts of the "Truck-amortization and Computer-amortization" now. The "Computers" account has three one-level subaccounts of the computer1 (two years, straight line, and half first month of $33.33), the computer server (two years, straight line, and half first month of $37.5), and the POS system (three years, straight line, and half first month of $30.56). Therefore, for the "Computer" account, its "Amortization expenses" account should have three two-level subaccounts. Their multi-subaccounts are:

  "Computer1- amortization< Computer - amortization",

  "Computer server1 - amortization< Computer - amortization",

  "POS system1 - amortization< Computer - amortization".

The parent account of the "Accumulated amortization: Computer" should be under the parent account "Computer" whose row number is the "174", so its row number should be the "175". It has three one-level subaccounts which are also the multi-subaccounts:

Computer1- accumulated amortization

Computer server1- accumulated amortization

POS system1- accumulated amortization

- On the same day, the RR Company pays $376.47 cash to Mike Newsome (Office department) for taxi expenses $298.69 and the other expenses $77.78.

- On the same day, the RR Company pays $280.70 cash for the utility expenses.

  The Utility expenses is recorded the one-level subaccount of the parent account "Administrative expenses". The related tables must be updated

- On the same day, the RR Company pays $1500 cash for the office rent expenses.

  For recording this transaction, I should create a table X503 for the parent account Office rent expenses. The Office supplies expenses account has no multi-subaccount. The related tables must be updated

- On the same day, the RR Company records the note payable's interest expenses $3,000 and the accrued interest payable (500,000*8%/12*27/30).

I have completed the first month transactions so far. The same things basically are repeated in the following months. The Table 2-1 to the Table 2-33 show all tables which record these transactions. After checking these tables in three steps, I will introduce how to build up the income statement, balance sheet, cash flows statement, and account flows statement.

In the sixth cabinet, there are the following tables. The Table 2-1 General equation is on the door of this cabinet.

Table 2-1 General equation

GeID	TransDate	General Equation	Left Amount	Right Amount	Explanation	Enter Date
1	2021-1-2	Cash(1): 10000 = Share capital(3): 4000 + Capital(3): 3000 + Capital(3): 3000	100000	100000	Ping Wang, Hua Li and Mike Newsome decide to open a RR trade business	2021-1-4
2	2021-1-3	Cash(1): -193 + Office supplies(1): 193 = 0	0	0	Purchase of Office supplies	2021-1-4
3	2021-1-3	Cash(1): -47 = Administrative expenses (5): -47	-47	-47	Cash payments for Hua Li's taxi fee expense	2021-1-4
4	2021-1-5	Cash(1): -670 + Inventory(1): 3670 + HST recoverable (1): 477.10 = Account payable(2): 3477.10	3477.10	3477.10	RR purchases $3,670 inventory by $670 cash and other on credit from A1 company (phone number: 987654321)	2021-1-6
5	2021-1-5	Cash(1): 300 + Inventory(1): -1900 + Account receivable(1): 2558.90 = HST payable(2): 328.90 + Sales(4): 2530 + Cost of sales (5): -1900	958.90	958.90	RR sells $1,900 inventory to B1 Company (phone number: 123456789) for sales of $2,530 and receives $300 cash	2021-1-6
6	2021-1-7	Cash(1): 1500 + Account receivable(1): -1500 = 0	0	0	RR Company receives $1,500 cash from B1 Company (phone number: 123456789) with the General ID 5	2021-1-8
7	2021-1-7	Cash (1): 500000 = Note payable (2): 500000	500000	500000	RR Company raises funds of $500,000 cash with interest rate 8% (paying interest at the end of each year) and two years from TD bank on January 7, 2014.	2021-1-8
8	2021-1-7	Cash (1): -450000 + Land (1): 450000 = 0	0	0	RR Company purchases two lands (Land1, Downtown for $270,000; Land2, North York for $180,000) for $450,000 cash as available for sale	2021-1-8
9	2021-1-8	Cash (1): -45000 + Truck (1): 45000 = 0	0	0	RR Company purchases a truck for $45,000 cash	2021-1-9
10	2021-1-8	Cash (1): -367 = Administrative expenses (5): -367	-367	-367	RR Company pays $367 cash to Ping Wang (Office department) for opening company expenses	2021-1-9
11	2021-1-9	Cash(1): -2000 + Inventory(1): 25000 + HST recoverable(1) 3250 = Account payable(2): 26250	26250	26250	RR Company purchases $25,000 inventory for $2,000 cash and $23,000 on credit from C1 Company (phone number: 987654322).	2021-1-10
12	2021-1-9	Inventory(1): 12000 + HST recoverable(1) 1560 = Account payable(2): 13560	13560	13560	RR Company purchases $12,000 inventory on credit from D1 Company (phone number: 987654323)	2021-1-10
13	2021-1-11	Cash(1): 3500 + Inventory(1): -17700 + Account receivable(1): 29835 = HST payable(2): 3835 + Sales(4): 29500 + Cost of sales (5): -17700	15635	15635	Xiao Zhou sales $17,700 inventory for $3,500 cash and $26,000 on credit to E1 Company (phone number: 123456788)	2021-1-12
14	2021-1-15	Inventory(1): -13200 + Account receivable(1): 24521 = HST	11321	11321	ZhenDao Yuan sales $13,200 inventory for $21,700 on	2021-1-16

		payable(2): 2821 + Sales(4): 21700 + Cost of sales (5): -13200			credit to F1 Company (phone number: 123456787)	
15	2021-1-17	Inventory(1): 12500 + HST recoverable (1): 1625 = Account payable(2): 14125	14125	14125	RR Company purchases $12,500 inventory on credit from G1 Company (phone number: 987654324)	2021-1-18
16	2021-1-17	Cash(1): 21000 + Account receivable: -21000 = 0	0	0	Receive $21,000 cash from E1 Company (phone number: 123456788) with the General ID 13	2021-1-18
17	2021-1-21	Cash (1) -14000 = Account payable(2): -14000	-14000	-14000	Pay $14,000 cash to C1 Company (phone number: 987654322) with the General ID 11	2021-1-22
18	2021-1-21	Cash (1) -6000 = Account payable(2): -6000	-6000	-6000	Pay $6,000 cash to D1 Company (phone number: 987654323) with the General ID 12	2021-1-22
19	2021-1-22	Inventory(1): 21500 + HST recoverable (1) 2795 = Account payable(2): 24295	24295	24295	RR Company purchases $21,500 inventory on credit from C1 Company (phone number: 987654322)	2021-1-23
20	2021-1-23	Inventory(1): -12000 + Account receivable(1): 22487 = HST payable(2): 2587 + Sales(4): 19900 + Cost of sales (5): -12000	10487	10487	Y Liu sales $12,000 inventory for $19,900 on credit to F1 Company (phone number: 123456787)	2021-1-24
21	2021-1-25	Inventory(1): -7500 + Account receivable: 15481 = HST payable(2): 1781 + Sales(4): 13700 + Cost of sales (5): -7500	7981	7981	ZhenDao Yuan sales $7,500 inventory for $13,700 on credit to H1 Company (phone number: 123456786)	2021-1-26
22	2021-1-28	Cash(1): -5600 + Computer(1): 1600 + Computer(1): 1800 – Computer(1): 2200 = 0	0	0	Purchase $5,600 computers equipment for $5,600 cash	2021-1-29
23	2021-1-29	Inventory(1): -3500 + Account receivable(1): 7006 = HST payable(2): 806 + Sales(4): 6200 + Cost of sales (5): -3500	3506	3506	Jun Wang sales $3,500 inventory for $6,200 on credit to B1 Company (phone number: 123456789)	2021-1-30
24	2021-1-30	Cash(1): 2558.90 + Account receivable(1): -828.90 + Account receivable: -1730 = 0	0	0	Receive $2558.90 cash from E1 Company (phone number: 123456789) with the General ID 5 ($828.9) and General ID 23 ($1730)	2021-1-30
25	2021-1-30	Cash(1): 15000 + Account receivable(1): -15000 = 0	0	0	Receive $15,000 cash from F1 Company (phone number: 123456787) with the General ID 14	2021-1-31
26	2021-1-30	Cash(1): 8475 + Account receivable(1): -8475 = 0	0	0	Receive $8,475 cash from H1 Company (phone number: 123456786) with the General ID 21	2021-1-31
27	2021-1-30	Cash (1) -7500 = Account payable(2): -7500	-7500	-7500	Pay $7,500 cash to C1Company (phone number: 987654322) with the General ID 11	2021-1-31
28	2021-1-30	Cash (1): -232.76 = Administrative expenses (5 : -178 + Administrative expenses (5): -54.76	-232.76	-232.76	Pay $232.76 cash to Dan Zhu (Purchase department) for the taxi expenses $178 and the mobile expenses$54.76	2021-1-31
29	2021-1-30	Cash (1): -221.30 = Administrative expenses (5: -	-221.30	-221.30	Pay $221.30 cash to Hua Li (Purchase department) for	2021-1-31

		135.12 + Administrative expenses (5): -86.18			the taxi expenses $135.12 and the other expenses $86.18	
30	2021-1-30	Cash (1): -339.52 = Administrative expenses (5): -243 + Administrative expenses (5): -96.52	-339.52	-339.52	RR Company pays $339.52 cash to Xiao Zhou (Sales department) for the taxi expenses $243 and the other expenses $96.52	2021-1-31
31	2021-1-30	Cash (1): -132.26 = Administrative expenses (5): -132.26	-132.26	-132.26	RR Company pays $132.26 cash to Jun Wang (Sales department) for the other expenses	2021-1-31
32	2021-1-30	Cash (1): -82.33 = Administrative expenses (5): -82.33	-82.33	-82.33	RR Company pays $82.33 cash to Zhendao Yuan (Sales department) for the other expenses	2021-1-31
33	2021-1-31	Cash(1): 13000 + Account receivable(1): -13000 = 0	0	0	RR Company receives $13,000 cash from F1Company (phone number: 123456787) with the General ID 20	2021-1-31
34	2021-1-31	Cash (1) -8000 = Account payable(2): -8000	-8000	-8000	RR Company pays $8,000 cash to G1Company (phone number: 987654324) with the General ID 15	2021-1-31
35	2021-1-31	Cash (1): -419.55 = Administrative expenses (5): -347.70 + Administrative expenses (5): -71.85	-419.55	-419.55	RR Company pays $419.55 cash to Yi Liu (Sales department) for the taxi expenses $347.7 and the other expenses$71.85	2021-1-31
36	2021-1-31	Office supplies(1): -88 = Administrative expenses(5): -88	-88	-88	RR Company records the Office supplies expenses $88	2021-1-31
37	2021-1-31	Cash (1): -18756 = Salary expenses (5): -18756	-18756	-18756	RR Company pays $18,756 cash for all salary of January, 2014	2021-1-31
38	2021-1-31	Accumulated amortization: Truck(1): -750 = Amortization expenses(5): -750	-750	-750	Record truck's amortization expenses $750 one month (5 years, straight line, and full first month)	2021-1-31
39	2021-1-31	Accumulated amortization: Computer(1): -33.33 + Accumulated amortization: Computer(1): -37.5 + Accumulated amortization: Computer(1): -30.56 = -Amortization expenses(5): 33.33 - Amortization expenses(5): 37.5 - Amortization expenses(5): 30.56	-101.39	-101.39	RR Company records the computers' amortization expenses $101.39	2021-1-31
40	2021-1-31	Cash (1): -376.47 = Administrative expenses(5): -298.69 + Administrative expenses (5): -77.78	-376.47	-376.47	Pay $376.47 cash to Mike Newsome (Office department) for taxi expenses $298.69 and the other expenses $77.78	2021-1-31
41	2021-1-31	Cash (1): -280.70 = Administrative expenses (5): -280.70	-280.70	-280.70	RR Company pays $280.70 cash for the utility expenses	2021-1-31
42	2021-1-31	Cash (1): -1500 = Office rent expenses (5): -1500	-1500	-1500	RR Company pays $1500 cash for the office rent expenses	2021-1-31

43	2021-1-31	0 = Accrued interest payable (2): 3000 + Interest expenses (5): -3000	0	0	Record the note payable's interest expenses $3,000 and the accrued interest payable (500,000*8%/12*27/30)	2021-1-31
Total Amount			672401.72	672401.72		

Table 2-2 Reference

ID	Account Name (Subtotal Name)	Row	GeID	Balance
1	**Current assets**	**103**	**1**	**172653.11**
2	Cash	104	1	103616.01
3	Office supplies	106	2	105.00
4	Inventory	108	4	18870.00
5	HST recoverable	109	4	9707.10
6	Account receivable	110	5	40355.00
7	**Long term investments**	**141**	**8**	**450000.00**
8	Land	143	8	450000.00
9	**Equipment**	**171**	**9**	**49748.61**
10	Truck	173	8	45000.00
11	Accumulated amortization: truck	174	38	-750.00
12	Computers	175	22	5600.00
13	Accumulated amortization: computer	176	39	-101.39
14	**Current liabilities**	**203**	**4**	**61366.00**
15	Account payable	204	4	46207.10
16	HST payable	205	5	12158.90
17	Accrued interest payable	207	43	3000.00
18	**Long term liabilities**	**251**	**7**	**500000.00**
19	Note payable	252	7	500000.00
20	**Owners' capital**	**303**	**1**	**100000.00**
21	Share capital	304	1	100000.00
22	**Revenues**	**403**	**5**	**93530.00**
23	Sales	404	5	93530.00
24	**Cost**	**431**	**5**	**-55800.00**
25	Cost of sales	432	5	-55800.00
26	**Operating and administrative expenses**	**453**	**3**	**-26694.28**
27	Administrative expenses	454	3	-2586.89
28	Salary expenses	456	37	-18756.00
29	Amortization expenses	458	38	-851.39
30	Office rent expenses	459	42	-1500.00
31	Interest expenses	461	43	-3000.00

Table 2-3 Subtotal Name

ID	Subtotal Name	Row	GeID	Class
1	Current assets,103	103	1	1
2	Long term investments,141	141	8	1
3	Equipment	171	9	1De
4	Current liabilities,203	203	4	2
5	Long term liabilities,251	251	7	2
6	Owners' capital,303	303	1	3
7	Revenues,403	403	5	4
8	Cost,431	431	5	5
9	Operating and administrative expenses,453	453	3	5

Table 2-4 Multi-subaccounts

ID	Multi-subaccount Name	Parent Account	GeID	Class
1	Cash receipts from owners<Financing activities	Cash	1	1
2	Capital-Ping Wang	Share capital	1	3
3	Capital-Hua Li	Share capital	1	3
4	Capital-Mike Newsome	Share capital	1	3
5	Cash payments for operating expenses<Operating activities	Cash	2	1
6	N	Office supplies	2	1
7	Hua Li-taxi<Purchase department-taxi<Taxi expenses	Administrative expenses	3	5
8	Cash payments to suppliers<Operating activities	Cash	4	1
9	Inven111<Inven11<Inven1	Inventory	4	1
10	Inven112<Inven11<Inven1	Inventory	4	1
11	Inven121<Inven12<Inven1	Inventory	4	1
12	Inven122<Inven12<Inven1	Inventory	4	1
13	Inven13<Inven1	Inventory	4	1
14	987654321	Account payable	4	2
15	Cash receipts from customers<Operating activities	Cash	5	1
16	123456789	Account receivable	5	1
17	Xiao Zhou-sales	Sales	5	4
18	N	Cost of sales	5	5
19	Cash receipts from banks<Financing activities	Cash	7	1
20	N	Note payable	7	2
21	Cash payments for investment<Operating activities	Cash	8	1
22	Land1, Downtown	Land	8	1
23	Land2, North York	Land	8	1
24	Cash payments for machinery<Operating activities	Cash	9	1

25	Truck1	Truck	9	1
26	Ping Wang-open fees<Office department-open fees<Other expenses	Administrative expenses	10	5
27	Inven221<Inven22<Inven2	Inventory	11	1
28	Inven222<Inven22<Inven2	Inventory	11	1
29	PPUK parts<ASD parts<Inven2	Inventory	11	1
30	PPGH parts<ASD parts<Inven2	Inventory	11	1
31	Inven31<Inven3	Inventory	11	1
32	Inven32<Inven3	Inventory	11	1
33	987654322	Account payable	11	2
34	Inven331<Inven33<Inven3	Inventory	12	1
35	Inven332<Inven33<Inven3	Inventory	12	1
36	HGFCVB parts<QASXC parts<Inven3	Inventory	12	1
37	PPGHUP parts<ASDUP parts<Inven3	Inventory	12	1
38	987654323	Account payable	12	2
39	123456788	Account receivable	13	1
40	123456787	Account receivable	14	1
41	ZhenDao Yuan-sales	Sales	14	4
42	Inven411<Inven41<Inven4	Inventory	15	1
43	Inven412<Inven41<Inven4	Inventory	15	1
44	TTTCU parts<TTT parts<Inven4	Inventory	15	1
45	RRRHJK parts<Inven4	Inventory	15	1
46	987654324	Account payable	15	2
47	Yi Liu-sales	Sales	20	4
48	123456786	Account receivable	21	1
49	Computer1	Computers	22	1
50	Computer server1	Computers	22	1
51	POS system1	Computers	22	1
52	Jun Wang-sales	Sales	23	4
53	Dan Zhu-taxi<Purchase department-taxi<Taxi expenses	Administrative expenses	28	5
54	Dan Zhu-mobile<Purchase department-mobile<Mobile expenses	Administrative expenses	28	5
55	Hua Li-other<Purchase department-other<Other expenses	Administrative expenses	29	5
56	Xiao Zhou-taxi<Sales department-taxi<Taxi expenses	Administrative expenses	30	5
57	Xiao Zhou-other<Sales department-other<Other expenses	Administrative expenses	30	5
58	Jun Wang-other<Sales department-other<Other expenses	Administrative expenses	31	5
59	Zhendao Yuan-other<Sales department-other<Other expenses	Administrative expenses	32	5
60	Yi Liu-taxi<Sales department-taxi<Taxi expenses	Administrative expenses	35	5
61	Yi Liu-other<Sales department-other<Other expenses	Administrative expenses	35	5
62	Office supplies expenses	Administrative expenses	36	5
63	N	Salary expenses	37	5
64	Truck1-accumulated amortization	Accumulated amortization: truck	38	1

65	Truck1-amortization	Amortization expenses	38	5
66	Computer1-accumulated amortization	Accumulated amortization: Computer	39	1
67	Computer server1-accumulated amortization	Accumulated amortization: Computer	39	1
68	POS system1-accumulated amortization	Accumulated amortization: computer	39	1
69	Computer1-amortization<Computer-amortization	Amortization expenses	39	5
70	Computer server1-amortization<Computer-amortization	Amortization expenses	39	5
71	POS system1-amortization<Computer-amortization	Amortization expenses	39	5
72	Mike Newsome-taxi<Office department-taxi<Taxi expenses	Accumulated amortization: Computer	40	1
73	Mike Newsome-other<Office department-other<Other expenses	Accumulated amortization: computer	40	1
74	Utility expenses	Administrative expenses	41	5
75	N	Office supplies expenses	42	5
76	Note1-TD bank	Accrued interest payable	43	2

Table 2-5 Suppliers information

Suppliers

ID	Supplier Phone	Supplier Name	Address	E-mail	Postal Code	City	State	Country
1	987654321	A1	A2	A3	A4	A5	A6	A7
2	987654322	C1	C2	C3	C4	C5	C6	C7
3	987654323	D1	D2	D3	D4	D5	D6	D7
4	987654324	G1	G2	G3	G4	G5	G6	G7

Supplier A1: Account payable (X201)

ID	MultiName	Amount	Balance	Ref	GeID	TransDate
1	987654321	3477.10	3477.10		4	2021-1-5

Supplier C1: Account payable (X201)

ID	MultiName	Amount	Balance	Ref	GeID	TransDate
1	987654322	26250	26250		11	2021-1-9
2	987654322	-14000	12250	11	17	2021-1-21
3	987654322	24295	36545		19	2021-1-22
4	987654322	-7500	29045	11	27	2021-1-30

Supplier D1: Account payable (X201)

ID	MultiName	Amount	Balance	Ref	GeID	TransDate
1	987654323	13560	13560		12	2021-1-9
2	987654323	-6000	7560	12	18	2021-1-21

Supplier G1: Account payable (X201)

ID	MultiName	Amount	Balance	Ref	GeID	TransDate
1	987654324	14125	14125		15	2021-1-17
2	987654324	-8000	6125	**15**	34	2021-1-31

Table 2-6 Customers information

Customers

ID	Customer Phone	Customer Name	Address	E-mail	Postal Code	City	State	Country
1	123456789	B1	B2	B3	B4	B5	B6	B7
2	123456788	E1	E2	E3	E4	E5	E6	E7
3	123456787	F1	F2	F3	F4	F5	F6	F7
4	123456786	H1	H2	H3	H4	H5	H6	H7

Customer B1: Account receivable (X105)

ID	MultiName	Amount	Balance	Ref	GeID	TransDate
1	123456789	2558.90	2558.90		5	2021-1-5
2	123456789	-1500	1058.90	**5**	6	2021-1-7
3	123456789	7006	8064.90		23	2021-1-29
4	123456789	-828.90	7236	**5**	24	2021-1-30
5	123456789	-1730	5506	**23**	24	2021-1-30

Customer E1: Account receivable (X105)

ID	MultiName	Amount	Balance	Ref	GeID	TransDate
1	123456788	29835	29835		13	2021-1-11
2	123456788	-21000	8835	**13**	16	2021-1-17

Customer F1: Account receivable (X105)

ID	MultiName	Amount	Balance	Ref	GeID	TransDate

1	123456787	24521	24521		14	2021-1-15
2	123456787	22487	47008		20	2021-1-23
3	123456787	-15000	32008	**14**	25	2021-1-30
4	123456787	-13000	19008	**20**	33	2021-1-31

Customer H1: Account receivable (X105)

ID	MultiName	Amount	Balance	Ref	GeID	TransDate
1	123456786	15481	15481		21	2021-1-25
2	123456786	-8475	7006	**21**	26	2021-1-30

In the first cabinet, there are the following tables.

Table 2-7 Assets (X1) on the door

ID	Account Name (Mathematical Name)	Subtotal	Ref (Row)	Balance
1	Cash (X101)	Current assets,103	104	103616.01
2	Office supplies (X102)	Current assets,103	106	105.00
3	Inventory (X103)	Current assets,103	108	18870.00
4	HST recoverable (X104)	Current assets,103	109	9707.10
5	Account receivable (X105)	Current assets,103	110	40355.00
6	Land (X106)	Long term investments,141	143	450000.00
7	Truck (X107)	Equipment, 171	172	45000.00
8	Accumulated amortization: truck (X109)	Equipment, 171	173	-750.00
9	Computer (X108)	Equipment, 171	174	5600.00
10	Accumulated amortization: Computer (X110)	Equipment, 171	175	-101.39

Table 2-8 Parent account: Cash on a drawer

Cash (X101)

ID	MultiName	TransDate	Amount	Balance	GeID	SubFirst	SubSecond	SubThird
1	Cash receipts from owners<Financing activities	2021-1-2	100000	100000	1	Financing activities	Cash receipts from owners	
2	Cash payments for operating expenses<Operating activities	2021-1-3	-193	99807	2	Operating activities	Cash payments for operating expenses	

100

3	Cash payments for operating expenses<Operating activities	2021-1-3	-47	99760	3	Operating activities	Cash payments for operating expenses
4	Cash payments to suppliers< Operating activities	2021-1-5	-670	99090	4	Operating activities	Cash payments to suppliers
5	Cash receipts from customers< Operating activities	2021-1-5	300	99390	5	Operating activities	Cash receipts from customers
6	Cash receipts from customers< Operating activities	2021-1-7	1500	100890	6	Operating activities	Cash receipts from customers
7	Cash receipts from banks< Financing activities	2021-1-7	500000	600890	7	Cash receipts from banks	Financing activities
8	Cash payments for investment<Investing activities	2021-1-7	-450000	150890	8	Cash payments for investment	Investing activities
9	Cash payments for machinery<Operating activities	2021-1-8	-45000	105890	9	Cash payments for machinery	Operating activities
10	Cash payments for operating expenses<Operating activities	2021-1-8	-367	105523	10	Cash payments for operating expenses	Operating activities
11	Cash payments to suppliers< Operating activities	2021-1-9	-2000	103523	11	Operating activities	Cash payments to suppliers
12	Cash receipts from customers< Operating activities	2021-1-11	3500	107023	13	Operating activities	Cash receipts from customers
13	Cash receipts from customers< Operating activities	2021-1-17	21000	128023	16	Operating activities	Cash receipts from customers
14	Cash payments to suppliers< Operating activities	2021-1-21	-14000	114023	17	Operating activities	Cash payments to suppliers
15	Cash payments to suppliers< Operating activities	2021-1-21	-6000	108023	18	Operating activities	Cash payments to suppliers
16	Cash payments for machinery<Operating activities	2021-1-23	-5600	102423	22	Operating activities	Cash payments for machinery
17	Cash receipts from customers< Operating activities	2021-1-30	2558.90	104981.90	24	Operating activities	Cash receipts from customers
18	Cash receipts from customers< Operating activities	2021-1-30	15000	119981.90	25	Operating activities	Cash receipts from customers
19	Cash receipts from customers< Operating activities	2021-1-30	8475	128456.90	26	Operating activities	Cash receipts from customers
20	Cash payments to suppliers<Operating activities	2021-1-30	-7500	120956.9	27	Operating activities	Cash payments to suppliers
21	Cash payments for operating expenses<Operating activities	2021-1-30	-232.76	120724.14	28	Operating activities	Cash payments for operating expenses

ID	MultiName	TransDate	Amount	Balance	GeID		MultiName	
22	Cash payments for operating expenses<Operating activities	2021-1-30	-221.30	120502.84	29	Operating activities	Cash payments for operating expenses	
23	Cash payments for operating expenses<Operating activities	2021-1-30	-339.52	120163.32	30	Operating activities	Cash payments for operating expenses	
24	Cash payments for operating expenses<Operating activities	2021-1-30	-132.26	120031.06	31	Operating activities	Cash payments for operating expenses	
25	Cash payments for operating expenses<Operating activities	2021-1-30	-82.33	119948.73	32	Operating activities	Cash payments for operating expenses	
26	Cash receipts from customers< Operating activities	2021-1-31	13000	132948.73	33	Operating activities	Cash receipts from customers	
27	Cash payments to suppliers<Operating activities	2021-1-31	-8000	124948.73	34	Operating activities	Cash payments to suppliers	
28	Cash payments for operating expenses<Operating activities	2021-1-31	-419.55	124529.18	35	Operating activities	Cash payments for operating expenses	
29	Cash payments for operating expenses<Operating activities	2021-1-31	-18756	105773.18	37	Operating activities	Cash payments for operating expenses	
30	Cash payments for operating expenses<Operating activities	2021-1-31	-376.47	105396.71	40	Operating activities	Cash payments for operating expenses	
31	Cash payments for operating expenses<Operating activities	2021-1-31	-280.70	105116.01	41	Operating activities	Cash payments for operating expenses	
32	Cash payments for operating expenses<Operating activities	2021-1-31	-1500.00	103616.01	42	Operating activities	Cash payments for operating expenses	

One-level on a **large** card

Financing activities (X10101) < Parent account: Cash (X101)

ID	MultiName	Amount	Ref	GeID	TransDate	Balance
1	Cash receipts from owners<Financing activities	100000		1	2021-1-2	100000
2	Cash receipts from banks<Financing activities	500000		7	2021-1-2	600000

Two-level on a **medium** card

Cash receipts from owners (X1010101) << Parent account: Cash (X101)

ID	MultiName	Amount	Ref	GeID	TransDate	Balance
1	Cash receipts from owners<Financing activities	100000		1	2021-1-2	100000

Two-level on a **medium** card

Cash receipts from banks (X1010102) << Parent account: Cash (X101)

ID	MultiName	Amount	Ref	GeID	TransDate	Balance
1	Cash receipts from banks<Financing activities	500000		7	2021-1-7	500000

One-level on a **large** card

Operating activities (X10102) < Parent account: Cash (X101)

ID	MultiName	Amount	Ref	GeID	TransDate	Balance
1	Cash payments for operating expenses<Operating activities	-193		2	2021-1-3	-193
2	Cash payments for operating expenses<Operating activities	-47		3	2021-1-3	-240
3	Cash payments to suppliers<Operating activities	-670		4	2021-1-5	-910
4	Cash receipts from customers<Operating activities	300		5	2021-1-5	-610
5	Cash receipts from customers<Operating activities	1500		6	2021-1-7	890
6	Cash payments for machinery<Operating activities	-45000		9	2021-1-8	-44110
7	Cash payments for operating expenses<Operating activities	-367		10	2021-1-8	-44477
8	Cash payments to suppliers<Operating activities	-2000		11	2021-1-9	-46477
9	Cash receipts from customers<Operating activities	3500		13	2021-1-11	-42977
10	Cash receipts from customers<Operating activities	21000		16	2021-1-17	-21977
11	Cash payments to suppliers<Operating activities	-14000		17	2021-1-21	-35977
12	Cash payments to suppliers<Operating activities	-6000		18	2021-1-21	-41977
13	Cash payments for machinery<Operating activities	-5600		22	2021-1-28	-47577
14	Cash receipts from customers<Operating activities	2558.90		24	2021-1-30	-45018.10

15	Cash receipts from customers< Operating activities	15000		25	2021-1-30	-30018.10
16	Cash receipts from customers< Operating activities	8475		26	2021-1-30	-21543.10
17	Cash payments to suppliers< Operating activities	-7500		27	2021-1-30	-29043.10
18	Cash payments for operating expenses<Operating activities	-232.76		28	2021-1-30	-29275.86
19	Cash payments for operating expenses<Operating activities	-221.30		29	2021-1-30	-29497.16
20	Cash payments for operating expenses<Operating activities	-339.52		30	2021-1-30	-29836.68
21	Cash payments for operating expenses<Operating activities	-132.26		31	2021-1-30	-29968.94
22	Cash payments for operating expenses<Operating activities	-82.33		32	2021-1-30	-30051.27
23	Cash receipts from customers< Operating activities	13000		33	2021-1-31	-17051.27
24	Cash payments to suppliers< Operating activities	-8000		34	2021-1-31	-25051.27
25	Cash payments for operating expenses<Operating activities	-419.55		35	2021-1-31	-25470.82
26	Cash payments for operating expenses<Operating activities	-18756		37	2021-1-31	-44226.82
27	Cash payments for operating expenses<Operating activities	-376.47		40	2021-1-31	-44603.29
28	Cash payments for operating expenses<Operating activities	-280.70		41	2021-1-31	-44883.99
29	Cash payments for operating expenses<Operating activities	-1500		42	2021-1-31	-46383.99

Two-level on a **medium** card

Cash payments for operating expenses (X1010201) << Parent account: Cash (X101)

ID	MultiName	Amount	Ref	GeID	TransDate	Balance
1	Cash payments for operating expenses<Operating activities	-193		2	2021-1-3	-193
2	Cash payments for operating expenses<Operating activities	-47		3	2021-1-3	-240
3	Cash payments for operating expenses<Operating activities	-367		10	2021-1-8	-607
4	Cash payments for operating expenses<Operating activities	-232.76		28	2021-1-30	-839.76
5	Cash payments for operating expenses<Operating activities	-221.30		29	2021-1-30	-1061.06
6	Cash payments for operating expenses<Operating activities	-339.52		30	2021-1-30	-1400.58
7	Cash payments for operating expenses<Operating activities	-132.26		31	2021-1-30	-1532.84
8	Cash payments for operating expenses<Operating activities	-82.33		32	2021-1-30	-1615.17
9	Cash payments for operating expenses<Operating activities	-419.55		35	2021-1-31	-2034.72
10	Cash payments for operating expenses<Operating activities	-18756		37	2021-1-31	-20790.72

11	Cash payments for operating expenses<Operating activities	-376.47		40	2021-1-31	-21167.19
12	Cash payments for operating expenses<Operating activities	-280.70		41	2021-1-31	-21447.89
13	Cash payments for operating expenses<Operating activities	-1500		42	2021-1-31	-22947.89

Two-level on a **medium** card

Cash payments to suppliers (X1010202) << Parent account: Cash (X101)

ID	MultiName	Amount	Ref	GeID	TransDate	Balance
1	Cash payments to suppliers<Operating activities	-670		4	2021-1-5	-670
2	Cash payments to suppliers<Operating activities	-2000		11	2021-1-9	-2670
3	Cash payments to suppliers<Operating activities	-14000		17	2021-1-21	-16670
4	Cash payments to suppliers<Operating activities	-6000		18	2021-1-21	-22670
5	Cash payments to suppliers<Operating activities	-7500		27	2021-1-30	-30170
6	Cash payments to suppliers<Operating activities	-8000		34	2021-1-31	-38170

Two-level on a **medium** card

Cash receipts from customers (X1010203) << Parent account: Cash (X101)

ID	MultiName	Amount	Ref	GeID	TransDate	Balance
1	Cash receipts from customers<Operating activities	300		5	2021-1-5	300
2	Cash receipts from customers<Operating activities	1500		6	2021-1-7	1800
3	Cash receipts from customers<Operating activities	3500		13	2021-1-11	5300
4	Cash receipts from customers<Operating activities	21000		16	2021-1-17	26300
5	Cash receipts from customers<Operating activities	2558.90		24	2021-1-30	28858.90
6	Cash receipts from customers<Operating activities	15000		25	2021-1-30	43858.90
7	Cash receipts from customers<Operating activities	8475		26	2021-1-30	52333.90
8	Cash receipts from customers<Operating activities	13000		33	2021-1-31	65333.90

Two-level on a **medium** card

Cash payments for machinery (X1010204) << Parent account: Cash (X101)

ID	MultiName	Amount	Ref	GeID	TransDate	Balance
1	Cash payments for machinery< Operating activities	-45000		9	2021-1-8	-45000
2	Cash payments for machinery< Operating activities	-5600		22	2021-1-28	-50600

One-level on a **large** card

Investing activities (X10103) < Parent account: Cash (X101)

ID	MultiName	Amount	Ref	GeID	TransDate	Balance
1	Cash payments for investment<Investing activities	-450000		8	2021-1-7	-450000

Two-level on a **medium** card

Cash payments for investment (X1010301) << Parent account: Cash (X101)

ID	MultiName	Amount	Ref	GeID	TransDate	Balance
1	Cash payments for investment<Investing activities	-45000		8	2021-1-7	-45000

Table 2-9 Parent account: Office supplies on a drawer

Office supplies (X102)

ID	MultiName	TransDate	Amount	Balance	GeID	SubFirst	SubSecond	SubThird
1	N	2021-1-3	193	193	2			
2	N	2021-1-31	-88	105	36			

Table 2-10 Parent account: Inventory on a drawer

Inventory (X103)

ID	MultiName	TransDate	Amount	Balance	GeID	SubFirst	SubSecond	SubThird	Unit
1	Inven111<Inven11<Inven1	2021-1-5	1650	1650	4	Inven1	Inven11	Inven111	165

2	Inven112<Inven11<Inven1	2021-1-5	900	2550	4	Inven1	Inven11	Inven112	225
3	Inven121<Inven12<Inven1	2021-1-5	520	3070	4	Inven1	Inven12	Inven121	650
4	Inven122<Inven12<Inven1	2021-1-5	330	3400	4	Inven1	Inven12	Inven122	66
5	Inven13<Inven1	2021-1-5	270	3670	4	Inven1	Inven13		9
6	Inven111<Inven11<Inven1	2021-1-5	-910	2760	5	Inven1	Inven11	Inven111	-91
7	Inven112<Inven11<Inven1	2021-1-5	-520	2240	5	Inven1	Inven11	Inven112	-130
8	Inven121<Inven12<Inven1	2021-1-5	-300	1940	5	Inven1	Inven12	Inven121	-375
9	Inven122<Inven12<Inven1	2021-1-5	-170	1770	5	Inven1	Inven12	Inven122	-34
10	Inven221<Inven22<Inven2	2021-1-9	3200	4970	11	Inven2	Inven22	Inven221	320
11	Inven222<Inven22<Inven2	2021-1-9	5000	9970	11	Inven2	Inven22	Inven221	1000
12	PPUK parts<ASD parts<Inven2	2021-1-9	4800	14770	11	Inven2	ASD parts	PPUK parts	1200
13	PPGH parts<ASD parts<Inven2	2021-1-9	3800	18570	11	Inven2	ASD parts	PPUK parts	1900
14	Inven31<Inven3	2021-1-9	5300	23870	11	Inven3	Inven31		530
15	Inven32<Inven3	2021-1-9	2900	26770	11	Inven3	Inven32		580
16	Inven331<Inven33<Inven3	2021-1-9	2700	29470	12	Inven3	Inven33	Inven331	1350
17	Inven332<Inven33<Inven3	2021-1-9	3100	32570	12	Inven3	Inven33	Inven332	620
18	HGFCVB parts<QASXC parts<Inven3	2021-1-9	4900	37470	12	Inven3	QASXC parts	HGFCVB parts	490
19	PPGHUP parts<ASDUP parts<Inven3	2021-1-9	1300	38770	12	Inven3	ASDUP parts	PPGHUP parts	130
20	Inven221<Inven22<Inven2	2021-1-11	-2900	35870	13	Inven2	Inven22	Inven221	-290
21	Inven222<Inven22<Inven2	2021-1-11	-4700	31170	13	Inven2	Inven22	Inven222	-940
22	PPUK parts<ASD parts< Inven2	2021-1-11	-2600	28570	13	Inven2	ASD parts	PPUK parts	-650
23	Inven32<Inven3	2021-1-11	-1900	26670	13	Inven3	Inven32		-380
24	HGFCVB parts<QASXC parts<Inven3	2021-1-11	-4800	21870	13	Inven3	QASXC parts	HGFCVB parts	-480
25	PPGHUP parts<ASDUP parts<Inven3	2021-1-11	-800	21070	13	Inven3	ASDUP parts	PPGHUP parts	-80
26	PPGH parts<ASD parts<Inven2	2021-1-15	-3100	17970	14	Inven2	ASD parts	PPUK parts	-1550
27	Inven31<Inven3	2021-1-15	-5000	12970	14	Inven3	Inven31		-500
28	Inven331<Inven33<Inven3	2021-1-15	-2200	10770	14	Inven3	Inven33	Inven331	-1100
29	Inven332<Inven33<Inven3	2021-1-15	-2900	7870	14	Inven3	Inven33	Inven332	-580
30	Inven411<Inven41<Inven4	2021-1-17	5100	12970	15	Inven4	Inven41	Inven411	1020

31	Inven412<Inven41<Inven4	2021-1-17	3700	16670	15	Inven4	Inven41	Inven412	1850
32	TTTCU parts<TTT parts<Inven4	2021-1-17	2300	18970	15	Inven4	TTT parts	TTTCU parts	1150
33	RRRHJK parts< Inven4	2021-1-17	1400	20370	15	Inven4	RRRHJK parts		700
34	PPUK parts<ASD parts<Inven2	2021-1-22	6500	26870	19	Inven2	ASD parts	PPUK parts	1625
35	PPGH parts<ASD parts<Inven2	2021-1-22	6000	32870	19	Inven2	ASD parts	PPGH parts	3000
36	Inven31<Inven3	2021-1-22	5300	38170	19	Inven3	Inven31		530
37	Inven32<Inven3	2021-1-22	3700	41870	19	Inven3	Inven32		740
38	PPUK parts<ASD parts<Inven2	2021-1-23	-3300	38570	20	Inven2	ASD parts	PPUK parts	-825
39	PPGH parts<ASD parts<Inven2	2021-1-23	-3900	34670	20	Inven2	ASD parts	PPGH parts	-1950
40	Inven31<Inven3	2021-1-23	-2500	32170	20	Inven3	Inven31		-250
41	Inven32<Inven3	2021-1-23	-2300	29870	20	Inven3	Inven32		-460
42	PPUK parts<ASD parts<Inven2	2021-1-25	-3000	26870	21	Inven2	ASD parts	PPUK parts	-750
43	PPGH parts<ASD parts<Inven2	2021-1-25	-1800	25070	21	Inven2	ASD parts	PPGH parts	-900
44	Inven31<Inven3	2021-1-25	-2700	22370	21	Inven3	Inven31		-270
45	PPUK parts<ASD parts<Inven2	2021-1-29	-2200	20170	23	Inven2	ASD parts	PPUK parts	-550
46	Inven32<Inven3	2021-1-29	-1300	18870	23	Inven3	Inven32		-260

One-level on a **large** card

Inven1 (X10301) < Parent account: Inventory (X103)

ID	MultiName	Amount	Unit	GeID	TransDate	Balance
1	Inven111<Inven11<Inven1	1650	165	4	2021-1-5	1650
2	Inven112<Inven11<Inven1	900	225	4	2021-1-5	2550
3	Inven121<Inven12<Inven1	520	650	4	2021-1-5	3070
4	Inven122<Inven12<Inven1	330	66	4	2021-1-5	3400
5	Inven13<Inven1	270	9	4	2021-1-5	3670
6	Inven111<Inven11<Inven1	-910	-91	5	2021-1-5	2760
7	Inven112<Inven11<Inven1	-520	-130	5	2021-1-5	2240
8	Inven121<Inven12<Inven1	-300	-375	5	2021-1-5	1940
9	Inven122<Inven12<Inven1	-170	-34	5	2021-1-5	1770

Two-level on a **medium** card

Inven11 (X1030101) << Parent account: Inventory (X103)

ID	MultiName	Amount	Unit	GeID	TransDate	Balance

1	Inven111<Inven11<Inven1	1650	165	4	2021-1-5	1650
2	Inven112<Inven11<Inven1	900	225	4	2021-1-5	2550
3	Inven111<Inven11<Inven1	-910	-91	4	2021-1-5	1640
4	Inven112<Inven11<Inven1	-520	-123	4	2021-1-5	1120

Three-level on a **small** card

Inven111 (X103010101) <<< Parent account: Inventory (X103)

ID	MultiName	Amount	Unit	GeID	TransDate	Balance
1	Inven111<Inven11<Inven1	1650	165	4	2021-1-5	1650
2	Inven111<Inven11<Inven1	-910	-91	5	2021-1-5	740

Three-level on a **small** card

Inven112 (X103010102) <<< Parent account: Inventory (X103)

ID	MultiName	Amount	Unit	GeID	TransDate	Balance
1	Inven112<Inven11<Inven1	900	225	4	2021-1-5	900
2	Inven112<Inven11<Inven1	-520	-123	5	2021-1-5	380

Two-level on a **medium** card

Inven12 (X1030102) << Parent account: Inventory (X103)

ID	MultiName	Amount	Unit	GeID	TransDate	Balance
1	Inven121<Inven12<Inven1	520	650	4	2021-1-5	520
2	Inven122<Inven12<Inven1	330	66	4	2021-1-5	850
3	Inven121<Inven12<Inven1	-300	-375	5	2021-1-5	550
4	Inven122<Inven12<Inven1	-170	-34	5	2021-1-5	380

Three-level on a **small** card

Inven121 (X103010201) <<< Parent account: Inventory (X103)

ID	MultiName	Amount	Unit	GeID	TransDate	Balance
1	Inven121<Inven12<Inven1	520	650	4	2021-1-5	520
2	Inven121<Inven12<Inven1	-300	-375	5	2021-1-5	220

Three-level on a **small** card

Inven122 (X103010202) <<< Parent account: Inventory (X103)

ID	MultiName	Amount	Unit	GeID	TransDate	Balance
1	Inven122<Inven12<Inven1	330	66	4	2021-1-5	330
2	Inven122<Inven12<Inven1	-170	-34	5	2021-1-5	160

Two-level on a **medium** card

Inven13 (X1030103) << Parent account: Inventory (X103)

ID	MultiName	Amount	Unit	GeID	TransDate	Balance
1	Inven13<Inven1	270	9	4	2021-1-5	270

One-level on a **large** card

Inven2 (X10302) < Parent account: Inventory (X103)

ID	MultiName	Amount	Unit	GeID	TransDate	Balance
1	Inven221<Inven22<Inven2	3200	320	11	2021-1-9	3200
2	Inven222<Inven22<Inven2	5000	1000	11	2021-1-9	8200
3	PPUK parts<ASD parts<Inven2	4800	1200	11	2021-1-9	13000
4	PPGH parts<ASD parts<Inven2	3800	1900	11	2021-1-9	16800
5	Inven221<Inven22<Inven2	-2900	-290	13	2021-1-11	13900
6	Inven222<Inven22<Inven2	-4700	-940	13	2021-1-11	9200
7	PPUK parts<ASD parts<Inven2	-2600	-650	13	2021-1-11	6600
8	PPGH parts<ASD parts<Inven2	-3100	-1550	14	2021-1-15	3500
9	PPUK parts<ASD parts<Inven2	6500	1625	19	2021-1-22	10000
10	PPGH parts<ASD parts<Inven2	6000	3000	19	2021-1-22	16000
11	PPUK parts<ASD parts<Inven2	-3300	-825	20	2021-1-23	12700
12	PPGH parts<ASD parts<Inven2	-3900	-1950	20	2021-1-23	8800
12	PPUK parts<ASD parts<Inven2	-3000	-750	21	2021-1-25	5800
14	PPGH parts<ASD parts<Inven2	-1800	-900	21	2021-1-25	4000
15	PPUK parts<ASD parts<Inven2	-2200	-550	23	2021-1-29	1800

Two-level on a **medium** card

Inven22 (X1030202) << Parent account: Inventory (X103)

ID	MultiName	Amount	Unit	GeID	TransDate	Balance
1	Inven221<Inven22<Inven2	3200	320	11	2021-1-9	3200

2	Inven222<Inven22< Inven2	5000	1000	11	2021-1-9	8200
3	Inven221<Inven22<Inven2	-2900	-290	13	2021-1-11	5300
4	Inven222<Inven22<Inven2	-4700	-940	13	2021-1-11	600

Three-level on a **small** card

Inven221 (X103020201) <<< Parent account: Inventory (X103)

ID	MultiName	Amount	Unit	GeID	TransDate	Balance
1	Inven221<Inven22<Inven2	3200	320	11	2021-1-9	3200
2	Inven221<Inven22<Inven2	-2900	-290	13	2021-1-11	300

Three-level on a **small** card

Inven222 (X103020202) <<< Parent account: Inventory (X103)

ID	MultiName	Amount	Unit	GeID	TransDate	Balance
1	Inven222<Inven22<Inven2	5000	1000	11	2021-1-9	5000
2	Inven222<Inven22<Inven2	-4700	-940	13	2021-1-11	300

Two-level on **medium** card

ASD parts (X1030203) << Parent account: Inventory (X103)

ID	MultiName	Amount	Unit	GeID	TransDate	Balance
1	PPUK parts<ASD parts<Inven2	4800	1200	11	2021-1-9	4800
2	PPGH parts<ASD parts<Inven2	3800	1900	11	2021-1-9	8600
3	PPUK parts<ASD parts<Inven2	-2600	-650	13	2021-1-11	6000
4	PPGH parts<ASD parts<Inven2	-3100	-1550	14	2021-1-15	2900
5	PPUK parts<ASD parts<Inven2	6500	1625	19	2021-1-22	9400
6	PPGH parts<ASD parts<Inven2	6000	3000	19	2021-1-22	15400
7	PPUK parts<ASD parts<Inven2	-3300	-825	20	2021-1-23	12100
8	PPGH parts<ASD parts<Inven2	-3900	-1950	20	2021-1-23	8200
9	PPUK parts<ASD parts<Inven2	-3000	-750	21	2021-1-25	5200
10	PPGH parts<ASD parts<Inven2	-1800	-900	21	2021-1-25	3400
11	PPUK parts<ASD parts<Inven2	-2200	-550	23	2021-1-29	1200

Three-level on a **small** card

PPUK parts (X103020301) <<< Parent account: Inventory (X103)

ID	MultiName	Amount	Unit	GeID	TransDate	Balance
1	PPUK parts<ASD parts<Inven2	4800	1200	11	2021-1-9	4800
2	PPUK parts<ASD parts<Inven2	-2600	-650	13	2021-1-11	2200
3	PPUK parts<ASD parts<Inven2	6500	1625	19	2021-1-22	8700
4	PPUK parts<ASD parts<Inven2	-3300	-825	20	2021-1-23	5400
5	PPUK parts<ASD parts<Inven2	-3000	-750	21	2021-1-25	2400
6	PPUK parts<ASD parts<Inven2	-2200	-550	23	2021-1-29	200

Three-level on a **small** card

PPGH parts (X103020302) <<< Parent account: Inventory (X103)

ID	MultiName	Amount	Unit	GeID	TransDate	Balance
1	PPGH parts<ASD parts<Inven2	3800	1900	11	2021-1-9	3800
2	PPGH parts<ASD parts<Inven2	-3100	-1550	14	2021-1-15	700
3	PPGH parts<ASD parts<Inven2	6000	3000	19	2021-1-22	6700
4	PPGH parts<ASD parts<Inven2	-3900	-1950	20	2021-1-23	2800
5	PPGH parts<ASD parts<Inven2	-1800	-900	21	2021-1-25	1000

One-level on a **large** card

Inven3 (X10303) < Parent account: Inventory (X103)

ID	MultiName	Amount	Unit	GeID	TransDate	Balance
1	Inven31<Inven3	5300	530	11	2021-1-9	5300
2	Inven32<Inven3	2900	580	11	2021-1-9	8200
3	Inven331<Inven33<Inven3	2700	1350	12	2021-1-9	10900
4	Inven332<Inven33<Inven3	3100	620	12	2021-1-9	14000
5	HGFCVB parts<QASXC parts<Inven3	4900	490	12	2021-1-9	18900
6	PPGHUP parts<ASDUP parts<Inven3	1300	130	12	2021-1-9	20200
7	Inven32<Inven3	-1900	-380	13	2021-1-11	18300
8	HGFCVB parts<QASXC parts<Inven3	-4800	-480	13	2021-1-11	13500
9	PPGHUP parts<ASDUP parts<Inven3	-800	-80	13	2021-1-11	12700
10	Inven31<Inven3	-5000	-500	14	2021-1-15	7700
11	Inven331<Inven33<Inven3	-2200	-1100	14	2021-1-15	5500
12	Inven332<Inven33< Inven3	-2900	-580	14	2021-1-15	2600

13	Inven31<Inven3	5300	530	19	2021-1-22	7900
14	Inven32<Inven3	3700	740	19	2021-1-22	11600
15	Inven31<Inven3	-2500	-250	20	2021-1-23	9100
16	Inven32<Inven3	-2300	-460	20	2021-1-23	6800
17	Inven31<Inven3	-2700	-270	21	2021-1-25	4100
18	Inven32<Inven3	-1300	-260	23	2021-1-29	2800

Two-level on a **medium** card

Inven31 (X1030301) << Parent account: Inventory (X103)

ID	MultiName	Amount	Unit	GeID	TransDate	Balance
1	Inven31<Inven3	5300	530	12	2021-1-9	5300
2	Inven31<Inven3	-5000	-500	14	2021-1-15	300
3	Inven31<Inven3	5300	530	19	2021-1-22	5600
4	Inven31<Inven3	-2500	-250	20	2021-1-23	3100
5	Inven31<Inven3	-2700	-270	21	2021-1-25	400

Two-level on a **medium** card

Inven32 (X1030302) << Parent account: Inventory (X103)

ID	MultiName	Amount	Unit	GeID	TransDate	Balance
1	Inven32<Inven3	2900	580	12	2021-1-9	2900
2	Inven32<Inven3	-1900	-380	13	2021-1-11	1000
3	Inven32<Inven3	3700	740	19	2021-1-22	4700
4	Inven32<Inven3	-2300	-460	20	2021-1-23	2400
5	Inven32<Inven3	-1300	-260	23	2021-1-29	1100

Two-level on a **medium** card

Inven33 (X1030303) << Parent account: Inventory (X103)

ID	MultiName	Amount	Unit	GeID	TransDate	Balance
1	Inven331<Inven33<Inven3	2700	1350	12	2021-1-9	2700
2	Inven332<Inven33<Inven3	3100	620	12	2021-1-9	5800
3	Inven331<Inven33<Inven3	-2200	-1100	14	2021-1-15	3600
4	Inven332<Inven33<Inven3	-2900	-2900	14	2021-1-15	700

Three-level on a **small** card

Inven331 (X103030301) <<< Parent account: Inventory (X103)

ID	MultiName	Amount	Unit	GeID	TransDate	Balance
1	Inven331<Inven33<Inven3	2700	1350	12	2021-1-9	2700
2	Inven331<Inven33<Inven3	-2200	-1100	14	2021-1-15	500

Three-level on a **small** card

Inven332 (X103030302) << Parent account: Inventory (X103)

ID	MultiName	Amount	Unit	GeID	TransDate	Balance
1	Inven332<Inven33<Inven3	3100	620	12	2021-1-9	3100
2	Inven332<Inven33<Inven3	-2900	-580	14	2021-1-15	200

Two-level on a **medium** card

QASXC parts (X1030304) << Parent account: Inventory (X103)

ID	MultiName	Amount	Unit	GeID	TransDate	Balance
1	HGFCVB parts<QASXC parts<Inven3	4900	490	12	2021-1-9	4900
2	HGFCVB parts<QASXC parts<Inven3	-4800	-480	13	2021-1-11	100

Three-level on a **small** card

HGFCVB parts (X103030401) <<< Parent account: Inventory (X103)

ID	MultiName	Amount	Unit	GeID	TransDate	Balance
1	HGFCVB parts<QASXC parts<Inven3	4900	490	12	2021-1-9	4900
2	HGFCVB parts<QASXC parts<Inven3	-4800	-480	13	2021-1-11	100

Two-level on a **medium** card

ASDUP parts (X1030305) << Parent account: Inventory (X103)

ID	MultiName	Amount	Unit	GeID	TransDate	Balance
1	PPGHUP parts<ASDUP parts<Inven3	1300	130	12	2021-1-9	1300
2	PPGHUP parts<ASDUP parts<Inven3	-800	-80	13	2021-1-11	500

Three-level on a **small** card

PPGHUP parts (X103030501) <<< Parent account: Inventory (X103)

ID	MultiName	Amount	Unit	GeID	TransDate	Balance
1	PPGHUP parts<ASDUP parts<Inven3	1300	130	12	2021-1-9	1300
2	PPGHUP parts<ASDUP parts<Inven3	-800	-80	13	2021-1-11	500

One-level on a **large** card

Inven4 (X10304) < Parent account: Inventory (X103)

ID	MultiName	Amount	Unit	GeID	TransDate	Balance
1	Inven411<Inven41<Inven4	5100	1020	15	2021-1-17	5100
2	Inven412<Inven41<Inven4	3700	1850	15	2021-1-17	8800
3	TTTCU parts<TTT parts<Inven4	2300	1150	15	2021-1-17	11100
4	RRRHJK parts<Inven4	1400	700	15	2021-1-17	12500

Two-level on a **medium** card

Inven41 (X1030401) << Parent account: Inventory (X103)

ID	MultiName	Amount	Unit	GeID	TransDate	Balance
1	Inven411<Inven41<Inven4	5100	1020	15	2021-1-17	5100
2	Inven412<Inven41<Inven4	3700	1850	15	2021-1-17	8800

Three-level on a **small** card

Inven411 (X103040101) <<< Parent account: Inventory (X103)

ID	MultiName	Amount	Unit	GeID	TransDate	Balance
1	Inven411<Inven41<Inven4	5100	1020	15	2021-1-17	5100

Three-level on a **small** card

Inven412 (X103040102) <<< Parent account: Inventory (X103)

ID	MultiName	Amount	Unit	GeID	TransDate	Balance
1	Inven412<Inven41<Inven4	3700	1850	15	2021-1-17	3700

Two-level on a **medium** card

TTT parts (X1030402) << Parent account: Inventory (X103)

ID	MultiName	Amount	Unit	GeID	TransDate	Balance
1	TTTCU parts<TTT parts<Inven4	2300	1150	15	2021-1-17	2300

Three-level on a **small** card

TTTCU parts (X103040201) <<< Parent account: Inventory (X103)

ID	MultiName	Amount	Unit	GeID	TransDate	Balance
1	TTTCU parts<TTT parts<Inven4	2300	1150	15	2021-1-17	2300

Two-level on a **medium** card

RRRHJK parts (X1030403) << Parent account: Inventory (X103)

ID	MultiName	Amount	Unit	GeID	TransDate	Balance
1	RRRHJK parts<Inven4	1400	700	15	2021-1-17	1400

Table 2-11 Parent account: HST recoverable on a drawer

HST recoverable (X104)

ID	MultiName	TransDate	Amount	Balance	GeID	SubFirst	SubSecond	SubThird
1	N	2021-1-5	477.1	477.10	4			
2	N	2021-1-9	3250	3727.10	11			
3	N	2021-1-9	1560	5287.10	12			
4	N	2021-1-17	1625	6912.10	15			
5	N	2021-1-22	2795	9707.10	19			

Table 2-12 Parent account: Account receivable on a drawer

Account receivable (X105)

ID	MultiName	TransDate	Amount	Balance	GeID	SubFirst	SubSecond	SubThird	Ref
1	123456789	2021-1-5	2558.90	2558.90	5	123456789			
2	123456789	2021-1-7	-1500	1058.90	6	123456789			5

3	123456788	2021-1-11	29835	30893.90	13	123456788			
4	123456787	2021-1-15	24521	55414.90	14	123456787			
5	123456788	2021-1-17	-21000	34414.90	16	123456788			13
6	123456787	2021-1-23	22487	56901.90	20	123456787			
7	123456786	2021-1-25	15481	72382.90	21	123456786			
8	123456789	2021-1-29	7006	79388.90	23	123456789			
9	123456789	2021-1-30	-828.90	76830	24	123456789			5
10	123456789	2021-1-30	-1730	76830	24	123456789			23
11	123456787	2021-1-30	-15000	61830	25	123456787			14
12	123456786	2021-1-30	-8475	53355	26	123456786			21
13	123456787	2021-1-31	-13000	40355	33	123456787			20

One-level on a **large** card

123456789 (X10501) < Parent account: Account receivable (X105)

ID	MultiName	Amount	Ref	GeID	TransDate	Balance
1	123456789	2558.90		5	2021-1-5	2558.90
2	123456789	-1500	5	6	2021-1-7	1058.90
3	123456789	7006		23	2021-1-29	8064.9
4	123456789	-828.90	5	24	2021-1-30	7236
5	123456789	-1730	23	24	2021-1-30	5506

One-level on a **large** card

123456788 (X10502) < Parent account: Account receivable (X105)

ID	MultiName	Amount	Ref	GeID	TransDate	Balance
1	123456788	29835		13	2021-1-11	29835
2	123456788	-21000	13	16	2021-1-17	8835

One-level on a **large** card

123456787 (X10503) < Parent account: Account receivable (X105)

ID	MultiName	Amount	Ref	GeID	TransDate	Balance
1	123456787	24521		14	2021-1-15	24521
2	123456787	22487		20	2021-1-23	47008
3	123456787	-15000	14	25	2021-1-30	32008
4	123456787	-13000	20	33	2021-1-31	19008

One-level on a **large** card

123456786 (X10504) < Parent account: Account receivable (X105)

ID	MultiName	Amount	Ref	GeID	TransDate	Balance
1	123456786	15481		21	2021-1-25	15481
2	123456786	-8475	**21**	26	2021-1-30	7006

Table 2-13 Parent account: Land on a drawer

Land (X106)

ID	MultiName	TransDate	Amount	Balance	GeID	SubFirst	SubSecond	SubThird
1	Land1, Downtown	2021-1-7	270000	270000	8	Land1, Downtown		
2	Land2, North York	2021-1-7	180000	450000	8	Land2, North York		

One-level on a **large** card

Land1, Downtown (X10601) < Parent account: Land (X106)

ID	MultiName	Amount	Unit	GeID	TransDate	Balance
1	Land1, Downtown	270000	1	8	2021-1-7	270000

One-level on a **large** card

Land2, North York (X10602) < Parent account: Land (X106)

ID	MultiName	Amount	Unit	GeID	TransDate	Balance
1	Land2, North York	180000	1	8	2021-1-7	180000

Table 2-14 Parent account: Truck on a drawer

Truck (X107)

ID	MultiName	TransDate	Amount	Balance	GeID	SubFirst	SubSecond	SubThird
1	Truck1	2021-1-8	45000	45000	9	Truck1		

One-level on a **large** card

Truck1 (X10701) < Parent account: Truck (X107)

ID	MultiName	Amount	Unit	GeID	TransDate	Balance
1	Truck1	45000	1	9	2021-1-8	45000

Table 2-15 Parent account: Computer on a drawer

Computer (X108)

ID	MultiName	TransDate	Amount	Balance	GeID	SubFirst	SubSecond	SubThird
1	Computer1	2021-1-28	1600	1600	22	Computer1		
2	Computer server1	2021-1-28	1800	3400	22	Computer server1		
3	POS system1	2021-1-28	2200	5600	22	POS system1		

One-level on a **large** card

Computer1 (X10801) < Parent account: Computer (X108)

ID	MultiName	Amount	Unit	GeID	TransDate	Balance
1	Computer1	1600	1	22	2021-1-28	1600

One-level on a **large** card

Computer server1 (X10802) < Parent account: Computer (X108)

ID	MultiName	Amount	Unit	GeID	TransDate	Balance
1	Computer server1	1800	1	22	2021-1-28	1800

One-level on a **large** card

POS system1 (X10803) < Parent account: Computer (X108)

ID	MultiName	Amount	Unit	GeID	TransDate	Balance
1	POS system1	2200	1	22	2021-1-28	2200

Table 2-16 Parent account: Accumulated amortization: truck on a drawer

Accumulated amortization: truck (X109)

ID	MultiName	TransDate	Amount	Balance	GeID	SubFirst	SubSecond	SubThird
1	Truck1-accumulated amortization	2021-1-31	-750	-750	38	Truck1-accumulated amortization		

One-level on a **large** card

Truck1-accumulated amortization (X10901) < Parent account: Accumulated amortization: truck (X109)

ID	MultiName	Amount	Unit	GeID	TransDate	Balance
1	Truck1-accumulated amortization	-750	1	38	2021-1-31	-750

Table 2-17 Parent account: Accumulated amortization: computer on a drawer

Accumulated amortization: computer (X110)

ID	MultiName	TransDate	Amount	Balance	GeID	SubFirst	SubSecond	SubThird
1	Computer1-accumulated amortization	2021-1-31	-33.33	-33.33	39	Computer1-accumulated amortization		
2	Computer server1-accumulated amortization	2021-1-31	-37.50	-70.83	39	Computer server1-accumulated amortization		
3	POS system1-accumulated amortization	2021-1-31	-30.56	-101.39	39	POS system1-accumulated amortization		

One-level on a **large** card

Computer1-accumulated amortization (X1101) < Parent account: Accumulated amortization: computer (X110)

ID	MultiName	Amount	Unit	GeID	TransDate	Balance
1	Computer1-accumulated amortization	-33.33	1	39	2021-1-31	-33.33

One-level on a **large** card

Computer server1-accumulated amortization (X1102) < Parent account: Accumulated amortization: computer (X110)

ID	MultiName	Amount	Unit	GeID	TransDate	Balance
1	Computer server1-accumulated amortization	-37.5	1	39	2021-1-31	-37.5

One-level on a **large** card

POS system1-accumulated amortization (*10803) < Parent account: Accumulated amortization: computer (X110)

ID	MultiName	Amount	Unit	GeID	TransDate	Balance
1	POS system1-accumulated amortization	-30.56	1	39	2021-1-31	-30.56

In the second cabinet, there are the following tables.

Table 2-18 Liabilities (X2) on the door

ID	Account Name (Mathematical Name)	Subtotal	Ref (Row)	Balance
1	Account payable (X201)	Current liabilities,203	204	46207.10
2	HST payable (X202)	Current liabilities,203	205	12158.90
3	Note payable (X203)	Current liabilities,203	207	500000.00
4	Accrued interest payable (X204)	Long term liabilities,203	252	3000.00

Table 2-19 Parent account: Account payable on a drawer

Account payable (X201)

ID	MultiName	TransDate	Amount	Balance	GeID	SubFirst	SubSecond	SubThird	Ref
1	987654321	2021-1-5	3477.10	3477.10	4	987654321			
2	987654322	2021-1-9	26250	29727.10	11	987654322			
3	987654323	2021-1-9	13560	43287.10	12	987654323			
4	987654324	2021-1-17	14125	57412.10	15	987654324			
5	987654322	2021-1-21	-14000	43412.10	17	987654322			11
6	987654323	2021-1-21	-6000	37412.10	18	987654323			12
7	987654322	2021-1-22	24295	61707.10	19	987654322			
8	987654322	2021-1-30	-7500	5420410	27	987654322			11
9	987654324	2021-1-31	-8000	46207.10	34	987654324			15

One-level on a **large** card

987654321 (X20101) < Parent account: Account payable (X201)

ID	MultiName	Amount	Ref	GeID	TransDate	Balance
1	987654321	3477.10		4	2021-1-5	3477.10

One-level on a **large** card

987654322 (X20102) < Parent account: Account payable (X201)

ID	MultiName	Amount	Ref	GeID	TransDate	Balance
1	987654322	26250		11	2021-1-9	26250
2	987654322	-14000	**11**	18	2021-1-21	12250
3	987654322	24295		19	2021-1-22	36545
4	987654322	-7500	**11**	27	2021-1-30	29045

One-level on a **large** card

987654323 (X20103) < Parent account: Account payable (X201)

ID	MultiName	Amount	Ref	GeID	TransDate	Balance
1	987654323	13560		12	2021-1-9	13560
2	987654323	-6000	**12**	18	2021-1-21	7560

One-level on a **large** card

987654324 (X20104) < Parent account: Account payable (X201)

ID	MultiName	Amount	Ref	GeID	TransDate	Balance
1	987654324	14125		15	2021-1-17	14125
2	987654324	-8000	**15**	34	2021-1-31	6125

Table 2-20 Parent account: HST payable on a drawer

HST payable (X202)

ID	MultiName	TransDate	Amount	Balance	GeID	SubFirst	SubSecond	SubThird
1	N	2021-1-5	328.90	328.90	5			
2	N	2021-1-11	3835	4163.90	13			
3	N	2021-1-15	2821	6984.90	14			
4	N	2021-1-23	2587	9571.90	20			
5	N	2021-1-25	1781	11352.90	21			
6	N	2021-1-29	806	12158.9	23			

Table 2-21 Parent account: Note payable on a drawer

Note payable (X203)

ID	MultiName	TransDate	Amount	Balance	GeID	SubFirst	SubSecond	SubThird
1	N	2021-1-7	500000	500000	7			

Table 2-22 Parent account: Accrued interest payable on a drawer

Accrued interest payable (X204)

ID	MultiName	TransDate	Amount	Balance	GeID	SubFirst	SubSecond	SubThird
1	Note1-TD bank	2021-1-31	3000	3000	43	Note1-TD bank		

One-level on a **large** card

Note1-TD bank (X20401) < Parent account: Accrued interest payable (X204)

ID	MultiName	Amount	Ref	GeID	TransDate	Balance
1	Note1-TD bank	3000		43	2021-1-31	3000

In the third cabinet, there are the following tables.

Table 2-23 Shareholders' Equity (X3) on the door

ID	Account Name (Mathematical Name)	Subtotal	Ref (Row)	Balance
1	Share capital (X301)	Owners' Capital,303	304	100000

Table 2-24 Parent account: Share capital on a drawer

Share capital (X301)

ID	MultiName	TransDate	Amount	Balance	GeID	SubFirst	SubSecond	SubThird
1	Capital-Ping Wang	2021-1-2	40000	40000	1	Capital-Ping Wang		
2	Capital-Hua Li	2021-1-2	30000	70000	1	Capital-Hua Li		
3	Capital-Mike Newsome	2021-1-2	30000	100000	1	Capital-Mike Newsome		

One-level on a **large** card

Capital-Ping Wang (X30101) < Parent account: Share capital (X301)

ID	MultiName	Amount	Unit	GeID	TransDate	Balance
1	Capital-Ping Wang	40000	1	1	2021-1-2	40000

One-level on a **large** card

Capital- Hua Li (X30102) < Parent account: Share capital (X301)

ID	MultiName	Amount	Unit	GeID	TransDate	Balance
1	Capital-Hua Li	30000	1	1	2021-1-2	30000

One-level on a **large** card

Capital-Mike Newsome (X30103) < Parent account: Share capital (X301)

ID	MultiName	Amount	Unit	GeID	TransDate	Balance
1	Capital- Mike Newsome	30000	1	1	2021-1-2	30000

In the fourth cabinet, there are following tables.

Table 2-25 Revenue (X4) on the door

ID	Account Name (Mathematical Name)	Subtotal	Ref (Row)	Balance
1	Sales (X401)	Owners' Capital,303	404	93530.00

Table 2-26 Parent accounts: Sales on a drawer

Sales (X401)

ID	MultiName	TransDate	Amount	Balance	GeID	SubFirst	SubSecond	SubThird
1	Xiao Zhou-sales	2021-1-5	2530	2530	5	Xiao Zhou-sales		
2	Xiao Zhou-sales	2021-1-11	29500	32030	13	Xiao Zhou-sales		
3	ZhenDao Yuan-sales	2021-1-15	21700	53730	14	ZhenDao Yuan-sales		
4	Yi Liu-sales	2021-1-23	19900	73630	20	Yi Liu-sales		
5	ZhenDao Yuan-sales	2021-1-25	13700	87330	21	ZhenDao Yuan-sales		
6	Jun Wang-sales	2021-1-29	6200	93530	23	Jun Wang-sales		

One-level on a **large** card

Xiao Zhou-sales (X40101) < Parent account: Sales (X401)

ID	MultiName	Amount	Unit	GeID	TransDate	Balance
1	Xiao Zhou-sales	2530	1	5	2021-1-5	2530
2	Xiao Zhou-sales	29500	1	13	2021-1-11	32030

One-level on a **large** card

ZhenDao Yuan-sales (X40102) < Parent account: Sales (X401)

ID	MultiName	Amount	Unit	GeID	TransDate	Balance
1	Xiao Zhou-sales	21700	1	14	2021-1-15	21700
2	Xiao Zhou-sales	13700	1	21	2021-1-25	35400

One-level on a **large** card

Yi Liu-sales (X40103) < Parent account: Sales (X401)

ID	MultiName	Amount	Unit	GeID	TransDate	Balance
1	Yi Liu-sales	19900	1	20	2021-1-23	19900

One-level on a **large** card

Jun Wang-sales (X40104) < Parent account: Sales (X401)

ID	MultiName	Amount	Unit	GeID	TransDate	Balance
1	Jun Wang-sales	6200	1	23	2021-1-29	6200

In the fifth cabinet, there are following tables.

Table 2-27 Expenses (X5) on the door

ID	Account Name (Mathematical Name)	Subtotal	Ref (Row)	Balance
1	Administrative expenses (X501)	Operating and administrative expenses,453	454	-2586.89
2	Cost of sales (X502)	Cost,431	432	-55800.00
3	Salary expenses (X503)	Operating and administrative expenses,453	459	-18756.00

4	Amortization expenses (X504)	Operating and administrative expenses,453	458	-851.39
5	Office rent expenses (X505)	Operating and administrative expenses,453	459	-1500
6	Interest expenses (X506)	Operating and administrative expenses,453	461	-3000.00

Table 2-28 Parent accounts: Administrative expenses on a drawer

Administrative expenses (X501)

ID	MultiName	TransDate	Amount	Balance	GeID	SubFirst	SubSecond	SubThird
1	Hua Li-taxi<Purchase department-taxi<Taxi expenses	2021-1-3	-47	-47	3	Taxi expenses	Purchase Department-taxi	Hua Li-taxi
2	Ping Wang-open company<Office department-open company<Other expenses	2021-1-8	-367	-414	10	Other expenses	Office department-open company	Ping Wang-open company
3	Dan Zhu-taxi< Purchase department-taxi<Taxi expenses	2021-1-30	-178	-592	28	Taxi expenses	Purchase department-taxi	Dan Zhu-taxi
4	Dan Zhu-mobile< Purchase department-mobile <Mobile expenses	2021-1-30	-54.76	-646.76	28	Mobile expenses	Purchase department-mobile	Dan Zhu-mobile
5	Hua Li-taxi<Purchase department-taxi<Taxi expenses	2021-1-30	-135.12	-781.88	29	Taxi expenses	Purchase department-taxi	Hua Li-taxi
6	Hua Li-other< Purchase department-other<Other expenses	2021-1-30	-86.18	-868.06	29	Other expenses	Purchase department-other	Hua Li-other
7	Xiao Zhou-taxi<Sales department-taxi<Taxi expenses	2021-1-30	-243	-1111.06	30	Taxi expenses	Sales department-taxi	Xiao Zhou-taxi
8	Xiao Zhou-other< Sales department-other<Other expenses	2021-1-30	-96.52	-1207.58	30	Other expenses	Purchase department-other	Xiao Zhou-other
9	Jun Wang-other< Sales department-other<Other expenses	2021-1-30	-132.26	-1339.84	31	Other expenses	Purchase department-other	Jun Wang-other
10	Zhendao Yuan-other<Sales department-other <Other expenses	2021-1-30	-82.33	-1422.17	32	Other expenses	Sales department-other	Zhendao Yuan-other
11	Yi Liu-taxi<Sales department-taxi<Taxi expenses	2021-1-30	-347.70	1769.87	35	Taxi expenses	Sales department-taxi	Yi Liu-taxi
12	Yi Liu-other<Sales department-other< Other expenses	2021-1-31	-71.85	-1841.72	35	Other expenses	Sales department-other	Yi Liu-other
13	Office supplies expenses	2021-1-31	-88	-1929.72	36	Office supplies expenses		

14	Mike Newsome-taxi<Office department-taxi<Taxi expenses	2021-1-31	-238.69	-2228.41	40	Taxi expenses	Office department-taxi	Mike Newsome-taxi
15	Mike Newsome-other<Office department-other<Other expenses	2021-1-31	-77.78	-2306.19	40	Other expenses	Office department-other	Mike Newsome-other
16	Utility expenses	2021-1-31	-280.70	-2586.89	41	Utility expenses		

One-level on a **large** card

Taxi expenses (X50101) < Parent account: Administrative expenses (X501)

ID	MultiName	Amount	Unit	GeID	TransDate	Balance
1	Hua Li-taxi<Purchase department-taxi<Taxi expenses	-47	1	3	2021-1-3	-47
2	Dan Zhu-taxi<Purchase department-taxi<Taxi expenses	-178	1	28	2021-1-30	-225
3	Hua Li-taxi<Purchase department-taxi<Taxi expenses	-135.12	1	29	2021-1-30	-360.12
4	Xiao Zhou-taxi<Sales department-taxi<Taxi expenses	-243	1	30	2021-1-30	-603.12
5	Yi Liu-taxi<Sales department-taxi<Taxi expenses	-347.70	1	35	2021-1-31	-950.82
6	Mike Newsome-taxi<Office department-taxi<Taxi expenses	-298.69	1	40	2021-1-31	-1249.51

Two-level on a **medium** card

Purchase department-taxi (X5010101) << Administrative expenses (X501)

ID	MultiName	Amount	Unit	GeID	TransDate	Balance
1	Hua Li-taxi<Purchase department-taxi<Taxi expenses	-47	1	3	2021-1-3	-47
2	Dan Zhu-taxi<Purchase department-taxi<Taxi expenses	-178	1	28	2021-1-30	-225
3	Hua Li-taxi<Purchase department-taxi<Taxi expenses	-135.12	1	29	2021-1-30	-360.12

Three-level on a **small** card

Hua Li-taxi (X501010101) <<< Administrative expenses (X501)

ID	MultiName	Amount	Unit	GeID	TransDate	Balance
1	Hua Li-taxi	-47	1	3	2021-1-3	-47
2	Hua Li-taxi	-135.12	1	29	2021-1-30	-182.12

Three-level on a **small** card

Dan Zhu-taxi (X501010102) <<< Administrative expenses (X501)

ID	MultiName	Amount	Unit	GeID	TransDate	Balance
1	Dan Zhu-taxi	-178	1	28	2021-1-30	-178

Two-level on a **medium** card

Sales department-taxi (X5010102) << Administrative expenses (X501)

ID	MultiName	Amount	Unit	GeID	TransDate	Balance
1	Xiao Zhou-taxi<Sales department-taxi<Taxi expenses	-243	1	30	2021-1-30	-243
2	Yi Liu-taxi<Sales department-taxi<Taxi expenses	-347.70	1	35	2021-1-31	-590.70

Three-level on a **small** card

Xiao Zhou-taxi (X501010201) <<< Administrative expenses (X501)

ID	MultiName	Amount	Unit	GeID	TransDate	Balance
1	Xiao Zhou-taxi<Sales department-taxi<Taxi expenses	-243	1	30	2021-1-30	-243

Three-level on a **small** card

Yi Liu-taxi (X501010202) <<< Administrative expenses (X501)

ID	MultiName	Amount	Unit	GeID	TransDate	Balance
1	Yi Liu-taxi<Sales department-taxi<Taxi expenses	-347.70	1	35	2021-1-31	-347.70

Two-level on a **medium** card

Office department-taxi (X5010103) << Administrative expenses (X501)

ID	MultiName	Amount	Unit	GeID	TransDate	Balance
1	Mike Newsome-taxi<Office department-taxi<Taxi expenses	-298.69	1	40	2021-1-31	-298.69

Three-level on a **small** card

Mike Newsome-taxi (X501010301) <<< Administrative expenses (X501)

ID	MultiName	Amount	Unit	GeID	TransDate	Balance
1	Mike Newsome-taxi<Office department-taxi<Taxi expenses	-298.69	1	40	2021-1-31	-298.69

One-level on a **large** card

Other expenses (X50102) < Parent account: Administrative expenses (X501)

ID	MultiName	Amount	Unit	GeID	TransDate	Balance
1	Ping Wang-open company<Office department-open company<Other expenses	-367	1	10	2021-1-8	-367
2	Hua Li-other<Purchase department-other<Other expenses	-86.18	1	29	2021-1-30	-453.18
3	Xiao Zhou-other<Sales department-other<Other expenses	-96.52	1	30	2021-1-30	-549.70
4	Jun Wang-other<Sales department-other<Other expenses	-132.26	1	31	2021-1-30	-681.96
5	Zhendao Yuan-other<Sales department-other<Other expenses	-82.33	1	32	2021-1-30	-764.29
6	Yi Liu-other<Sales department-other<Other expenses	-71.85	1	35	2021-1-31	-836.14
7	Mike Newsome-other<Office department-other<Other expenses	-77.78	1	40	2021-1-31	-913.92

Two-level on a **medium** card

Office department-open company (X5010201) << Administrative expenses (X501)

ID	MultiName	Amount	Unit	GeID	TransDate	Balance
1	Ping Wang-open company<Office department-open company<Other expenses	-367	1	10	2021-1-8	-367

Three-level on a **small** card

Ping Wang-open company (X501020101) <<< Administrative expenses (X501)

ID	MultiName	Amount	Unit	GeID	TransDate	Balance
1	Ping Wang-open company<Office department-open company<Other expenses	-367	1	10	2021-1-8	-367

Two-level on a **medium** card

Purchase department-other (X5010202) << Administrative expenses (X501)

ID	MultiName	Amount	Unit	GeID	TransDate	Balance
1	Hua Li-other<Purchase department-other<Other expenses	-86.18	1	29	2021-1-30	-86.18

Three-level on a **small** card

Hua Li-other (X501020201) <<< Administrative expenses (X501)

ID	MultiName	Amount	Unit	GeID	TransDate	Balance
1	Hua Li-other<Purchase department-other<Other expenses	-86.18	1	29	2021-1-30	-86.18

Two-level on a **medium** card

Sales department-other (X5010203) << Administrative expenses (X501)

ID	MultiName	Amount	Unit	GeID	TransDate	Balance
1	Xiao Zhou-other<Sales department-other<Other expenses	-96.52	1	30	2021-1-30	-96.53
2	Jun Wang-other<Sales department-other<Other expenses	-132.26	1	31	2021-1-30	-228.78
3	Zhendao Yuan-other<Sales department-other<Other expenses	-82.33	1	32	2021-1-30	-311.11
4	Yi Liu-other<Sales department-other<Other expenses	-71.85	1	35	2021-1-31	-382.96

Three-level on a **small** card

Xiao Zhou-other (X501020301) <<< Administrative expenses (X501)

ID	MultiName	Amount	Unit	GeID	TransDate	Balance
1	Xiao Zhou-other<Sales department-other<Other expenses	-96.52	1	30	2021-1-30	-96.52

Three-level on a **small** card

Jun Wang-other (X501020302) <<< Administrative expenses (X501)

ID	MultiName	Amount	Unit	GeID	TransDate	Balance
1	Jun Wang-other<Sales department-other<Other expenses	-132.26	1	31	2021-1-30	-132.26

Three-level on a **small** card

Zhendao Yuan-other (X501020303) <<< Administrative expenses (X501)

ID	MultiName	Amount	Unit	GeID	TransDate	Balance
1	Zhendao Yuan-other<Sales department-other<Other expenses	-82.33	1	32	2021-1-30	-82.23

Three-level on a **small** card

Yi Liu-other (X501020304) <<< Administrative expenses (X501)

ID	MultiName	Amount	Unit	GeID	TransDate	Balance
1	Yi Liu-other<Sales department-other<Other expenses	-71.85	1	35	2021-1-31	-71.85

Two-level on a **medium** card

Office department-other (X5010204) << Administrative expenses (X501)

ID	MultiName	Amount	Unit	GeID	TransDate	Balance
1	Mike Newsome-other<Office department-other<Other expenses	-77.78	1	40	2021-1-31	-77.78

Three-level on a **small** card

Mike Newsome-other (X501020401) <<< Administrative expenses (X501)

ID	MultiName	Amount	Unit	GeID	TransDate	Balance
1	Mike Newsome-other<Office department-other<Other expenses	-77.78	1	40	2021-1-31	-77.78

One-level on a **large** card

Mobile expenses(X50103) < Parent account: Administrative expenses (X501)

ID	MultiName	Amount	Unit	GeID	TransDate	Balance
1	Dan Zhu-mobile<Purchase department-mobile <Mobile expenses	-54.76	1	28	2021-1-30	-54.76

Two-level on a **medium** card

Purchase department-mobile (X5010301) << Administrative expenses (X501)

ID	MultiName	Amount	Unit	GeID	TransDate	Balance
1	Dan Zhu-mobile<Purchase department-mobile<Mobile expenses	-54.76	1	28	2021-1-30	-54.76

Three-level on a **small** card

Dan Zhu-mobile (X501030101) <<< Administrative expenses (X501)

ID	MultiName	Amount	Unit	GeID	TransDate	Balance
1	Dan Zhu-mobile<Purchase department-mobile<Mobile expenses	-54.76	1	28	2021-1-30	-54.76

One-level on a **large** card

Office supplies expenses (X50104) < Parent account: Administrative expenses (X501)

ID	MultiName	Amount	Unit	GeID	TransDate	Balance
1	Office supplies expenses	-88	1	36	2021-1-31	-88

One-level on a **large** card

Utility expenses (X50105) < Parent account: Administrative expenses (X501)

ID	MultiName	Amount	Unit	GeID	TransDate	Balance
1	Utility expenses	-280.70	1	41	2021-1-31	-280.70

Table 2-29 Parent accounts: Cost of sales on a drawer

Cost of sales (X502)

ID	MultiName	TransDate	Amount	Balance	GeID	SubFirst	SubSecond	SubThird
1	N	2021-1-5	-1900	-1900	5			
2	N	2021-1-11	-17700	-19600	13			
3	N	2021-1-15	-13200	-32800	14			
4	N	2021-1-23	-12000	-44800	20			
5	N	2021-1-25	-7500	-52300	21			
6	N	2021-1-29	-3500	-55800	23			

Table 2-30 Parent accounts: Salary expenses on a drawer

Salary expenses (X503)

ID	MultiName	TransDate	Amount	Balance	GeID	SubFirst	SubSecond	SubThird
1	n	2021-1-31	-18756	-18756	37			

Table 2-31 Parent accounts: Amortization expenses on a drawer

Amortization expenses (X504)

ID	MultiName	TransDate	Amount	Balance	GeID	SubFirst	SubSecond	SubThird
1	Truck1-amortization	2021-1-31	-750	-750	38	Truck1-amortization		
2	Computer1-amortization<Computer-amortization	2021-1-31	-33.33	-783.33	39	Computer-amortization	Computer1-amortization	
3	Computer server1-amortization<Computer-amortization	2021-1-31	-37.50	-820.83	39	Computer-amortization	Computer server1-amortization	
4	POS system1-amortization< Computer-amortization	2021-1-31	-30.56	-851.39	39	Computer-amortization	POS system1-amortization	

One-level on a **large** card

Truck1-amortization (X50401) < Parent account: Amortization expenses (X504)

ID	MultiName	Amount	Unit	GeID	TransDate	Balance
1	Truck1-amortization	-750	1	38	2021-1-31	-750

One-level on a **large** card

Computer-amortization (X50402) < Parent account: Amortization expenses (X504)

ID	MultiName	Amount	Unit	GeID	TransDate	Balance
1	Computer1-amortization<Computer-amortization	-33.33	1	39	2021-1-31	-33.33
2	Computer server1-amortization<Computer-amortization	-37.50	1	39	2021-1-31	-70.83
3	POS system1-amortization< Computer-amortization	-30.56	1	39	2021-1-31	-101.39

Two-level on a **medium** card

Computer1-amortization (X5040201) << Amortization expenses (X504)

ID	MultiName	Amount	Unit	GeID	TransDate	Balance
1	Computer1-amortization<Computer-amortization	-33.33	1	39	2021-1-31	-33.33

Two-level on a **medium** card

Computer server1-amortization (X5040202) << Amortization expenses (X504)

ID	MultiName	Amount	Unit	GeID	TransDate	Balance
1	Computer server1-amortization<Computer-amortization	-37.50	1	39	2021-1-31	-37.50

Two-level on a **medium** card

POS system1-amortization (X5040203) << Amortization expenses (X504)

ID	MultiName	Amount	Unit	GeID	TransDate	Balance
1	POS system1-amortization< Computer-amortization	-30.56	1	39	2021-1-31	-30.56

Table 2-32 Parent accounts: Office rent expenses on a drawer

Office rent expenses (X505)

ID	MultiName	TransDate	Amount	Balance	GeID	SubFirst	SubSecond	SubThird
1	N	2021-1-31	-1500	-1500	42			

Table 2-33 Parent accounts: Interest expenses on a drawer

Interest expenses (X506)

ID	MultiName	TransDate	Amount	Balance	GeID	SubFirst	SubSecond	SubThird
1	N	2021-1-31	-3000	-3000	43			

For checking whether the recording data is reliable and correct, I will do the following three calculations which also ensure integrity of the recorded data.

- Check whether the dynamic accounting equation is equal.

From the Table 2-1, I get the left balance $672,401.72 and the right balance $672,401.72 of the dynamic accounting equation on January 31, 2021 when the all general equations are added together. These two amounts are equal.

- Check whether the sum of all assets accounts' balances is equal to the sum of all liabilities accounts, all equity accounts, all incomes accounts, and all expenses accounts' balances.

For all Assets accounts:

From the Table 2-8, I get that the balance of the parent account "Cash" is $103,616.01.

From the Table 2-9, I get that the balance of the parent account "Office supplies" is $105.

From the Table 2-10, I get that the balance of the parent account "Inventory" is $18,870.

From the Table 2-11, I get that the balance of the parent account "HST recoverable" is $9707.10.

From the Table 2-12, I get that the balance of the parent account "Account receivable" is $40,355.

From the Table 2-13, I get that the balance of the parent account "Land" is $450,000.

From the Table 2-14, I get that the balance of the parent account "Truck" is $45,000.

From the Table 2-15, I get that the balance of the parent account "Computer" is $5,600.

From the Table 2-16, I get that the balance of the parent account "Accumulated amortization: truck" is -$750.

From the Table 2-17, I get that the balance of the parent account "Accumulated amortization: computer" is -$101.39

Therefore, the sum of the assets accounts' balances is $672,401.72 (= $103,616.01 + $105 + $18,870 + $9,707.10 + $40,355+ $450,000 + $45,000 + $5,600 - $750 - $101.39).

Of course, I can also get that the sum of the assets accounts' balances is $672,401.72 from the table "Assets (X1)" in the Table 2-7.

For all liabilities accounts:

From the Table 2-19, I get that the balance of the parent account "Account payable" is $46,207.10.

From the Table 2-20, I get that the balance of the parent account "HST payable" is $12,158.90.

From the Table 2-21, I get that the balance of the parent account "Note payable" is $500,000.

From the Table 2-22, I get that the balance of the parent account "Accrued interest payable" is $3,000

Therefore, the total sum of the liabilities accounts' balances is $561,366 (= $46,207.10 + $12,158.90 + $500,000 + $3,000).

Of course, I can also get that the sum of the liabilities accounts' balances is $561,366 from the table "Liabilities (X2)" in the Table 2-18.

For all Shareholders' equity accounts:

From the Table 2-24, I get that the balance of the parent account "Share capital" is $100,000.

Therefore, the sum of the shareholders' equity account's balance is $100,000.

Of course, I can also get that the sum of the "Shareholders' equity" account's balance is $100,000 from the table "Shareholders' equity (X3)" in the Table 2-23.

For all Revenues accounts:

From the Table 2-26, I get that the balance of the parent account "Sales" is $93.530.

Therefore, the sum of the revenues account's balance is $93,530.

Of course, I can also get that the sum of the revenues account's balance is $93,530 from the table "Revenues (X4)" in the Table 2-25.

For all Expenses accounts:

From the Table 2-28, I get that the balance of the parent account "Administrative expenses" is -$2,586.89.

From the Table 2-29, I get that the balance of the parent account "Cost of sales" is -$55,800.

From the Table 2-30, I get that the balance of the parent account "Salary expenses" is -$18,755.

From the Table 2-31, I get that the balance of the parent account "Amortization expenses" is -$851.39.

From the Table 2-32, I get that the balance of the parent account "Office rent expenses" is -$1,500.

From the Table 2-33, I get that the balance of the parent account "Interest expenses" is -$3,000.

Therefore, the sum of the expenses accounts' balances is -$82,494.28 (= -$2,586.89 - $55,800 - $18,756 - $851.39 - $1,500 - $3,000).

Of course, I can also get that the sum of the expenses accounts' balances is -$82,494.28 from the table "Expenses (X5)" in the Table 2-27.

The sum of all liabilities accounts, all shareholders' equity accounts, all revenues accounts, and all expenses accounts is $672,401.72 (= $561,366 + $100,000 + $93,530 - $82,494.28).

The sum of all assets accounts is also $672,401.72.

These two sum amounts are equal. They are $672,401.72.

- After the previous two steps are correct, I check whether the left (or right) amount of the dynamic accounting equation is equal to the sum of all assets accounts' balances (or the sum of all liabilities, all equity accounts, all incomes accounts, and all expenses accounts' balances).

     Obviously, the requirement is satisfied.

     The above three requirements are satisfied, so the mathematical accounting model is reliable and correct.

May you ask me why I do not check the subaccounts' tables? This is good question. The final goal of building mathematical accounting model is to program a software. I have researched and developped this mathematical accounting model and its MathAccounting software. When I enter all above transactions into a database by using of the MathAccounting software, the MathAccounting software does not create any subaccount's table. These subaccounts' tables are created in this database by using of the "New Query" of the SQL Server or the Oracle. If checking all tables in this database is right, then the created tables are also right.

     The financial statements are actually a summary of the economic events or performance of a company during a period. The RR Company has the tax rate of the 0.3. I will create the four tables of the Income Statement, the Balance Sheet, the Cash Flows, and the Account Flows.

     From the Table 2-2, I can get the some amounts of the Income Statement, seeing the following table 2-34.

Table 2-34 Income Statement

	Month ended on 1/31/2021	
1	Revenues	
2	Sales	$93,530.00
3	Cost	
4	Cost of sales	-$55,800.00
5	Gross Margin	$37,730.00

6		
7	Operating and administrative expenses	
8	Administrative expenses	-$2,586.89
9	Salary expenses	-$18,756.00
10	Amortization expenses	-$851.39
11	Office rent expenses	-$1,500.00
12	Interest expenses	-$3,000.00
13	Earnings Before Income Taxes	$11,035.72
14		
15	Tax	
16	Tax expenses	-$3310.72
17	Net Earnings	$7,725.00
18		
19	Retained Earnings, Beginning	$0.00
20	Retained Earnings, Ending	$7,725.00

From the Table 2-34, the amounts of the line 2 and the line 4 can be added together to get the amount of the line 5. The amounts of the line 5 and the line 8 to 12 can be added together to get the amount of the line 13. Then I can get the amount of the Tax expenses which is equal to -$3,310.72 (-$11,035.72*0.3 = -$3,310.72). Because I temporarily check the performance of the RR Company, I do not create the table of the Tax expenses. In other words, I do not enter the following transaction equation.

0 = Tax payable (2) 3310.72 + Tax expenses (5) -3310.72

Adding the amounts of the line 13 and the line 16 together, I get the amount of the Net Earnings (line 17) which is equal to $7,725. Obviously, the amount of the line 19 is equal to $0. Finally, I get the amount of the Retained Earnings, Ending (line 20) after adding the amounts of the line 17 and the line 19 together. It is equal to $7,725.

From the Table 2-2, I can get the some amounts of the Balance Sheet, seeing the following table 2-35.

Table 2-35 Balance Sheet

	As at 1/31/2021	
1	ASSETS	
2	Current assets	
3	Cash	$103,616.01
4	Office supplies	$105.00
5	Inventory	$18,870.00
6	HST recoverable	$9,707.10
7	Account receivable	$40,355.00
8		$172,653.11
9	Long term investments	
10	Land	$450,000.00
11	Equipment	
12	Truck	$45,000.00
13	Accumulated amortization: truck	-$750.00
14	Computer	$5,600.00
15	Accumulated amortization: computer	-$101.39
16		$49,748.61
17	Total Assets	$672,401.72
18		
19	LIABILITIES	
20	Current liabilities	
21	Account payable	$46207.10
22	HST payable	$12,158.90
23	Accrued interest payable	$3,000.00
24	Tax payable	$3,310.72
25		$64,676.72
26	Long term liabilities	
27	Note payable	$500,000.00
28	Total Liabilities	$564,676.72
29		
30	SHAREHOLDERS' EQUITY	
31	Owners' capital	
32	Share capital	$100,000.00
33	Retained earnings	$7,725.00
34	Total Shareholders' Equity	$107,725.00
35		
36	Total Liabilities and Shareholders' Equity	$672,401.72

From the Table 2-35, the amounts of the line 3 to the line 7 can be added together to get the amount of the line 8. The amounts of the line 12 to line 15 can be added together to get the amount of the line 16. Then I can get the amount of the Total Assets (line 17) after adding the amounts of the line 8, the line 10, and the line 16 together. It is equal to $672,401.72. Adding the amounts of the line 21 to the line 24 together, I get the amount of the line 25 which is equal to $64,676.72. Adding the amounts of the line 25 and the line 27 together, I get the amount of the Total Liabilities (line 28) which is equal to $564,676.72. Adding the amounts of the line 32 and the line 33 together, I get the amount of the Total Shareholders' Equity (line 34) which is equal to $107,725.00. Finally, adding the amounts of the line 28 and the line 34 together, I get the amount of the Total Liabilities and Shareholders' Equity (line 36). It is equal to $672,401.72.

From the Table 2-8, I can get the Cash Flows, seeing the following table 2-36.

Table 2-36 Cash Flows

	Month ended on 1/31/2021	
1	Operating activities	
2	Cash payments for machinery	-$50,600.00
3	Cash payments to suppliers	-$38,170.00
4	Cash payments for operating expenses	-$22,947.89
5	Cash receipts from customers	$65,333.90
6	Net cash provided by Operating activities	-$46,383.99
7		
8	Investing activities	
9	Cash payments for investment	-$450,000.00
10	Net cash provided by Investing activities	-$450,000.00
11		
12	Financing activities	
13	Cash receipts from owners	$500,000.00
14	Cash receipts from banks	$100,000.00
15	Net cash provided by Financing activities	$600,000.00
16		
17	Net change in cash	$103,616.01
18	Cash, Beginning	$0.00
19	Cash, Ending	$103,616.01

From the Table 2-8, the amounts of the line 2 to the line 5 in the Table 2-36 can be respectively gotten from the tables of the two-level subaccounts under the one-level subaccount: Operating activities. The amount of the line 6 can be gotten from the table of the one-level subaccount: Operating activities. Of course, this amount is also gotten after adding the amounts of the line 2 to the line 5 together. The amount of the line 9 can be gotten from the table of the two-level subaccount under the one-level subaccount: Investing activities. The amount of the line 10 can be gotten from the table of the one-level subaccount: Investing activities. The amounts of the line 13 to the line 14 can be respectively gotten from the tables of the two-level subaccounts under the one-level subaccount: Financing activities. The amount of the line 15 can be gotten from the table of the one-level subaccount: Financing activities. Adding the amounts of the line6, the line 10, and the line 15 together, I can get the amount of the Net change in cash (line 17). It is equal to $103,616.01. Finally, I can get the amount of the Cash, Ending (line 19) after adding the amounts of the line 17 and the line 18 together. It is equal to $103,616.01.

Now, I will introduce a new concept of the Account Flows. If a parent account has more than three one-level subaccounts, then I can create the Account Flows of this parent account, such as the Inventory account and Administrative expenses account. Here, I introduce the Inventory Flows. At the end of the fiscal year, I will introduce the Administrative expenses Flows. Because the Inventory account has four one-level subaccounts of the Inven1, the Inven2, the Inven3, and the Inven4, the Inventory Flows only shows the top three balances of the one-level subaccounts.

From the Table 2-10, I can get the Inventory Flows statement, seeing the following table 2-37. The process is the same as the Cash Flows statement.

Table 2-37 Inventory Flows

Inventory Flows, Month ended on 1/31/2021		
1	Inven4	
2	Inven41	$8,800.00
3	TTT parts	$2,300.00

4	RRRHJK parts	$1,400.00
5	Net inventory provided by Inven4	$12,500.00
6		
7	Inven3	
8	Inven31	$400.00
9	Inven32	$1,100.00
10	Inven33	$7000.00
11	QASXC parts	$100.00
12	ASDUP parts	$500.00
13	Net inventory provided by Inven3	$2,800.00
14		
15	Inven2	
16	ASD parts	$1,200.00
17	Inven22	$600.00
18	Net inventory provided by Inven2	$1,800.00
19		
20	Net change in Inventory	$17,100.00
21	Inventory, Beginning	$0.00
22	Inventory, Ending	$17,100.00
23		
24	Total Inventory, Ending	$18,870.00

The ending inventory for the top three one-level subaccounts is $17,100 while total ending inventory is $18,870. The difference between them is $1,770 which is the balance of the one-level subaccount Inven1.

The followings are the transactions for the second month:

- On February 1, the RR Company records the new balance of the HST payable account or the HST recoverable account.

  If the balance (XXX) of the HST payable account is smaller than the balance of the HST recoverable account, then RR Company does not pay anything and only records the following transaction.

  HST recoverable (1): -XXX = HST payable (2): -XXX

If the balance (XXX1) of the HST recoverable payable account is smaller than the balance (XXX2) of the HST payable account, then RR Company must pay the cash of their difference (XXX3 = XXX2 - XXX1) and records the two transactions.

Here, the XXX1 is equal to $9,707.10 and the XXX2 is equal to $12,158.90, so the RR Company records the following transactions.

> HST recoverable (1): -9707.10 = HST payable (2): -9707.10
> Cash (1): -2451.80 = HST payable (2): -2451.80

Problem: In what situations is there a fact that the balance of the HST payable account is smaller than the balance of the HST recoverable account at the end of a fiscal year?

- On February 1, 2021, the RR Company purchases the Office supplies for cash $103.3.
- On February 3, 2021, the RR Company purchases $91,000 inventory on credit from D1 Company (phone number: 987654323).

  The inventory's multi-subaccounts are:

  "HGFCVB parts<QASXC parts<Inven3" for $10*5960,

  "PPGHUP parts<ASDUP parts<Inven3" for $10*3140.

- On February 4, 2021, Jun Wang sales $91,200 inventory to E1 Company (phone number: 123456788) on credit $177,600.

  The inventory's multi-subaccounts are:

  "HGFCVB parts<QASXC parts<Inven3" of cost -$10*5960,

  "PPGHUP parts<ASDUP parts<Inven3" of cost -$10*3160.

- On February 8, 2021, the RR Company receives $5,000 cash from B1 Company (phone number: 123456789) with the General ID 23.
- On February 9, 2021, the RR Company receives $12,821 cash from F1 Company (phone: 123456787) with the General ID 14 ($9521) and the General ID 20 ($3300).

- On February 11, 2021, the RR Company receives $3,500 cash from H1 Company (phone number: 123456786) with the General ID 21.

- On February 13, 2021, the RR Company pays $2,500 cash to A1 Company (phone number: 987654321) with the General ID 4.

- On February 15, 2021, the RR Company pays $15,000 cash to C1 Company (phone number: 987654322) with the General ID 21.

- On February 17, 2021, the RR Company pays $4,000 cash to D1 Company (phone number: 987654323) with the General ID 12.

- On February 18, 2021, the RR Company sells land1 (downtown) for $360,000 cash. The transaction sub-equation is:

  Cash (1): 360000 + Land (1): -270000 = Investment income (4): 90000

  For the parent account "Investment income, the "Subtotal name" should be the "Other income, 475", so the parent account "Investment Income" row number is the "476".

- On the same day, the RR Company purchases 10,000 the MicroQQ Company shares for $35.67 each share. Total amount is $356,700.

- On February 25, 2021, the RR Company receives $120,000 cash from E1 Company (phone number: 123456788) with the General ID 48.

- On February 26, 2021, the RR Company pays $55,000 cash to D1 Company (phone number: 987654323) with the General ID 47.

- On February 28, 2021, the RR Company pays $55.32 cash to Dan Zhu (Purchase department) for the other expenses.

- On the same day, the RR Company pays $458.39 cash to Hua Li (Purchase department) for the taxi expenses $336.41 and the other expenses $121.98.

- On the same day, the RR Company pays $33.72 cash to Xiao Zhou (Sales department) for the other expenses.

- On the same day, the RR Company pays $152.31 cash to Jun Wang (Sales department) for the taxi expenses.

- On the same day, the RR Company pays $1,015.98 cash to Zhendao Yuan (Sales department) for the other expenses.

- On the same day, the RR Company pays $117.95 cash to Yi Liu (Sales department) for the taxi expenses $99.8 and the other expenses $18.15.

- On the same day, the RR Company records the Office supplies expenses $101.28.

- On the same day, the RR Company pays $18,756 cash for all salary of February, 2014.

- On the same day, the RR Company records the truck's amortization expenses $750 one month (5 years, straight line, and second month).

- On the same day, the RR Company records the second month computers' amortization expenses ($202.78).

The computer account has three one-level subaccounts of the computer1 ($66.67), the computer server ($75), and the POS system ($61.11). The transaction sub-equation is:

Accumulated amortization: computer (1) -66.67 + Accumulated amortization: computer (1) -75 + Accumulated amortization: computer (1) -61.11 = - Amortization expenses (5) 66.67 - Amortization expenses (5) 75 - amortization expenses (5) 61.11

The left three items of the equation belong to the same account. It has three one-level subaccounts which are the "Computer1-accumulated amortization", the "Computer server-accumulated amortization", and the "POS system-accumulated amortization".

The right three items of the equation have respectively their two-level subaccounts which are the "Computer1-amortization<Computer- amortization", the "Computer server-amortization<Computer-amortization", and the "POS system - amortization

Computer- amortization". The Figure 3-7 shows the detail information of the subaccount "POS system- accumulated amortization".

- On the same day, the RR Company pays $293.37 cash for the utility expenses.
- On the same day, the RR Company pays $1,500 cash for the office rent expenses.
- On the same day, the RR Company records the note payable's interest expenses $3,333.33 and the accrued interest payable (500,000*8%/12).

If RR Company ends its first fiscal year on February 28, 2021 and begins a new fiscal year on March 1, 2021, then I need enter the following transactions.

- On February 28, 2021, the RR Company records the tax expenses $48,199.59 and the tax payable $48,199.59.

    From the Table A-2 in the Appendixes A, I get the earnings before income taxes ($160,665.29). It is equal to sum of the amounts of the line 27, the line 29, the line 31 to 35, and the line 37. If the income tax rate is 0.3, then the Tax expenses and the Tax payable are all equal to $48,199.59 (=160,665.29*0.3), and the net earrings is equal to $112,465.70 (=$160,665.29 - $48,199.59).

    After entering the transaction, the net earnings will transfer into the end retained earnings.

- On the same day, the RR Company records the land's unrealized holding gain or loss. The land (land2, North York) has fair price of $210,000.

    Due to the land being the AFS investment, I must calculate the unrealized holding gain or loss (OCI) and the accumulated other comprehensive income (AOCI). A similar method of dealing with the accumulated amortization account can be used for dealing with the accumulated other comprehensive income (AOCI) account. So the accumulated other comprehensive income (AOCI) account is also a contra account of the land account.

    The Unrealized holding gain or loss account, which is the difference between the fair price and the cost price, will be put into the fourth class accounts. If the amount of this account is negative, it means the unrealized holding loss. The fair price is $210,000 and the cost is $180,000, so the sub-equation is:

Accumulated other comprehensive income of land (1): 30000 = Unrealized holding gain or loss (4): 30000

Here, you must pay attention that the increase of the "Accumulated other comprehensive income (AOCI)" means the "+" because I put the "Unrealized holding gain or loss" into the fourth class accounts.

If you wish put the "Unrealized holding gain or loss" into the fifth class accounts, then the meaning of the "Accumulated other comprehensive income (AOCI)" account's increasing or decreasing is as same as the "Accumulated amortization" account's.

The "Accumulated other comprehensive income: land" account and the "Unrealized holding gain or loss" account all have the one-level subaccounts, and their Subtotal names are the "Long term investments, 141" and the "Other comprehensive income, 713" respectively.

- On the same day, the RR Company records the share's unrealized holding gain or loss. The share's market price is $35.21 each share.

The transaction is the same as the previous transaction. The unrealized holding gain or loss of the MicroQQ share is -$4,600. The transaction sub-equation is:

Accumulated other comprehensive income: share (1): -4600 = Unrealized holding gain or loss (4): -4600

All tables of the Table A-1 to the Table A-40 on February 28, 2021 are showed in the Appendixes A.

For checking whether the recording data is reliable and correct again, I will do the following three calculations which also ensure integrity of the recorded data.

- Check whether the cynamic accounting equation is equal.

  From the Table A-1, I get the left balance $888,023.72 and the right balance $888,023.72 of the dynamic accounting equation on February 31, 2021 when the all general equations are added together. These two amounts are equal.

- Check whether the sum of all assets accounts' balances is equal to the sum of all liabilities accounts, all equity accounts, all incomes accounts, and all expenses accounts' balances.

For all Assets accounts:

From the Table A-8, I get that the balance of the parent account "Cash" is $146,798.87.

From the Table A-9, I get that the balance of the parent account "Office supplies" is $107.02.

From the Table A-10, I get that the balance of the parent account "Inventory" is $18,670.

From the Table A-11, I get that the balance of the parent account "HST recoverable" is $11,830.

From the Table A-12, I get that the balance of the parent account "Account receivable" is $99,722.

From the Table A-13, I get that the balance of the parent account "Land" is $180,000.

From the Table A-14, I get that the balance of the parent account "Truck" is $45,000.

From the Table A-15, I get that the balance of the parent account "Computer" is $5,600.

From the Table A-16, I get that the balance of the parent account "Accumulated amortization: truck" is -$1,500.

From the Table A-17, I get that the balance of the parent account "Accumulated amortization: computer" is -$304.17.

From the Table A-18, I get that the balance of the parent account "Share" is $356,700.

From the Table A-19, I get that the balance of the parent account "AOCI of land" is $30,000.

From the Table A-20, I get that the balance of the parent account "AOCI of share" is -$4,600.

Therefore, the sum of the assets accounts' balances is $888,023.72 (= $146,798.87 + $107.02 + $18,670 + $11,830 + $99,722+ $180,000 + $45,000 + $5,600 - $1,500 - $304.17 + $356,700 + $30,000 - $4,600).

Of course, I can also get that the sum of the assets accounts' balances is $888,023.72 from the table "Assets (X1)" in the Table A-7.

For all liabilities accounts:

From the Table A-22, I get that the balance of the parent account "Account payable" is $72,537.10.

From the Table A-23, I get that the balance of the parent account "HST payable" is $23,088.

From the Table A-24, I get that the balance of the parent account "Note payable" is $500,000.

From the Table A-25, I get that the balance of the parent account "Accrued interest payable" is $6,333.33.

From the Table A-26, I get that the balance of the parent account "Tax payable" is $48,199.59.

Therefore, the total sum of the liabilities accounts' balances is $650,158.02 (= $72,537.10 + $23,088 + $500,000 + $6,333.33 + $48,199.59).

Of course, I can also get that the sum of the liabilities account's balance is $650,158.02 from the table "Liabilities (X2)" in the Table B-21.

For all Shareholders' equity accounts:

From the Table A-28, I get that the balance of the parent account "Share capital" is $100,000.

Therefore, the sum of the shareholders' equity account's balance is $100,000.

Of course, I can also get that the sum of the shareholders' equity account's balance is $100,000 from the table "Shareholders' equity (X3)" in the Table 2-27.

For all Revenues accounts:

From the Table A-30, I get that the balance of the parent account "Sales" is $271,130.

From the Table A-31, I get that the balance of the parent account "Investment income" is $90,000.

From the Table A-32, I get that the balance of the parent account "Unrealized holding gain or loss" is $25,400.

Therefore, the sum of the revenues accounts' balances is $386,530 (= $271,130 + $90,000 + $25,400).

Of course, I can also get that the sum of the revenues accounts' balances is $386,530 from the table "Revenues (X4)" in the Table A-29.

For all Expenses accounts:

From the Table A-34, I get that the balance of the parent account "Administrative expenses" is -$4,815.21.

From the Table A-35, I get that the balance of the parent account "Cost of sales" is -$147,000.

From the Table A-36, get that the balance of the parent account "Salary expenses" is -$37,512.

From the Table A-37, I get that the balance of the parent account "Amortization expenses" is -$1,804.17.

From the Table A-38, I get that the balance of the parent account "Office rent expenses" is -$3,000.

From the Table A-39, I get that the balance of the parent account "Interest expenses" is -$6,333.33.

From the Table A-40, I get that the balance of the parent account "Tax expenses" is -$48,199.59.

Therefore, the sum of the expenses accounts' balances is -$248,664.30 (= -$4,815.21 - $147,000 - $37,512 - $1,804.17 - $3,000 - $6,333.33 - $48,199.59).

Of course, I can also get that the sum of the expenses accounts' balances is -$248,722.71 from the table "Expenses (X5)" in the Table A-27.

The sum of all liabilities accounts, all shareholders' equity accounts, all revenues accounts, and all expenses accounts is $888,023.72 (= $650,158.02 + $100,000 + $386,530 - $248,664.30).

The sum of all assets accounts is also $888,023.72.

These two sum amounts are equal. They are $888,023.72.

- After the previous two steps are correct, I check whether the left (or right) amount of the dynamic accounting equation is equal to the sum of all assets accounts' balances (or the sum of all liabilities, all equity accounts, all incomes accounts, and all expenses accounts' balances).

    Obviously, the requirement is satisfied.

    The above three requirements are satisfied, so the mathematical accounting model is reliable and correct.

From the Table A-2 in the Appendixes A, I can get the some amounts of the Income Statement, seeing the following table 2-38.

Table 2-38 Income Statement

	Year ended on 2/28/2021	
1	Revenues	
2	Sales	$271,130.00
3	Cost	
4	Cost of sales	-$147,000.00
5	Gross Margin	$124,130.00
6		
7	Operating and administrative expenses	
8	Administrative expenses	-$4,815.21
9	Salary expenses	-$37,512.00
10	Amortization expenses	-$1,804.17
11	Office rent expenses	-$3,000.00
12	Interest expenses	-$6,333.33
13	Earnings Before Income Taxes	$160,665.29
14		
15	Tax	
16	Tax expenses	-$48,199.59
17	Net Earnings	$112,465.70
18		
19	Retained Earnings, Beginning	$0.00
20	Retained Earnings, Ending	$112,465.70

From the Table 2-38, the amounts of the line 2 and the line 4 can be added together to get the amount of the line 5. The amounts of the line 5 and the line 8 to 12 can be added together to get the amount of the line 13. Adding the amounts of the line 13 and the line 16 together, I get the amount of the Net Earnings which is equal to $112,465.70. Obviously, the amount of the line 19 is equal to $0. Finally, adding the amounts of the line 17 and the line 19 together, I get the amount of the Retained Earnings, Ending (line 20). Itis equal to $112,465.70.

From the Table A-2 in the Appendixes A, I can get the some amounts of the Balance Sheet, seeing the table 2-39 on the next page.

Table 2-39 Balance Sheet

	As at 2/28/2021	
1	ASSETS	
2	Current assets	
3	Cash	$146,798.87
4	Office supplies	$107.02
5	Inventory	$18,670.00
6	HST recoverable	$11,830.00
7	Account receivable	$99,722.00
8		$277,127.89
9	Long term investments	
10	Land	$180,000.00
11	AOCI of land	$30,000.00
12	Share	$356,700.00
13	AOCI of share	-$4,600.00
14		$562,100.00
15	Equipment	
16	Truck	$45,000.00
17	Accumulated amortization: truck	-$1,500.00
18	Computer	$5,600.00
19	Accumulated amortization: computer	-$304.17
20		$48,795.83
21	Total Assets	$888,023.72
22		
23	LIABILITIES	
24	Current liabilities	
25	Account payable	$72,537.10
26	HST payable	$23,088.00
27	Accrued interest payable	$6,333.33
28	Tax payable	$48,199.59
29		$150,158.02
30	Long term liabilities	
31	Note payable	$500,000.00
32	Total Liabilities	$650,158.02
33		
34	SHAREHOLDERS' EQUITY	
35	Owners' capital	
36	Share capital	$100,000.00
37	Retained earnings	$112,465.70
38	Accumulated other comprehensive income	$25,400.00

39	Total Shareholders' Equity	$237,865.70
40		
41	Total Liabilities and Shareholders' Equity	$888,023.72

From the Table 2-39, the amounts of the line 3 to the line 7 can be added together to get the amount of the line 8. The amounts of the line 10 to line 13 can be added together to get the amount of the line 14. The amounts of the line 16 to line 19 can be added together to get the amount of the line 20. Then I can get the amount of the Total Assets (line 17) after adding the amounts of the line 8, the line 14, and the line 20 together. It is equal to $888,023.72. Adding the amounts of the line 25 to the line 28 together, I get the amount of the line 29 which is equal to $150,158.02. Adding the amounts of the line 29 and the line 31 together, I get the amount of the Total Liabilities (line 32) which is equal to $$650,158.02. Adding the amounts of the line 36, the line 37, and the line 38 together, I get the amount of the Total Shareholders' Equity (line 39) which is equal to $237,865.70. Finally, adding the amounts of the line 32 and the line 39 together, I get the amount of the Total Liabilities and Shareholders' Equity (line 41). It is equal to $888,023.72.

From the Table A-8 in the Appendixes A, I can get the Cash Flows statement, seeing the following table 2-40.

Table 2-40 Cash Flows

Year ended on 2/28/2021		
1	Operating activities	
2	Cash payments for machinery	-$50,600.00
3	Cash payments to suppliers	-$114,670.00
4	Cash payments for operating expenses	-$47,886.03
5	Cash receipts from customers	$566,654.90
6	Net cash provided by Operating activities	$353,498.87
7		
8	Investing activities	
9	Cash payments for investment	-$806,700.00
10	Net cash provided by Investing activities	-$806,700.00

11		
12	Financing activities	
13	Cash receipts from owners	$500,000.00
14	Cash receipts from banks	$100,000.00
15	Net cash provided by Financing activities	$600,000.00
16		
17	Net change in cash	$146,798.87
18	Cash, Beginning	$0.00
19	Cash, Ending	$146,798.87

From the Table A-8, the amounts of the line 2 to the line 5 in the table 2-40 can be respectively gotten from the tables of the two-level subaccounts under the one-level subaccount: Operating activities. The amount of the line 6 can be gotten from the table of the one-level subaccount: Operating activities. Of course, this amount is also gotten after adding the amounts of the line 2 to the line 5 together. The amount of the line 9 can be gotten from the table of the two-level subaccount under the one-level subaccount: Investing activities. The amount of the line 10 can be gotten from the table of the one-level subaccount: Investing activities. The amounts of the line 13 to the line 14 can be respectively gotten from the tables of the two-level subaccounts under the one-level subaccount: Financing activities. The amount of the line 15 can be gotten from the table of the one-level subaccount: Financing activities. Adding the amounts of the line6, the line 10, and the line 15, I can get the amount of the Net change in cash (line 17). It is equal to $146,798.87. Finally, I can get the amount of the Cash, Ending (line 19) after adding the amounts of the line 17 and the line 18. It is equal to $146,798.87.

Now, I will introduce the Administrative expenses Flows. The Administrative expenses account has five one-level subaccounts of the Taxi expenses, the Other expenses, the Mobile expenses, the Office supplies expenses, and the Utility expenses, so the Administrative expenses Flows only shows the top three absolute balances of the one-level subaccounts.

From the Table A-10, I can get the Administrative expenses Flows statement, seeing the following table 2-41. The process is the same as the Cash Flows statement.

Table 2-41 Administrative expenses Flows

	Administrative expenses Flows, Year ended on 2/28/2021	
1	Other expenses	
2	Office department-open fees	-$367.00
3	Office department-other	-$77.73
4	Purchase department-other	-$263.43
5	Sales department-other	-$1,450.81
6	Net Administrative expenses provided by Other expenses	-$2,159.07
7		
8	Taxi expenses	
9	Purchase department-taxi	-$696.53
10	Sales department-taxi	-$842.81
11	Office department-taxi	-$298.69
12	Net Administrative expenses provided by Taxi expenses	-$1,838.03
13		
14	Utility expenses	
15		-$574.07
16	Net Administrative expenses provided by Utility expenses	-$574.07
17		
18	Net change in Administrative expenses	-$4,571.17
19	Administrative expenses, Beginning	$0.00
20	Administrative expenses, Ending	-$4,571.17
21		
22	Total Administrative expenses, Ending	-$4,815.21

The ending administrative expenses for the top three one-level subaccounts is -$4,571.17 while total ending inventory is -$4,815.21. The difference between them is -$244.04 which is the sum of the one-level subaccount Mobile expenses (-$54.76) and Office supplies expenses (-$189.28).

The Table 2-42 shows the total unrealized holding gain or loss $25,400 which is consisted of the land's unrealized holding gain or loss $30,000 and the MicroQQ share's unrealized holding gain or loss -$4,500.

Table 2-42 Comprehensive income statement

	Year ended on 2/28/2021	
1	Net income	$112,465.70
2		
3	Other comprehensive income	
4	Unrealized holding gain or loss, net of tax	$25,400.00
5		
6	Comprehensive income	$137,865.70

From the tables of the one-level subaccounts under the Table A-12 and the Table A-6, I can get every Account receivable age on March 3, 2021, seeing the following Table 2-43. For example, when the RR Company sold some inventories to the B1 Company on January 5, 2021, the amount of the Account receivable is $2,558.90 and its GeID is 5. Later, the RR Company respectively received cash $1,500 with the Ref **5** and the GeID 6 on January 7, 2021 and cash $828.90 with the Ref **5** and the GeID 24 on January 30, 2021, so the balance of the Account receivable with the GeID 5 is equal to $230 (= $2,558.90 - $1,500 - $828.90).

Table 2-43 Account receivable age

ID	Customer Name	TransDate	Phone No. (MultiName)	Day	GeID	Amount (Sub-Balance)	Balance
1	B1	2021-1-5	123456789	57	5	230	230
2	B1	2021-1-29	123456789	33	23	276	506
3	E1	2021-1-11	123456788	51	13	8835	9341
4	E1	2021-2-4	123456788	27	48	80688	90029
5	F1	2021-1-23	123456787	39	20	6187	96216
6	H1	2021-1-25	123456787	37	21	3506	99722

From the tables of the one-level subaccounts under the Table A-22 and the Table A-5, I can get every Account payable age on March 3, 2021, seeing the following Table 2-44. For example, when the RR Company purchased some inventories from the A1 Company on January 4, 2021, the amount of the Account payable is $3477.10 and its GeID is 4. Later, the RR Company paid cash $2,500 with the Ref **4** and the GeID 52 on February 13, 2021 to A1

Company, so the balance of the Account payable with the GeID 4 is equal to $977.10 (= $3,477.10 - $2,500).

Table 2-44 Account payable age

ID	Supplier Name	TransDate	Phone No. (MultiName)	Day	GeID	Amount (Sub-Balance)	Balance
1	A1	2021-1-4	987554321	**58**	4	977.10	977 10
2	C1	2021-1-9	987554322	**53**	11	4750	5727.10
3	C1	2021-1-22	987554322	**40**	19	9295	15022.10
4	D1	2021-1-9	987554323	**53**	12	3560	18582.10
5	D1	2021-2-3	987554323	**28**	47	47830	66412.10
6	G1	2021-1-17	987654324	**45**	15	6125	72537.10

For beginning a new fiscal year, a technical problem for the parent accounts of the class 4 and the class 5 must be dealt with. There are two methods to resolve this problem. First, I will keep these cards and continue to record the new transactions in the new fiscal year. When I check performance of the RR Company during a period, the difference of the last transaction's balance at the ending day of this fiscal year and the last transaction's balance at the ending day of last fiscal year for all parent accounts of the class 4 and class 5 was used. Second, I will clear these cards of the parent accounts of the class 4 and class 5 (including their subaccounts' cards) and only keep their empty tables. In this book, I use the second method.

2.2 Beginning second fiscal year

In the new fiscal year, I will enter the following transactions.

- On March 1, 2021, the RR Company records the new balance of the HST payable account or the HST recoverable account.

  If the balance (XXX) of the HST payable account is smaller than the balance of the HST recoverable account, then RR Company does not pay anything and only records the following transaction.

HST recoverable (1): -XXX = HST payable (2): -XXX

If the balance (XXX1) of the HST recoverable payable account is smaller than the balance (XXX2) of the HST payable account, then RR Company must pay the cash of their difference (XXX3 = XXX2 - XXX1) and records the two transactions.

Here, the XXX1 is equal to $11,830 and the XXX2 is equal to $23,088, so the RR Company records the following transactions.

HST recoverable (1): -11830 = HST payable (2): -11830

Cash (1): -11258 = HST payable (2): -11258

- On March 2, 2021, the RR Company purchases the Office supplies for cash $123.87.
- On March 3, 2021, the RR Company purchases the $85,360 inventory on credit from G1 Company (phone number: 987654324).

  The inventory's multi-subaccounts are:

  "TTTCU parts<TTT parts<Inven4" for $2*33105,

  "RRRHJK parts<Inven4" for $ 2*9575.
- On March 4, 2021, Yi Liu sales $85,200 inventory to F1 Company (phone number: 123456787) on credit $154,800.

  The inventory's multi-subaccounts are:

  "TTTCU parts<TTT parts<Inven4" of cost -$2*33035,

  "RRRHJK parts<Inven4" of cost -$2*9565.
- On March 10, 2021, the RR Company receives $52,000 cash from E1 Company (phone number: 123456788) with the General ID 48.
- On March 12, 2021, the RR Company receives $506 cash from B1 Company (phone number: 123456789) with the General ID 5 ($230) and the General ID 25 ($276).
- On March 13, 2021, the RR Company receives $2,200 cash from H1 Company (phone number: 123456786) with the General ID 23.

- On March 14, 2021, the RR Company pays $977.1 cash to A1 Company (phone number: 987654321) with the General ID 4.

- On March 15, 2021, the RR Company pays $4,500 cash to C1 Company (phone number: 987654322) with the General ID 11.

- On March 17, 2021, the RR Company pays $30,000 cash to D1 Company (phone number: 987654323) with the General ID 47.

- On March 28, 2021, the RR Company pays $153.72 cash to Mike Newsome (Office department) for the other expenses.

- On March 29, 2021, the RR Company receives $120,000 cash from F1 Company (phone number: 123456787) with the General ID 78.

- On same day, the RR Company pays $82,360 cash to G1 Company (phone number: 987654324) with the General ID 77.

- On the same day, the RR Company pays $171.63 cash to Hua Li (Purchase department) for tax expenses $101.33 and the other expenses $70.30.

- On the same day, the RR Company pays $52.17 cash to Xiao Zhou (Sales department) the other expenses.

- On the same day, the RR Company pays $129.34 cash to Jun Wang (Sales department) for the taxi expenses.

- On the same day, the RR Company pays $111.93 cash to Zhendao Yuan (Sales department) for the other expenses.

- On March 30, 2021, the RR Company pays $1,210.91 cash to Yi Liu (Sales department) for the taxi expenses $1132.56 and the other expenses $78.35.

- On the same day, the RR Company pays $201.99 cash to Ping Wang (Office department) for the other expenses.

- On the same day, the RR Company pays $48,199.59 cash to the Canada Revenue Agency.

- On March 31, 2021, the RR Company records the Office supplies expenses $101.28.

- On the same day, the RR Company pays $23,790 cash for all salary of March, 2014.

- On the same day, the RR Company records the truck's amortization expenses $750 one month (5 years, straight line, and third month).

- On the same day, the RR Company records the computers' amortization expenses ($202.78).

  The computer account has three one-level subaccounts of the computer1 ($66.67), the computer server ($75), and the POS system ($61.11).

- On the same day, the RR Company pays $323.14 cash for the utility expenses.

- On the same day, the RR Company pays $1,500 cash for the office rent expenses.

- On the same day, the RR Company records the note payable's interest expenses $3,333.33 and the accrued interest payable (500,000*8%/12).

- On the same day, the RR Company pays $48,199.59 cash for the Tax expenses.

- On the same day, the RR Company decides to return $20,000 to the owners.

Problem: What is this transaction equation?

If I will begin a new fiscal year on April 1, 2014 to check performance of the RR Company, I must enter following transactions.

- On March 31, 2021, the RR Company records the tax expenses $11,270.33 and tax payable $11,270.33, and the net earnings will transfer into the ending retained earnings. This amount can be gotten form the Table B-2 in the Appendixes B.

- On the same day, the RR Company records the land's unrealized holding gain or loss. The land (land2, North York) has fair price of $235,000.

  The Unrealized holding gain or loss account is now the difference between the fair price and the carrying value. The fair price is $235,000 and the carrying value is $210,000, so the transaction sub-equation is:

  Accumulated other comprehensive income: land (1): 25000 = Unrealized holding gain or loss (4): 25000

The "Accumulated other comprehensive income: Land" and the "Unrealized holding gain or loss" accounts all have the one-level subaccounts.

- On the same day, the RR Company records the share's market price is $39.78 each share.

The transaction is the same as the previous transaction. The unrealized holding gain or loss of MicroQQ is $45,700, and the transaction sub-equation is:

Accumulated other comprehensive income: share (1): 45700 = Unrealized holding gain or loss (4): 45700

All tables of the Table B-1 to the Table B-40 on March 31, 2021 are showed in the Appendixes B.

For checking whether the recording data is reliable and correct again, I will do the following three calculations which also ensure integrity of the recorded data.

- Check whether the dynamic accounting equation is equal.

From the Table B-1, I get the left balance $907,080.94 and the right balance $907,080.94 of the dynamic accounting equation on March 31, 2021 when the all general equations are added together. These two amounts are equal.

- Check whether the sum of all assets accounts' balances is equal to the sum of all liabilities accounts, all equity accounts, all incomes accounts, and all expenses accounts' balances.

For all Assets accounts:

From the Table B-8, I get that the balance of the parent account "Cash" is $96,441.48.

From the Table B-9, I get that the balance of the parent account "Office supplies" is $129.61.

From the Table B-10, I get that the balance of the parent account "Inventory" is $18,830.

From the Table B-11, I get that the balance of the parent account "HST recoverable" is $11,096.80.

From the Table B-12, I get that the balance of the parent account "Account receivable" is $99,940.

From the Table B-13, I get that the balance of the parent account "Land" is $180,000.

From the Table B-14, I get that the balance of the parent account "Truck" is $45,000.

From the Table B-15, I get that the balance of the parent account "Computer" is $5,600.

From the Table -16, I get that the balance of the parent account "Accumulated amortization: truck" is -$2,250.

From the Table B-17, I get that the balance of the parent account "Accumulated amortization: computer" is -$506.95.

From the Table B-18, I get that the balance of the parent account "Share" is $356,700.

From the Table B-19, I get that the balance of the parent account "AOCI of land" is $55,000.

From the Table B-20, I get that the balance of the parent account "AOCI of share" is $41,100.

Therefore, the sum of the assets accounts' balances is $907,080.94 (= $96,441.48 + $129.61 + $18,830 + $11,096.80 + $99,940 + $180,000 + $45,000 + $5,600 - $2,250 - $506.95 + $356,700 + $55,000 + $41,100).

Of course, I can also get that the sum of the assets accounts' balances is $907,080.94 from the table "Assets (X1)" in the Table B-7.

For all liabilities accounts:

From the Table B-22, I get that the balance of the parent account "Account payable" is $51,156.80.

From the Table B-23, I get that the balance of the parent account "HST payable" is $20,124.

From the Table B-24, I get that the balance of the parent account "Note payable" is $500,000.

From the Table B-25, I get that the balance of the parent account "Accrued interest payable" is $9,666.66.

From the Table B-26, I get that the balance of the parent account "Tax payable" is $11,270.33.

Therefore, the total sum of the liabilities accounts' balances is $592,217.79 (= $51,156.80 + $20,124 + $500,000 + $9,666.66 + $11,270.33).

Of course, I can also get that the sum of the liabilities account's balance is $592,217.79 from the table "Liabilities (X2)" in the Table B-21.

For all Shareholders' equity accounts:

From the Table B-28, I get that the balance of the parent account "Share capital" is $80,000.

There are some Retained earnings and Accumulated other comprehensive income at last fiscal year, so I can get that the Retained earnings is $112,465.70 and the Accumulated other comprehensive income is $ $25,400 from the Table 2-39.

Therefore, the sum of the shareholders' equity accounts' balances is $217,865.70 (= $80,000 + $112,465.70 + $25,400).

Of course, I can also get that the sum of the shareholders' equity account's balance is $80,000 from the table "Shareholders' equity (X3)" in the Table B-27.

For all Revenues accounts:

From the Table B-30, I get that the balance of the parent account "Sales" is $154,800.

From the Table B-31, I get that the balance of the parent account "Investment income" is $0.

From the Table B-32, I get that the balance of the parent account "Unrealized holding gain or loss" is $70,700.

Therefore, the sum of the revenues accounts' balances is $225,500 (= $154,800 + $0 + $70,700).

Of course, I can also get that the sum of the revenues accounts' balances is $386,530 from the table "Revenues (X4)" in the Table B-29.

For all Expenses accounts:

From the Table B-34, I get that the balance of the parent account "Administrative expenses" is -$2,456.11.

From the Table B-35, I get that the balance of the parent account "Cost of sales" is -$85,200.

From the Table B-36, I get that the balance of the parent account "Salary expenses" is -$23,790.

From the Table B-37, I get that the balance of the parent account "Amortization expenses" is -$952.78.

From the Table B-38, I get that the balance of the parent account "Office rent expenses" is -$1,500.

From the Table B-39, I get that the balance of the parent account "Interest expenses" is -$3,333.33.

From the Table B-40, I get that the balance of the parent account "Tax expenses" is -$11,270.33.

Therefore, the sum of the expenses accounts' balances is -$128,502.55 (= -

$2,456.11 - $85,200 - $23,790 - $952.78 - $1,500 - $3,333.33 - $11,270.33).

Of course, I can also get that the sum of the expenses accounts' balances is - $128,502.55 from the table "Expenses (X5)" in the Table A-27.

The sum of all liabilities accounts, all shareholders' equity accounts, all revenues accounts, and all expenses accounts is $907,080.94 (= $592,217.79 + $217,865.70 + $225,500 - $128,502.55).

The sum of all assets accounts is also $907,080.94.

These two sum amounts are equal. They are $907,080.94.

- After the previous two steps are correct, I check whether the left (or right) amount of the dynamic accounting equation is equal to the sum of all assets accounts' balances (or the sum of all liabilities, all equity accounts, all incomes accounts, and all expenses accounts' balances).

Obviously, the requirement is satisfied.

The above three requirements are satisfied, so the mathematical accounting model is reliable and correct.

From the Table B-2 in the Appendixes B, I can get the some amounts of the Income Statement, seeing the following table 2-45.

Table 2-45 Income Statement

	Year ended on 3/31/2021	
1	Revenues	
2	Sales	$154,800.00
3	Cost	
4	Cost of sales	-$85,200.00
5	Gross Margin	$69,600.00
6		
7	Operating and administrative expenses	
8	Administrative expenses	-$2,456.11
9	Salary expenses	-$23,790.00
10	Amortization expenses	-$952.78

167

11	Office rent expenses	-$1,500.00
12	Interest expenses	-$3,333.33
13	Earnings Before Income Taxes	$37,567.78
14		
15	Tax	
16	Tax expenses	-$11,270.33
17	Net Earnings	$26,297.45
18		
19	Retained Earnings, Beginning	$112.465.70
20	Retained Earnings, Ending	$138,763.15

From the Table 2-45, the amounts of the line 2 and the line 4 can be added together to get the amount of the line 5. The amounts of the line 5 and the line 8 to 12 can be added together to get the amount of the line 13. Adding the amounts of the line 13 and the line 16 together, I get the amount of the Net Earnings which is equal to $26,297.45. Obviously, the amount of the line 19 is equal to $112.465.70 which is the Retained earnings, Ending of the last fiscal year. Finally, adding the amounts of the line 17 and the line 19 together, I get the amount of the Retained Earnings, Ending (line 20). Itis equal to $138,763.15.

From the Table B-2 in the Appendixes B, I can get the some amounts of the Balance Sheet, seeing the following table 2-46.

Table 2-46 Balance Sheet

	As at 3/31/2021	
1	ASSETS	
2	Current assets	
3	Cash	$96,441.48
4	Office supplies	$129.61
5	Inventory	$18,830.00
6	HST recoverable	$11,096.80
7	Account receivable	$99,940.00
8		$226,437.89
9	Long term investments	
10	Land	$180,000.00

11	AOCI of land	$55,000.00
12	Share	$356,700.00
13	AOCI of share	$41,100.00
14		$632,800.00
15	Equipment	
16	Truck	$45,000.00
17	Accumulated amortization: truck	-$2,250.00
18	Computer	$5,600.00
19	Accumulated amortization: computer	-$506.95
20		$47,843.05
21	Total Assets	$907,080.94
22		
23	LIABILITIES	
24	Current liabilities	
25	Account payable	$51,156.80
26	HST payable	$20,124.00
27	Accrued interest payable	$9,666.66
28	Tax payable	$11,270.33
29		$92,217.79
30	Long term liabilities	
31	Note payable	$500,000.00
32	Total Liabilities	$592,217.79
33		
34	SHAREHOLDERS' EQUITY	
35	Owners' capital	
36	Share capital	$80,000.00
37	Retained earnings	$138,763.15
38	Accumulated other comprehensive income	$96,100.00
39	Total Shareholders' Equity	$314,863.15
40		
41	Total Liabilities and Shareholders' Equity	$907,080.94

From the Table 2-46, the amounts of the line 3 to the line 7 can be added together to get the amount of the line 8. The amounts of the line 10 to line 13 can be added together to get the amount of the line 14. The amounts of the line 16 to line 19 can be added together to get the amount of the line 20. Then I can get the amount of the Total Assets (line 17) after adding the amounts of the line 8, the line 14, and the line 20 together. It is equal to

$907,080.94. Adding the amounts of the line 25 to the line 28 together, I get the amount of the line 29 which is equal to $150,158.02. Adding the amounts of the line 29 and the line 31 together, I get the amount of the Total Liabilities (line 32) which is equal to $$650,158.02. Adding the amounts of the line 36, the line 37, and the line 38 together, I get the amount of the Total Shareholders' Equity (line 39) which is equal to $47,843.05. Finally, adding the amounts of the line 32 and the line 39 together, I get the amount of the Total Liabilities and Shareholders' Equity (line 41). It is equal to $888,023.72.

From the Table B-8 in the Appendixes B, I can get the Cash Flows statement, seeing the following table 2-47.

Table 2-47 Cash Flows

	Year ended on 3/31/2021	
1	Operating activities	
2	Cash payments for machinery	-$0
3	Cash payments to suppliers	-$117,837.10
4	Cash payments for operating expenses	-$87,226.29
5	Cash receipts from customers	$174,706.00
6	Net cash provided by Operating activities	-$30,357.39
7		
8	Investing activities	
9	Cash payments for investment	$0
10	Net cash provided by Investing activities	$0
11		
12	Financing activities	
13	Cash receipts from owners	-$20,000.00
14	Cash receipts from banks	
15	Net cash provided by Financing activities	-$20,000.00
16		
17	Net change in cash	-$50,357.39
18	Cash, Beginning	$146,798.87
19	Cash, Ending	$96,441.48

From the Table B-8, the amounts of the line 2 to the line 5 in the Table 2-47 can be respectively gotten from the tables of the two-level subaccounts under the one-level subaccount: Operating activities. The amount of the line 6 can be gotten from the table of the one-level subaccount: Operating activities. Of course, this amount is also gotten after adding the amounts of the line 2 to the line 5 together. The amount of the line 9 can be gotten from the table of the two-level subaccount under the one-level subaccount: Investing activities. The amount of the line 10 can be gotten from the table of the one-level subaccount: Investing activities. The amounts of the line 13 to the line 14 can be respectively gotten from the tables of the two-level subaccounts under the one-level subaccount: Financing activities. The amount of the line 15 can be gotten from the table of the one-level subaccount: Financing activities. Adding the amounts of the line 6, the line 10, and the line 15, I can get the amount of the Net change in cash (line 17). It is equal to -$50,357.39. Finally, I can get the amount of the Cash, Ending (line 19) after adding the amounts of the line 17 and the line 18. It is equal to $96,441.48.

Now, I will introduce the Administrative expenses Flows. The Administrative expenses account has five one-level subaccounts of the Taxi expenses, the Other expenses, the Mobile expenses, the Office supplies expenses, and the Utility expenses, so the Administrative expenses Flows only shows the top three absolute balances of the one-level subaccounts.

From the Table B-10, I can get the Administrative expenses Flows statement, seeing the following table 2-48. The process is the same as the Cash Flows statement.

Table 2-48 Administrative expenses Flows

	Administrative expenses Flows, Year ended on 3/31/2021	
1	Taxi expenses	
2	Purchase department-taxi	-$101.33
3	Sales department-taxi	-$1,261.90
4	Office department-taxi	-$0
5	Net Administrative expenses provided by Taxi expenses	-$1,363.23
6		
7	Other expenses	
8	Office department-other	-$355.71
9	Purchase department-other	-$70.30

10	Sales department-other	-$242.45
11	Net Administrative expenses provided by Other expenses	-$668.46
12		
13	Utility expenses	
14		-$323.14
15	Net Administrative expenses provided by Utility expenses	-$323.14
16		
17	Net change in Administrative expenses	-$2,354.83
18	Administrative expenses, Beginning	$0.00
19	Administrative expenses, Ending	-$2,354.83
20		
21	Total Administrative expenses, Ending	-$2,456.11

The ending administrative expenses for the top three one-level subaccounts is -$2,354.83 while total ending inventory is -$2,456.11. The difference between them is -$101.28 which is the balance of the Office supplies expenses (-$101.28).

The Table 2-49 shows the total unrealized holding gain or loss $25,400 which is consisted of the land's unrealized holding gain or loss $30,000 and the MicroQQ share's unrealized holding gain or loss -$4,600.

Table 2-49 Comprehensive income statement

	Year ended on 3/31/2021	
1	Net income	$26,297.45
2		
3	Other comprehensive income	
4	Unrealized holding gain or loss, net of tax	$70,700.00
5		
6	Comprehensive income	$96,997.45

From the tables of the one-level subaccounts under the Table B-12 and the Table B-6, I can get every Account receivable age on April 5, 2021, seeing the following Table 2-50. For example, when the RR Company sold some inventories to the E1 Company on February 4,

2021, the amount of the Account receivable is $200,688 and its GeID is 48. Later, the RR Company respectively received cash $120,000 with the Ref **48** and the GeID 57 on February 25, 2021 and cash $52,000 with the Ref **48** and the GeID 80 on March 10, 2021, so the balance of the Account receivable with the GeID 48 is equal to $28,688 (=$200,688 - $120,000 - $52,000).

Table 2-50 Account receivable age

ID	Customer Name	TransDate	Fhone No. (MultiName)	Day	GeID	Amount (Sub-Balance)	Balance
1	B1	2021-1-5	123456789	0	5	0	0
2	B1	2021-1-29	123456789	0	23	0	0
3	E1	2021-1-11	123456788	84	13	8835	8835
4	E1	2021-2-4	123456788	60	48	28688	37523
5	F1	2021-1-23	123456787	72	20	6187	43710
6	F1	2021-3-4	123456787	32	79	54924	98634
7	H1	2021-1-25	123456787	70	21	1306	99940

From the tables of the one-level subaccounts under the Table B-22 and the Table B-5, I can get every Account payable age on April 5, 2021, seeing the following Table 2-51. For example, when the RR Company purchased some inventories from the C1 Company on January 9, 2021, the amount of the Account payable is $26,250 and its GeID is 11. Later, the RR Company paid cash $14,000 with the Ref **11** and the GeID 17 on January 21, 2021 to C1 Company. The RR Company paid cash $7,500 with the Ref **11** and the GeID 27 on January 30, 2021 to C1 Company. The RR Company paid cash $4,500 with the Ref **11** and the GeID 84 on March 15, 2021 to C1 Company. Therefore, the balance of the Account payable with the GeID 11 is equal to $250 (=$26,250 - $14,000 - $7,500 - $4,500).

Table 2-51 Account payable age

ID	Supplier Name	TransDate	Fhone No. (MultiName)	Day	GeID	Amount (Sub-Balance)	Balance
1	A1	2021-1-4	987654321	0	4	0	0
2	C1	2021-1-9	987654322	86	11	250	25C

3	C1	2021-1-22	987654322	73	19	9295	9545
4	D1	2021-1-9	987654323	81	12	3560	13105
5	D1	2021-2-3	987654323	61	47	17830	30935
6	G1	2021-1-17	987654324	78	15	6125	37060
7	G1	2021-3-3	987654324	33	78	14096.8	51156.80

Now, I complete the three financial statements for the different three periods. Please notice the changes of the AOCI, the Accumulated amortization, the Cash (Beginning), the Cash (Ending), the Retained earnings (Beginning), and Retained earnings (Ending) in the above tables.

2.3 Convert to mathematical accounting model during fiscal year

If a company will like to use the mahematical accounting model during its current fiscal year, it is easy to begin to use the mathematical accounting model. For any company, the balances of all accounts must be satisfied a dynamic accounting equation, so you may enter a transaction which includes all the accounts and their related information to complete the transference in theory. However, for clear and conveniance, you should divide the dynamic accounting equation into the N sub-equations. No matter how you combine the accounts in a transaction, the only requirement is that each sub-equation must be balanced exception of the "Account receivable" and the "Account payable" accounts.

Because you need the transaction dates of the "Account receivable" and the "Account payable" accounts later, only the same transaction date of the "Account receivable" account and the "Account payable" account can be combined into a new transaction in the conversion. The following is an example.

For a customer (phone number: 567891234), the detail information of its account receivable account is:

Trancaction date: Janurary 3, 2021, amount: $980,

Trancaction date: Janurary 19, 2021, amount: $1,230,

Trancaction date: Feruary 27, 2021, amount: $5,500.

For a supplier (phone number: 123498765), the detail information of its account payable account is:

Trancaction date: Janurary 8, 2021, amount: $1,400,

Trancaction date: January 19, 2021, amount: $1,860,

Trancaction date: Feruary 28, 2021, amount: $6,900.

Then, the account receivable and account payable with the same transaction date can be combined into a new transaction ir the conversion. The new transaction sub-equation is:

Account receivable (1): 1230 + Cash (1): 630 = Account payable (2): 1860

Here, cash $630 is only the part of the cash account's balance. Of course, you can add more items to the sub-equation if you wish.

Chapter 3

Accounting Future

Finally, I will introduce three concepts of the great accounting, the digital currency, and the internet of things simply. Theses concept are based on the mathematical accounting model and the wealth conservation law.

3.1 Great accounting

In the great data time, centered management of accounting is an inexorable trend. Every business company can login in a government's centered database by using of its business number. In addition, there is a famous law of the "Energy conservation law" in natural science. The every different exposition of this law has promoted science development. The most famous exposition of the law is atomic theory. Similarly, I think that there is a law of the "Wealth conservation law" in social science. All companies and organizations in the world will follow the law of the "Wealth conservation law". For a company or an organization, every department can do part work of the accounting about itself duty. All works of the company or the organization's departments will be made up of the financial statements. The great accounting has many advantages, such as being difficult to draw up false accounts and to evade a tax.

Now, the accounting department is too powerful. It not only manages cash, but also is responsible of being made up of the financial statements. However, many accounting data are the second data which come from other departments. There may be some problems in the financial statements under the special circumstances. The accounting department's duty should be to manage the cash. Every department in a company or an organization can do part work of the accounting about itself duty. All works of the company or the organization's departments will be made up of the financial statements which are more reliable and correct

The many expenses are related to every employee in a company or an organization, but the salary expenses is the most expense for every employee. Therefore, the form of the multi-subaccount name of the "Salary expenses" account should also be the same as the many expenses' accounts in the great accounting.

If a company or an organization has 99 factories in the different places and the maximum number of every department's employees in a factory is 9999, then the three-level subaccount of the "Salary expenses" account is every employee ID which may be every employee's name, or phone number, or social insurance number. Its multi-subaccount's form is the "Employee ID<Different department<Different factory". If a company or an organization has only different departments, the multi-subaccount's form of the "Salary expenses" account is the "Employee ID<Different department".

The other many expenses can be distinguished from the salary expenses by adding a symbol of the "-xxxx". Its multi-subaccount's form is the "Employee ID-xxxx<Different department-xxxx<Different factory-xxxx". For example, the multi-subaccount's form of the "Administrative expenses" account is the "Employee name-other<Different department-other<Other expenses" in the Chapter 2.

A typical company or organization structure may have fifteen departments: accounting department, office department, human resource department, production department, equipment department, purchases department, sales department, inventory management department, research development department, and other departments. I will introduce a few of the departments' duty in the great accounting.

3.1.1 Accounting department

Accounting department duty is only to pay the cash according to the other departments' requirement except for recording itself salary expenses according to actual attendance and miscellaneous expenses.

Every employee's salary expenses is planned by the human resource department. According to actual attendance, some employees' actual salary expenses of the accounting department may be corrected by the accounting department.

3.1.2 Human resource department

The Human Resource department's main duty is to build every employee's profile including planned salary expenses and salary payable at beginning of every month. Of course, it also records itself salary expenses according to actual attendance and its miscellaneous expenses.

The "Salary expenses" account has the three-level subaccounts. Its multi-subaccount form should be the "Employee ID-salary<Different department-salary<Different factory-salary". However, the "Salary expenses" is the most expenses in all employee's expenses, so I define its multi-subaccount form as the "Employee ID<Different department<Different factory". The "Salary payable" account has the two-level subaccounts. Its multi-subaccount form is the "Employee ID-xxxx<XXXX payable". Here, I use social insurance number as the employee ID. In fact, the "Administrative expenses" account in the Chapter 2 uses the employee's name as the employee ID.

3.1.3 Office department

Office department duty is to record itself salary expenses according to actual attendance and its miscellaneous expenses.

3.1.4 Production department

Production department duty is to record the inventory in production process except for recording itself salary expenses according to actual attendance and its miscellaneous expenses.

3.1.5 Equipment department

Equipment department duty is to record the amortization expenses and accumulated amortization except for recording itself salary expenses according to actual attendance and its miscellaneous expenses.

3.1.6 Purchases department

Purchase department duty is to record and manage the account payable and the suppliers' information except for recording itself salary expenses according to actual attendance and its miscellaneous expenses.

3.1.7 Sales department

Sales department duty is to record and manage the account receivable and the customers' information except for recording itself salary expenses according to actual attendance and its miscellaneous expenses.

3.1.8 Inventory department

Inventory department duty is to record and manage the inventory according to other departments' needs except for recording itself salary expenses according to actual attendance and its miscellaneous expenses.

3.1.9 Research development department

Research development department duty is to record the research development expenses except for recording itself salary expenses according to actual attendance and its miscellaneous expenses.

3.2 Digital currency

3.2.1 Digital Currency Definition

The digital currency may have other definition. However, I give the digital currency a new definition in this essay. Based on the mathematical accounting model, the digital currency is the electric extension of the traditional money and has an important character which is that every dollar in circulating process is embedded an ID. The IDs of all members of a society will be embedded in the circulating money because all members of a society will touch money. The most advantage of digital currency is that the Canada Revenue Agency can get the cash flows statement of any organization or company by using of data which is provided by other related organizations or companies. In this situation, drawing up false accounts, tax evasion, and money laundering will be impossible to occur.

For recording the detail information of all circulating money (data), I design a table, seeing the Figure 3-1, which is a public table. The table will record cash received and paid by all social members (all organizations and all individuals). The detail information of a social member (an organization or an individual) in this table is recorded by other different organizations, so the data is fair, reliable, and correct. In other words, an organization can build itself cash flows statement by using of itself data while the administrators of the Canada Revenue Agency can build this organization's cash flows statement by using of other organizations' data recorded in this table. Of course, this table is in the Canada Revenue Agency.

ID	Amount	Symbol	MultiSubaccount Names	Transaction Date	Recorder

Figure 3-1 Cash Received and Paid by All Social Members

Cash can be divided into two classes of cash receipts and cash payments and can be distinguished by the symbols of the "+" and "-". For every social member, the sum of cash receipts and cash payments is his or her balance of cash he or she holds. The cash receipts can be divided into three classes of the taxable receipts, the no taxable receipts, and the deposits. The cash payments can also be divided into four classes of investment, consumption, not deductible expenses, and deposits. The two deposits can be merged and have the same two-level subaccount and one-level subaccount names (Cash receipts from customers deposits < Operating activities). Therefore, the balance of cash held by a member is different from the balance of asset owned by the same member. For getting the cash or asset detail information of every member, I design a table to explain the meanings of these symbols, seeing the Figure 3-2 on the next page.

Cash (**Symbol**)	Symbols	Meanings	Examples
Receipts (+)	-t	Taxable income	Salary, Dividend, Investment income, and Sales
Receipts (+)	-n	No taxable income	Transfer between friends, OSAP, and Other
Receipts (+)	-d	Deposit	Deposits in business bank
Payments (-)	-i	Investment	Open company, buy shares, and buy bonds
Payments (-)	-c	Consumption	Buy machinery or Operating expenses. Reference of MultiSubaccount Names in Figure 1
Payments (-)	-m	Not deductible expenses	Fine fees
Payments (-)	-d	Deposit	Deposits in business bank

Figure 3-2   Meanings of Symbols Table

3.2.2 Technical Support and Security of Digital Currency

The most advantage of the the mathematical accounting model is that it can embed an ID into every dollar in the process of money circulation regardless of the cash receipts and the cash payments. Therefore, the the mathematical accounting model is the strong technical support and security of the digital currency. All members of the society in the world will touch money and the digital currency is the electric extend of the traditional money, so all IDs of society members can be embedded in the money.

To embed an ID into every dollar will be achieved by adding a three-level subaccount of the ID to the parent account Cash. The ID is opposite social member's ID in a transaction. There is an exception for the symbol "d". The ID is this social member's ID itself in a transaction. When a company records a cash receipt from a customer, this customer will be recorded a cash payment and the customer's cash will decrease; when a company records a cash payments to suppliers, this supplier will be recorded a cash receipt and the supplier's cash will increase. Because a social member may occur many different cash transactions in an organization, a suffix of the "-xxxx" must be added into the ID to distinguish them. The multi-subaccount name should be the "ID-symbol-xxxx<Cash receipts from XXXX or Cash payments for (to) XXXX<Financial activities (Investment activities or Operating activities).

The Figure 3-3 shows all possible multi-subaccounts of the Cash parent account in this paper. When two-level subaccounts are the lowest-level subaccount of the Cash account, they are sole. Please pay attention. If adding a three-level subaccount of the "ID-symbol-xxxx" to the multi-subaccount name of the Cash account, then the two-level subaccount will not be sole again. Obviously, an employee can repeatedly occur the "Salary expenses" fees.

Order	Cash receipts	Cash payments
1	Cash receipts from banks < Financial activities	Cash payments for investments < Investing activities
2	Cash receipts from customers < Operating activities	Cash payments for machinery < Operating activities
3	Cash receipts from investments < Investing activities	Cash payments for operating expenses < Operating activities
4	Cash receipts from owners < Financial activities	Cash payments to suppliers < Operating activities
5	Cash receipts from customers deposits < Operating activities	Cash payments to owners < Financial activities
6	Cash receipts from issued bonds < Financial activities	Cash payments to note lenders < Operating activities
7	Cash receipts from note accrued interest (customers) < Operating activities	Cash payments to bond holders < Operating activities
8	Cash receipts from central bank budgets < Financial activities	-

Figure 3-3　Two-Level Subaccount Names of Cash

Simple digital currency means that there is not any paper money in the process of money circulation. Obviously, it is an ideal society and the MathAccounting software will be a perfect solution of the digital currency. When every organization (company) of a society uses the MathAccounting software to record their business transactions, the Canada Revenue Agency will get every member's (including individuals) detail information of the cash received and paid. In this situation, drawing up false accounts, tax evasion, and money laundering will be impossible to occur.

3.2.3 Sample of a Small Society Model

If there is a small society with the 10 organizations and the 30 persons, its conceptual framework of all society members is showed in the Figure 3-4 on the next page.

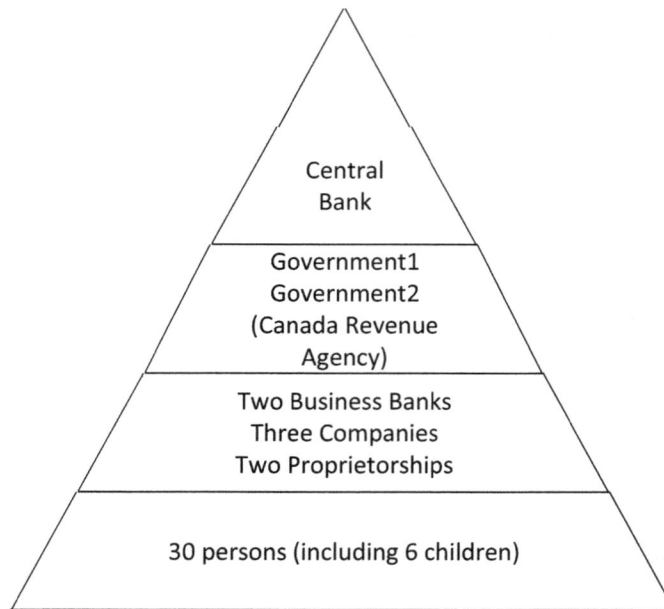

Figure 3-4   Pyramid Pattern of Small Society

After completing the conversion on December 31, 2019 and entering all transactions of all organizations (companies) in an accounting fiscal year 2020, I can get a public table which includes the detail information of all social members.

3.2.4 Analysis and Conclusion

By using of the public table, I can get the following perfect financial information of all individuals in the society.

1. Cash Balances of all individuals.
2. Taxation information of all individuals.
3. Investment information of all individuals
4. Consuming information of all individuals
5. No taxable incomes information of all individuals

I can also get the following financial information of all organizations in this society. Moreover, the financial information is not provided by one social member itself, but is provided by other social members

1. Cash Balances of of organizations.

2. Cash Flows statements of organizations.

3. Investment information of organizations.

4. Taxation information of organizations (Part).

3.3 Internet of things

3.3.1 Internet of Things Definition

Because the data of the cash in all banks is recorded by using of all smart cards automatically, the customers' data of the cash in these banks is the most trustworthy. The data of the cash in the banks can be regarded as a standard or a ruler of measuring other data of the cash. From this idea, I have developed a new concept of the digital currency. Based on this concept and the great accounting cycle including the interior transactions, I have developed and extended a concept of the digital inventory. The inventory account is a concomitant of the cash account or the account receivable (account payable) account in the same transaction. There are two classes of transaction sub-equations for different combinations of the three accounts.

First, there are the cash account and the inventory account in a transaction sub-equation. The transaction sub-equations are respectively:

Cash (1): xxx + Inventory (1): -xxx = HST payable (2) xxx + Sales (4): xxx + Cost of goods sold (5): -xxx

Or   Cash (1): xxx + Inventory (1): -xxx + Account receivable (1): xxx = HST payable (2) xxx + Sales (4): xxx + Cost of goods sold (5): -xxx

Or   Cash (1): -xxx + Inventory (1): xxx + HST recoverable (1) xxx = 0

Or   Cash (1): -xxx + Inventory (1): xxx + HST recoverable (1) xxx = Account payable (2): xxx

Or Cash (1): xxx + Inventory (1): -xxx + HST recoverable (1) -xxx = 0 (Return)

Or Cash (1): xxx + Inventory (1): -xxx = 0 (Conversation)

When the cash is embedded in a social member identity, the inventory is also embedded in this social member identity.

Second, there is not the cash account and is only the account receivable (account payable) account with the inventory account in a transaction sub-equation. The transaction sub-equations are respectively:

Inventory (1): -xxx + Account receivable (1): xxx = Sales (4): xxx + Cost of goods sold (5): -xxx

Or Inventory (1): xxx = Account payable (2): xxx

The lowest multi-subaccount of the account receivable (account payable) account is the customer (supplier) telephone number, and there is a relationship of one to one between the telephone number and the social member identity in the two tables of the customers' information and the suppliers' information. Therefore, when a transaction sub-equation only include the account receivable (account payable) account and the inventory account, the inventory is also embedded in this social member identity.

There is an exception of the interior transaction. When a company (an organization) has produced some products which are the sources of all other companies' inventories, the identity embedded in these inventories is obviously the identity of the producer itself. When a company (an organization) uses the purchased inventories as the some equipment or some parts to produce itself products or as the consumables to consume, the identities embedded in these purchased inventories do not change. For distinguishing the interior transactions, I give the recorder's identity as these inventories' identities. These interior transaction sub-equations respectively are:

Inventory (1): xxx + Working-in-process inventory (1): xxx = 0

Or   Inventory (1): -xxx + Different equipment (1): xxx = 0

Or   Inventory (1): -xxx = Cost of goods manufactured (5): -xxx

Or   Inventory (1): -xxx = Administrative expenses (5): -xxx

These accounts of the Cash, the Account payable, the Account receivable, the Working-in-process inventory, the Equipment, the Cost of goods manufactured, and the XXX expenses are defined as the judging accounts. When correcting a transaction which includes a judging account, the transaction sub-equation must include a judging account even if its amount is zero. However, the judging accounts are too many to deal with, so I take another method to solve this problem.

When there is an Inventory account in a transaction sub-equation, the identity of the Inventory is defaulted as the recorder's identity. If there is any Cash account, or the Account payable account, or the Account receivable account in the same transaction sub-equation, the identity of the Inventory will be set as the Cash's identity automatically. In this situation, there are only the four judging accounts of the Cash, the Account payable, the Account receivable, and the Inventory. The four judging accounts must be the same for all users.

If I wish that there is the detail information of the Inventory account on the balance sheet, then the form of the Inventory account is the "Inventory-xxxx".

By tracking the embedded identity, the parts of this inventory and their product codes or their product batches will be detected. All inventories embedded in all social members' identities and information of their parts will be consisted of digital inventory. The combination of internet and the digital inventory is the Internet of Things. The Internet of Things will realize the intelligent recognition, tracking, monitoring and management of all inventories. In this situation, counterfeit and shoddy products will be impossible to occur.

For recording the detail information of all circulating inventory (data), I design a table, seeing the Figure 3-6. The table will record inventory purchased and sold by all social members (all organizations and all individuals) through the mathematical accounting model. The detail information of a social member (an organization or an individual) in this table is recorded by other different organizations, so the data is fair, reliable, and correct.

In other words, an organization can build itself inventory flows statement by using of itself data while the Canada Revenue Agency can build this organization's inventory flows statement by using of other organizations' data recorded in this table. Of course, this table is in the Canada Revenue Agency.

ID	Amount	Symbol	Multi-subaccount Names	Transaction Date	Recorder	Unit

Figure 3-6   Inventory Purchased and Sold by All Social Members

Inventory can be divided into two classes of inventory purchased and inventory sold and can be distinguished by the symbols of the "+" and "-". For every social member, the sum of inventory purchased and inventory sold is his or her balance of inventory he or she holds. The individuals may not sell the inventories to other social members, but they may return some inventories to their suppliers.

The Figure 3-7 shows the meanings of the inventory's symbols in the transactions of including the account receivable or the account payable and the interior transactions.

Inventory	Symbols	Meanings	Examples
Including Cash or only Account receivable	-c	Sold to customers to consume	Cash or Account receivable
Including Cash or only Account payable	-t	Purchased from suppliers	Cash or Account payable
In interior transactions	-p	Produced products (Sources)	Working-in-process inventory
In interior transactions	-e	Equipment	Vehicle, Computer, Airplane, Buildings, Machine, Ship, and so on
In interior transactions	-f	Transfer into other product	Cost of goods manufactured
In interior transactions	-s	Consumption	Office supply expenses

Figure 3-7   Meanings of Symbols Table

3.3.2 Technical Support and Security of Digital Inventory

The mathematical accounting model is the strong technical support and security of the digital currency. The inventory account is a concomitant of the cash account or the account receivable (account payable) account in the same transaction. When I record the cata of the cash account, I also records the relevant information of the inventory account. In addition, for the multi-subaccount name of the inventory account, every company (organization) can build the different one-level and two-level subaccounts and only need to ensure that the three-level subaccounts are sole for all companies (organizations). Therefore, the digital inventory is feasible and reliable.

3.3.3 Sample of a Small Society Model

Digital currency and digital inventory are a pair of twins, so digital inventory is also based on the simple (pure) digital currency model. The sole difference is that the lowest multi-subaccount of the inventory account must be included a product codes or a product batch or other information.

3.3.4 Analysis and Conclusion

Based on the Table dcj200, the Canada Revenue Agency can get cash, investment, and taxation information of all social members (including all organizations and all individuals), the financial information, which are not provided by one social member himself, are provided by other relevant social members. By using of the Table 3-xx, I can get the Inventory Flows and realize function of the Internet of Things: intelligent recognition, tracking, monitoring and management of all inventories.

3.4 MathAccounting software

Maybe, you asked that the mathematical accounting model is so complicated. Yes. If a business company has many subaccounts, it is very difficult to record these transactions.

However, we are lucky With development of computer and database technology, the most work in the mathematical accounting model can be done by the computer. I have developed a MathAccounting software based on the mathematical accounting model. By using of the MathAccounting software, it is very easy to record these transactions. The only parent accounts' tables are created in the database and all subaccounts' tables will be gotten by using of the database query in the MathAccounting software, so what you must know is just to fill in the original proof of a transaction. It is easy? Meanwhile, I can easily get reliable and correct financial statements and achieve the goals of the Digital currency and the Interent of things by using of the MathAccounting software.

Moreover, the MathAccounting software is a powerful container. In my opnion, all management software can be contained in this container by using of the different multi-subaccounts.

Appendixes A

In the sixth cabinet, there are the following tables.

Table A-1 General equation

GeID	TransDate	General Equation	Left Amount	Right Amount	Explanation	Enter Date
1	2021-1-2	Cash(1): 10000 = Share capital(3): 4000 + Capital(3): 3000 + Capital(3): 3000	100000	100000	Ping Wang, Hua Li and Mike Newsome decide to open a RR trade business	2021-1-4
2	2021-1-3	Cash(1): -193 + Office supplies(1): 193 = 0	0	0	Purchase of Office supplies	2021-1-4
3	2021-1-3	Cash(1): -47 = Administrative expenses (5): -47	-47	-47	Cash payments for Hua Li's taxi fee expense	2021-1-4
4	2021-1-5	Cash(1): -670 + Inventory(1): 3670 + HST recoverable(1): 477.10 = Account payable(2): 3477.10	3477.10	3477.10	RR purchases $3,670 inventory by $670 cash and other on credit from A1 company (phone number: 987654321)	2021-1-6
5	2021-1-5	Cash(1): 300 + Inventory(1): -1900 + Account receivable(1): 2558.90 = HST payable(2): 328.90 + Sales(4): 2530 + Cost of sales (5): -1900	958.90	958.90	RR sells $1,900 inventory to B1 Company (phone number: 123456789) for sales of $2,530 and receives $300 cash	2021-1-6
6	2021-1-7	Cash(1): 1500 + Account receivable(1): -1500 = 0	0	0	RR Company receives $1,500 cash from B1 Company (phone number: 123456789) with the General ID 5	2021-1-8
7	2021-1-7	Cash (1): 500000 = Note payable (2): 500000	500000	500000	RR Company raises funds of $500,000 cash with interest rate 8% (paying interest at the end of each year) and two years from TD bank on January 7, 2014.	2021-1-8
8	2021-1-7	Cash (1): -450000 + Land (1): 450000 = 0	0	0	RR Company purchases two lands (Land1, Downtown for $270,000; Land2, North York for $180,000) for $450,000 cash as available for sale	2021-1-8
9	2021-1-8	Cash (1): -45000 + Truck (1): 45000 = 0	0	0	RR Company purchases a truck for $45,000 cash	2021-1-9
10	2021-1-8	Cash (1): -367 = Administrative expenses (5): -367	-367	-367	RR Company pays $367 cash to Ping Wang (Office department) for opening company expenses	2021-1-9
11	2021-1-9	Cash(1): -2000 + Inventory(1): 25000 + HST recoverable(1): 3250 = Account payable(2): 26250	26250	26250	RR Company purchases $25,000 inventory for $2,000 cash and $23,000 on credit from C1 Company (phone number: 987654322).	2021-1-10
12	2021-1-9	Inventory(1): 12000 + HST recoverable(1): 1560 = Account payable(2): 13560	13560	13560	RR Company purchases $12,000 inventory on credit from D1 Company (phone number: 987654323)	2021-1-10

13	2021-1-11	Cash(1): 3500 + Inventory(1): -17700 + Account receivable(1): 29835 = HST payable(2): 3835 + Sales(4): 29500 + Cost of sales (5): -17700	15635	15635	Xiao Zhou sales $17,700 inventory for $3,500 cash and $26,000 on credit to E1 Company (phone number: 123456788)	2021-1-12
14	2021-1-15	Inventory(1): -13200 + Account receivable(1): 24521 = HST payable(2): 2821 + Sales(4): 21700 + Cost of sales (5): -13200	11321	11321	ZhenDao Yuan sales $13,200 inventory for $21,700 on credit to F1 Company (phone number: 123456787)	2021-1-16
15	2021-1-17	Inventory(1): 12500 + HST recoverable(1): 1625 = Account payable(2): 14125	14125	14125	RR Company purchases $12,500 inventory on credit from G1 Company (phone number: 987654324)	2021-1-18
16	2021-1-17	Cash(1): 21000 + Account receivable: -21000 = 0	0	0	Receive $21,000 cash from E1 Company (phone number: 123456788) with the General ID 13	2021-1-18
17	2021-1-21	Cash (1) -14000 = Account payable(2): -14000	-14000	-14000	Pay $14,000 cash to C1 Company (phone number: 987654322) with the General ID 11	2021-1-22
18	2021-1-21	Cash (1) -6000 = Account payable(2): -6000	-6000	-6000	Pay $6,000 cash to D1 Company (phone number: 987654323) with the General ID 12	2021-1-22
19	2021-1-22	Inventory(1): 21500 + HST recoverable(1): 2795 = Account payable(2): 24295	24295	24295	RR Company purchases $21,500 inventory on credit from C1 Company (phone number: 987654322)	2021-1-23
20	2021-1-23	Inventory(1): -12000 + Account receivable(1): 22487 = HST payable(2): 2587 + Sales(4): 19900 + Cost of sales (5): -12000	10487	10487	Yi Liu sales $12,000 inventory for $19,900 on credit to F1 Company (phone number: 123456787)	2021-1-24
21	2021-1-25	Inventory(1): -7500 + Account receivable(1): 15481 = HST payable(2): 1781 + Sales(4): 13700 + Cost of sales (5): -7500	7981	7981	ZhenDao Yuan sales $7,500 inventory for $13,700 on credit to H1 Company (phone number: 123456786)	2021-1-26
22	2021-1-28	Cash(1): -5600 + Computer(1): 1600 + Computer(1): 1800 + Computer(1): 2200 = 0	0	0	Purchase $5,600 computers equipment for $5,600 cash	2021-1-29
23	2021-1-29	Inventory(1): -3500 + Account receivable(1): 7006 = HST payable(2): 806 + Sales(4): 6200 + Cost of sales (5): -3500	3506	3506	Jun Wang sales $3,500 inventory for $6,200 on credit to B1 Company (phone number: 123456789)	2021-1-30
24	2021-1-30	Cash(1): 2558.90 + Account receivable(1): -828.90 + Account receivable(1): -1730 = 0	0	0	Receive $2558.90 cash from B1 Company (phone number: 123456789) with the General ID 5 ($828.9) and General ID 23 ($1730)	2021-1-30
25	2021-1-30	Cash(1): 15000 + Account receivable(1): -15000 = 0	0	0	Receive $15,000 cash from F1 Company (phone number: 123456787) with the General ID 14	2021-1-31
26	2021-1-30	Cash(1): 8475 + Account receivable(1): -8475 = 0	0	0	Receive $8,475 cash from H1 Company (phone number: 123456786) with the General ID 21	2021-1-31
27	2021-1-30	Cash (1) -7500 = Account payable(2): -7500	-7500	-7500	Pay $7,500 cash to C1Company (phone number:	2021-1-31

					987654322) with the General ID 11	
28	2021-1-30	Cash (1): -232.76 = Administrative expenses(5): -178 + Administrative expenses (5): -54.76	-232.76	-232.76	Pay $232.76 cash to Dan Zhu (Purchase department) for the taxi expenses $178 and the mobile expenses$54.76	2021-1-31
29	2021-1-30	Cash (1): -221.30 = Administrative expenses(5): -135.12 + Administrative expenses (5): -85.18	-221.30	-221.30	Pay $221.30 cash to Hua Li (Purchase department) for the taxi expenses $135.12 and the other expenses $36.18	2021-1-31
30	2021-1-30	Cash (1): -339.52 = Administrative expenses(5): -243 + Administrative expenses (5): -96.52	-339.52	-339.52	RR Company pays $339.52 cash to Xiao Zhou (Sales department) for the taxi expenses $243 and the other expenses $96.52	2021-1-31
31	2021-1-30	Cash (1): -132.26 = Administrative expenses(5): -132.26	-132.26	-132.26	RR Company pays $132.26 cash to Jun Wang (Sales department) for the other expenses	2021-1-31
32	2021-1-30	Cash (1): -82.33 = Administrative expenses(5): -82.33	-82.33	-82.33	RR Company pays $82.33 cash to Zhendao Yuan (Sales department) for the other expenses	2021-1-31
33	2021-1-31	Cash(1): 13000 + Account receivable(1): -13000 = 0	0	0	RR Company receives $13,000 cash from F1Company (phone number: 123456787) with the General ID 20	2021-1-31
34	2021-1-31	Cash (1) -8000 = Account payable(2): -8000	-8000	-8000	RR Company pays $8,000 cash to G1Company (phone number: 987654324) with the General ID 15	2021-1-31
35	2021-1-31	Cash (1): -419.55 = Administrative expenses (5): -347.70 + Administrative expenses (5): -71.85	-419.55	-419.55	RR Company pays $419.55 cash to Yi Liu (Sales department) for the taxi expenses $347.7 and the mobile expenses$71.85	2021-1-31
36	2021-1-31	Office supplies(1): -88 = Administrative expenses(5): -88	-88	-88	RR Company records the Office supplies expenses $88	2021-1-31
37	2021-1-31	Cash (1): -18756 = Salary expenses (5): -18756	-18756	-18756	RR Company pays $18,756 cash for all salary of January, 2014	2021-1-31
38	2021-1-31	Accumulated amortization: Truck(1): -750 = Amortization expenses(5): -750	-750	-750	Record truck's amortization expenses $750 one month (5 years, straight line, and full first month)	2021-1-31
39	2021-1-31	Accumulated amortization: Computer(1): -33.33 + Accumulated amortization: Computer(1): -37.5 + Accumulated amortization: Computer(1): -30.56 = - Amortization expenses(5): 33.33 - Amortization expenses(5): 37.5 - Amortization expenses(5): 30.56	-101.39	-101.39	RR Company records the computers' amortization expenses $101.39	2021-1-31
40	2021-1-31	Cash (1): -376.47 = Administrative expenses (5): -298.69 + Administrative expenses(5): -77.78	-376.47	-376.47	Pay $376.47 cash to Mike Newsome (Office department) for taxi	2021-1-31

					expenses $298.69 and the mobile expenses$77.78	
41	2021-1-31	Cash (1): -280.70 = Administrative expenses(5): -280.70	-280.70	-280.70	RR Company pays $280.70 cash for the utility expenses	2021-1-31
42	2021-1-31	Cash (1): -1500 = Office rent expenses (5): -1500	-1500	-1500	RR Company pays $1500 cash for the office rent expenses	2021-1-31
43	2021-1-31	0 = Accrued interest payable (2): 3000 + Interest expenses (5): -3000	0	0	Record the note payable's interest expenses $3,000 and the accrued interest payable (500,000*8%/12*27/30)	2021-1-31
44	2021-2-1	HST recoverable (1) -9707.10 = HST payable(2): -9707.10	-9707.10	-9707.10	RR Company records the new balance of the HST payable	2021-2-1
45	2021-2-1	Cash (1) -2451.80 = Account payable(2): -2451.80	-2451.80	-2451.80	RR Company pays the cash of the new balance of the HST payable	2021-2-1
46	2021-2-1	Cash (1): -103.3 + Office supplies (1): 103.3 = 0	0	0	RR Company purchases the Office supplies for cash $103.3	2021-2-2
47	2021-2-3	Inventory(1): 91000 + HST recoverable (1) 11830 = Account payable(2): 102830	102830	102830	RR Company purchases $91,000 inventory on credit from D1 Company (phone number: 987654323)	2021-2-10
48	2021-2-4	Inventory(1): -91200 + Account receivable(1): 200688 = HST payable(2): 23088 + Sales(4): 177600 + Cost of sales (5): -91200	109488	109488	Jun Wang sales $91,200 inventory to E1 Company (phone number: 123456788) on credit $177,600	2021-2-10
49	2021-2-8	Cash(1): 5000 + Account receivable(1): -5000 = 0	0	0	RR Company receives $5,000 cash from B1 Company (phone number: 123456789) with the General ID 23	2021-2-10
50	2021-2-9	Cash(1): 12821 + Account receivable(1): -9521 + Account receivable(1): -3300 = 0	0	0	RR Company receives $12,821 cash from F1 Company (phone number: 123456787) with the General ID 14 ($9521) and the General ID 20 ($3300)	2021-2-10
51	2021-2-11	Cash(1): 3500 + Account receivable(1): -3500 = 0	0	0	RR Company receives $3,500 cash from H1 Company (phone number: 123456786) with the General ID 21	2021-2-20
52	2021-2-13	Cash (1) -2500 = Account payable(2): -2500	-2500	-2500	RR Company pays $2,500 cash to A1 Company (phone number: 987654321) with the General ID 4	2021-2-20
53	2021-2-15	Cash (1) -15000 = Account payable(2): -15000	-15000	-15000	RR Company pays $15,000 cash to C1 Company (phone number: 987654322) with the General ID 19	2021-2-20
54	2021-2-17	Cash (1) -4000 = Account payable(2): -4000	-4000	-4000	RR Company pays $4,000 cash to D1 Company (phone number: 987654323) with the General ID 12	2021-2-20

55	2021-2-18	Cash (1): 360000 + Land(1): -270000 = Investment income (4): 90000	90000	90000	RR Company sells land1 (downtown) for $360,000 cash	2021-2-20
56	2021-2-18	Cash(1): -356700 + Share(1): 356700 = 0	0	0	RR Company purchases 10,000 the MicroQQ Company shares for $35.67 each share. Total amount is $356,700	2021-2-20
57	2021-2-25	Cash(1): 120000 + Account receivable(1): -120000 = 0	0	0	RR Company receives $120,000 cash from E1 Company (phone number: 123456788) with the General ID 48	2021-2-28
58	2021-2-26	Cash (1) -55000 = Account payable(2): -55000	-55000	-55000	RR Company pays $55,000 cash to D1 Company (phone number: 987654323) with the General ID 47	2021-2-28
59	2021-2-28	Cash (1): -55.32 = Administrative expenses(5): -55.32	-55.32	-55.32	RR Company pays $55.32 cash to Dan Zhu (Purchase department) for the other expenses	2021-2-28
60	2021-2-28	Cash (1): -458.39 = Administrative expenses(5): -336.41 + Administrative expenses(5): -121.98	-458.39	-458.39	RR Company pays $458.39 cash to Hua Li (Purchase department) for the taxi expenses $336.41 and the other expenses $121.98	2021-2-28
61	2021-2-28	Cash (1): -33.72 = Administrative expenses(5): -33.72	-33.72	-33.72	RR Company pays $33.72 cash to Xiao Zhou (Sales department) for the other expenses	2021-2-28
62	2021-2-28	Cash (1): -152.31 = Administrative expenses(5): -152.31	-152.31	-152.31	RR Company pays $152.31 cash to Jun Wang (Sales department) for the taxi expenses	2021-2-28
63	2021-2-28	Cash (1): -1015.98 = Administrative expenses(5): -1015.98	-1015.98	-1015.98	RR Company pays $1,015.98 cash to Zhendao Yuan (Sales department) for the other expenses	2021-2-28
64	2021-2-28	Cash (1): -117.95 = Administrative expenses(5): -117.95	-117.95	-117.95	RR Company pays $117.95 cash to Yi Liu (Sales department) for the taxi expenses $99.8 and the other expenses $18.15	2021-2-28
65	2021-2-28	Office supplies (1): -101.28 = Office supplies expenses(5): -101.28	-101.28	-101.28	RR Company records the Office supplies expenses $101.28	2021-2-28
66	2021-2-28	Cash (1): -18756 = Salary expenses(5): -18756	-18756	-18756	RR Company pays $18,756 cash for all salary of February, 2014	2021-2-28
67	2021-2-28	Accumulated amortization: Truck(1): -750 = Amortization expenses(5): -750	-750	-750	Record truck's amortization expenses $750 one month (5 years, straight line, and full first month)	2021-2-28
68	2021-2-28	Accumulated amortization: Computer(1): -66.67 + Accumulated amortization: Computer(1): -75 + Accumulated amortization: Computer(1): -61.11 = - Amortization expenses(5): 66.67 –	-202.78	-202.78	RR Company records the computers' amortization expenses $101.39	2021-2-28

		Amortization expenses(5): 75 – Amortization expenses(5): 61.11				
69	021-2-28	Cash (1): -293.37 = Utility expenses(5): -293.37	-293.37	-293.37	RR Company pays $293.37 cash for the utility expenses	2021-2-28
70	2021-2-28	Cash (1): -1500 = Office rent expenses(5): -1500	-1500	-1500	RR Company pays $1,500 cash for the office rent expenses	2021-2-28
71	2021-2-28	0 = Accrued interest payable (2): 3333.33 + Interest expenses (5): -3333.33	0	0	RR Company records the note payable's interest expenses $3,333.33 and the accrued interest payable (500,000*8%/12)	2021-2-28
72	2021-2-28	0 = Tax payable (2): 48199.59 + Tax expenses (5): -48199.59	0	0	RR Company records the tax expenses $48,199.59 and the tax payable $48,199.59	2021-2-28
73	2021-2-28	Accumulated other comprehensive income of land (1): 30000 = Unrealized holding gain or loss (4): 30000	30000	30000	RR Company records the land's unrealized holding gain or loss	2021-2-28
74	2021-2-8	Accumulated other comprehensive income: share (1): -4600 = Unrealized holding gain or loss (4): -4600	-4600	-4600	RR Company records the share's unrealized holding gain or loss	2021-2-28
Total Amount			888023.72	888023.72		

Table A-2 Reference

ID	Account Name (Subtotal Name)	Row	GeID	Balance
1	**Current assets**	**103**	**1**	**277624.89**
2	Cash	104	1	147298.87
3	Office supplies	106	2	107.02
4	Inventory	108	4	18670.00
5	HST recoverable	109	4	11830.00
6	Account receivable	110	5	99722.00
7	**Long term investments**	**141**	**8**	**450000.00**
8	Land	143	8	450000.00
9	AOCI of land	144	73	30000.00
10	Shares	145	56	356700.00
11	AOCI of share	146	74	-4600.00
12	**Equipment**	**171**	**9**	**48795.83**
13	Truck	173	8	45000.00
14	Accumulated amortization: truck	174	38	-1500.00
15	Computers	175	22	5600.00
16	Accumulated amortization: computer	176	39	-304.17
17	**Current liabilities**	**203**	**4**	**150658.02**
18	Account payable	204	4	73037.10
19	HST payable	205	5	23088.00

20	Accrued interest payable	207	43	6333.33
21	Tax payable	209	75	48199.59
22	**Long term liabilities**	**251**	**7**	**500000.00**
23	Note payable	252	7	500000.00
24	**Owners' capital**	**303**	**1**	**100000.00**
25	Share capital	304	1	100000.00
26	**Revenues**	**403**	**5**	**271130.00**
27	Sales	404	5	271130.00
28	**Cost**	**431**	**5**	**-147000.00**
29	Cost of sales	432	5	-147000.00
30	**Operating and administrative expenses**	**453**	**3**	**-53464.71**
31	Administrative expenses	454	3	-4815.21
32	Salary expenses	456	37	-37512.00
33	Amortization expenses	458	38	-1804.17
34	Office rent expenses	459	42	-3000.00
35	Interest expenses	461	43	-6333.33
36	**Other income**	**475**	**55**	**90000.00**
37	Investment income	476	55	90000.00
38	**Tax**	**600**	**72**	**-48199.59**
39	Tax expenses	602	72	-48199.59
40	**Other comprehensive income**	**713**	**73**	**25400.00**
41	Unrealized holding gain or loss	715	73	25400.00

Table A-3 Subtotal Name

ID	Subtotal Name	Row	GeID	Class
1	Current assets,103	103	1	1
2	Long term investments,141	141	8	1
3	Equipment	171	9	1
4	Current liabilities,203	203	4	2
5	Long term liabilities,251	251	7	2
6	Owners' capital,303	303	1	3
7	Revenues,403	403	5	4
8	Cost,431	431	5	5
9	Operating and administrative expenses,453	453	3	5
10	Other income,475	475	55	4
11	Tax,600	600	75	5
12	Other comprehensive income,713	713	73	4

Table A-4 Multi-subaccounts

ID	Multi-subaccount Name	Parent Account	GeID	Class
1	Cash receipts from owners<Financing activities	Cash	1	1
2	Capital-Ping Wang	Share capital	1	3
3	Capital-Hua Li	Share capital	1	3
4	Capital-Mike Newsome	Share capital	1	3
5	Cash payments for operating expenses<Operating activities	Cash	2	1
6	N	Office supplies	2	1
7	Hua Li-taxi<Purchase department-taxi<Taxi expenses	Administrative expenses	3	5
8	Cash payments to suppliers<Operating activities	Cash	4	1
9	Inven111<Inven11<Inven1	Inventory	4	1
10	Inven112<Inven11<Inven1	Inventory	4	1
11	Inven121<Inven12<Inven1	Inventory	4	1
12	Inven122<Inven12<Inven1	Inventory	4	1
13	Inven13<Inven1	Inventory	4	1
14	987654321	Account payable	4	2
15	Cash receipts from customers<Operating activities	Cash	5	1
16	123456789	Account receivable	5	1
17	Xiao Zhou-sales	Sales	5	4
18	N	Cost of sales	5	5
19	Cash receipts from banks<Financing activities	Cash	7	1
20	N	Note payable	7	2
21	Cash payments for investment<Operating activities	Cash	8	1
22	Land1, Downtown	Land	8	1
23	Land2, North York	Land	8	1
24	Cash payments for machinery<Operating activities	Cash	9	1
25	Truck1	Truck	9	1
26	Ping Wang-open fees<Office department-open fees<Other expenses	Administrative expenses	10	5
27	Inven221<Inven22<Inven2	Inventory	11	1
28	Inven222<Inven22<Inven2	Inventory	11	1
29	PPUK parts<ASD parts<Inven2	Inventory	11	1
30	PPGH parts<ASD parts<Inven2	Inventory	11	1
31	Inven31<Inven3	Inventory	11	1
32	Inven32<Inven3	Inventory	11	1
33	987654322	Account payable	11	2
34	Inven331<Inven33<Inven3	Inventory	12	1
35	Inven332<Inven33<Inven3	Inventory	12	1
36	HGFCVB parts<QASXC parts<Inven3	Inventory	12	1
37	PPGHUP parts<ASDUP parts<Inven3	Inventory	12	1

38	987654323	Account payable	12	2
39	123456788	Account receivable	13	1
40	123456787	Account receivable	14	1
41	ZhenDao Yuan-sales	Sales	14	4
42	Inven411<Inven41<Inven4	Inventory	15	1
43	Inven412<Inven41<Inven4	Inventory	15	1
44	TTTCU parts<TTT parts<Inven4	Inventory	15	1
45	RRRHJK parts<Inven4	Inventory	15	1
46	987654324	Account payable	15	2
47	Yi Liu-sales	Sales	20	4
48	123456786	Account receivable	21	1
49	Computer1	Computers	22	1
50	Computer server1	Computers	22	1
51	POS system1	Computers	22	1
52	Jun Wang-sales	Sales	23	4
53	Dan Zhu-taxi<Purchase department-taxi<Tax expenses	Administrative expenses	28	5
54	Dan Zhu-mobile<Purchase department-mobile<Mobile expenses	Administrative expenses	28	5
55	Hua Li-other<Purchase department-other<Other expenses	Administrative expenses	29	5
56	Xiao Zhou-taxi<Sales department-taxi<Taxi expenses	Administrative expenses	30	5
57	Xiao Zhou-other<Sales department-other<Other expenses	Administrative expenses	30	5
58	Jun Wang-other<Sales department-other<Other expenses	Administrative expenses	31	5
59	Zhendao Yuan-other<Sales department-other<Other expenses	Administrative expenses	32	5
60	Yi Liu-taxi<Sales department-taxi<Taxi expenses	Administrative expenses	35	5
61	Yi Liu-other<Sales department-other<Other expenses	Administrative expenses	35	5
62	Office supplies expenses	Administrative expenses	36	5
63	N	Salary expenses	37	5
64	Truck1-accumulated amortization	Accumulated amortization: truck	38	1
65	Truck1-amortization	Amortization expenses	38	5
66	Computer1-accumulated amortization	Accumulated amortization: Computer	39	1
67	Computer server1-accumulated amortization	Accumulated amortization: Computer	39	1
68	POS system1-accumulated amortization	Accumulated amortization: computer	39	1
69	Computer1-amortization<Computer-amortization	Amortization expenses	39	5
70	Computer server1-amortization<Computer-amortization	Amortization expenses	39	5
71	POS system1-amortization<Computer-amortization	Amortization expenses	39	5
72	Mike Newsome-taxi<Office department-taxi<Taxi expenses	Accumulated amortization: Computer	40	1
73	Mike Newsome-other<Office department-other<Other expenses	Accumulated amortization: computer	40	1
74	Utility expenses	Administrative expenses	41	5
75	N	Office supplies expenses	42	5
76	Note1-TD bank	Accrued interest payable	43	2

77	MicroQQ-share	Share	56	1
78	Dan Zhu-other<Purchase department-other<Other expenses	Administrative expenses	59	5
79	Jun Wang-taxi<Sales department-taxi<Taxi expenses	Administrative expenses	62	5
80	AOCI-land2, North York	AOCI of land	73	1
81	Unrealized holding gain or loss-land	Unrealized holding gain or loss	73	4
82	AOCI-microQQ	AOCI of share	74	1
83	Unrealized holding gain or loss-share	Unrealized holding gain or loss	74	4
84	N	Tax expenses	75	5

Table A-5 Suppliers information

Suppliers

ID	Supplier Phone	Supplier Name	Address	E-mail	Postal Code	City	State	Country
1	987654321	A1	A2	A3	A4	A5	A6	A7
2	987654322	C1	C2	C3	C4	C5	C6	C7
3	987654323	D1	D2	D3	D4	D5	D6	D7
4	987654324	G1	G2	G3	G4	G5	G6	G7

Supplier A1: Account payable (X201)

ID	MultiName	Amount	Balance	Ref	GeID	TransDate
1	987654321	3477.10	3477.10		4	2021-1-5
2	987654321	-2500.00	977.10	4	52	2021-2-13

Supplier C1: Account payable (X201)

ID	MultiName	Amount	Balance	Ref	GeID	TransDate
1	987654322	26250	26250		11	2021-1-9
2	987654322	-14000	12250	11	17	2021-1-21
3	987654322	24295	36545		19	2021-1-22
4	987654322	-7500	29045	11	27	2021-1-30
5	987654322	-15000	14045	19	53	2021-2-15

Supplier D1: Account payable (X201)

ID	MultiName	Amount	Balance	Ref	GeID	TransDate
1	987654323	13560	13560		12	2021-1-9
2	987654323	-6000	7560	12	18	2021-1-21

3	987654323	102830	110390		47	2021-2-3
4	987654323	-4000	106390	12	54	2021-2-17
5	987654323	-55000	51390	47	58	2021-2-26

Supplier G1: Account payable (X201)

ID	MultiName	Amount	Balance	Ref	GeID	TransDate
1	987654324	14125	14125		15	2021-1-17
2	987654324	-8000	6125	15	34	2021-1-31

Table A-6 Customers information

Customers

ID	Customer Phone	Customer Name	Address	E-mail	Postal Code	City	State	Country
1	123456789	B1	B2	B3	B4	B5	B6	B7
2	123456788	E1	E2	E3	E4	E5	E6	E7
3	123456787	F1	F2	F3	F4	F5	F6	F7
4	123456786	H1	H2	H3	H4	H5	H6	H7

Customer B1: Account receivable (X105)

ID	MultiName	Amount	Balance	Ref	GeID	TransDate
1	123456789	2558.90	2558.90		5	2021-1-5
2	123456789	-1500	1058.90	5	6	2021-1-7
3	123456789	7006	8064.90		23	2021-1-29
4	123456789	-828.90	7236	5	24	2021-1-30
5	123456789	-1730	5506	23	24	2021-1-30
6	123456789	-5000	506	23	49	2021-2-8

Customer E1: Account receivable (X105)

ID	MultiName	Amount	Balance	Ref	GeID	TransDate
1	123456788	29835	29835		13	2021-1-11
2	123456788	-21000	8835	13	16	2021-1-17
3	123456788	200688	109523		48	2021-2-4
4	123456788	-120000	89523	48	57	2021-2-25

Customer F1: Account receivable (X105)

ID	MultiName	Amount	Balance	Ref	GeID	TransDate
1	123456787	24521	24521		14	2021-1-15
2	123456787	22487	47008		20	2021-1-23
3	123456787	-15000	32008	**14**	25	2021-1-30
4	123456787	-13000	19008	**20**	33	2021-1-31
5	123456787	-9521	9487	**14**	50	2021-2-9
6	123456787	-3300	6187	**20**	50	2021-2-9

Customer H1: Account receivable (X105)

ID	MultiName	Amount	Balance	Ref	GeID	TransDate
1	123456786	15481	15481		21	2021-1-25
2	123456786	-8475	7006	**21**	26	2021-1-30
3	123456786	-3500	3506	**21**	51	2021-2-11

In the first cabinet, there are the following tables.

Table A-7 Assets (X1) on the door

ID	Account Name (Mathematical Name)	Subtotal	Ref (Row)	Balance
1	Cash (X101)	Current assets,103	104	146798.87
2	Office supplies (X102)	Current assets,103	106	107.02
3	Inventory (X103)	Current assets,103	108	18670.00
4	HST recoverable (X104)	Current assets,103	109	11830.00
5	Account receivable (X105)	Current assets,103	110	99722.00
6	Land (X106)	Long term investments,141	143	180000.00
7	Truck (X107)	Equipment, 171	172	45000.00
8	Accumulated amortization: truck (X109)	Equipment, 171	173	-1500.00
9	Computer (X108)	Equipment, 171	174	5600.00
10	Accumulated amortization: Computer (X110)	Equipment, 171	175	-304.17
11	AOCI of land (X111)	Long term investments,141	144	30000.00
12	Shares (X112)	Long term investments,141	145	356700.00
13	AOCI of share (X113)	Long term investments,141	146	-4600.00

Table A-8 Parent account: Cash on a drawer

Cash (X101)

ID	MultiName	TransDate	Amount	Balance	GeID	SubFirst	SubSecond	SubThird
1	Cash receipts from owners<Financing activities	2021-1-2	100000	100000	1	Financing activities	Cash receipts from owners	
2	Cash payments for operating expenses<Operating activities	2021-1-3	-193	99807	2	Operating activities	Cash payments for operating expenses	
3	Cash payments for operating expenses<Operating activities	2021-1-3	-47	99760	3	Operating activities	Cash payments for operating expenses	
4	Cash payments to suppliers< Operating activities	2021-1-5	-670	99090	4	Operating activities	Cash payments to suppliers	
5	Cash receipts from customers< Operating activities	2021-1-5	300	99390	5	Operating activities	Cash receipts from customers	
6	Cash receipts from customers< Operating activities	2021-1-7	1500	100890	6	Operating activities	Cash receipts from customers	
7	Cash receipts from banks< Financing activities	2021-1-7	500000	600890	7	Cash receipts from banks	Financing activities	
8	Cash payments for investment<Investing activities	2021-1-7	-450000	150890	8	Cash payments for investment	Investing activities	
9	Cash payments for machinery<Operating activities	2021-1-8	-45000	105890	9	Cash payments for machinery	Operating activities	
10	Cash payments for operating expenses<Operating activities	2021-1-8	-367	105523	10	Cash payments for operating expenses	Operating activities	
11	Cash payments to suppliers< Operating activities	2021-1-9	-2000	103523	11	Operating activities	Cash payments to suppliers	
12	Cash receipts from customers< Operating activities	2021-1-11	3500	107023	13	Operating activities	Cash receipts from customers	
13	Cash receipts from customers< Operating activities	2021-1-17	21000	128023	16	Operating activities	Cash receipts from customers	
14	Cash payments to suppliers< Operating activities	2021-1-21	-14000	114023	17	Operating activities	Cash payments to suppliers	
15	Cash payments to suppliers< Operating activities	2021-1-21	-6000	108023	18	Operating activities	Cash payments to suppliers	
16	Cash payments for machinery<Operating activities	2021-1-28	-5600	102423	22	Operating activities	Cash payments for machinery	
17	Cash receipts from customers< Operating activities	2021-1-30	2558.90	104981.90	24	Operating activities	Cash receipts from customers	

18	Cash receipts from customers< Operating activities	2021-1-30	15000	119981.90	25	Operating activities	Cash receipts from customers	
19	Cash receipts from customers< Operating activities	2021-1-30	8475	128456.90	26	Operating activities	Cash receipts from customers	
20	Cash payments to suppliers<Operating activities	2021-1-30	-7500	120956.9	27	Operating activities	Cash payments to suppliers	
21	Cash payments for operating expenses<Operating activities	2021-1-30	-232.76	120724.14	28	Operating activities	Cash payments for operating expenses	
22	Cash payments for operating expenses<Operating activities	2021-1-30	-221.30	120502.84	29	Operating activities	Cash payments for operating expenses	
23	Cash payments for operating expenses<Operating activities	2021-1-30	-339.52	120163.32	30	Operating activities	Cash payments for operating expenses	
24	Cash payments for operating expenses<Operating activities	2021-1-30	-132.26	120031.06	31	Operating activities	Cash payments for operating expenses	
25	Cash payments for operating expenses<Operating activities	2021-1-30	-82.33	119948.73	32	Operating activities	Cash payments for operating expenses	
26	Cash receipts from customers< Operating activities	2021-1-31	13000	132948.73	33	Operating activities	Cash receipts from customers	
27	Cash payments to suppliers<Operating activities	2021-1-31	-8000	124948.73	34	Operating activities	Cash payments to suppliers	
28	Cash payments for operating expenses<Operating activities	2021-1-31	-419.55	124529.18	35	Operating activities	Cash payments for operating expenses	
29	Cash payments for operating expenses<Operating activities	2021-1-31	-18756	105773.18	37	Operating activities	Cash payments for operating expenses	
30	Cash payments for operating expenses<Operating activities	2021-1-31	-376.47	105396.71	40	Operating activities	Cash payments for operating expenses	
31	Cash payments for operating expenses<Operating activities	2021-1-31	-280.70	105116.01	41	Operating activities	Cash payments for operating expenses	
32	Cash payments for operating expenses<Operating activities	2021-1-31	-1500.00	103616.01	42	Operating activities	Cash payments for operating expenses	
33	Cash payments for operating expenses<Operating activities	2021-2-1	-2451.80	101164.21	45	Operating activities	Cash payments for operating expenses	
34	Cash payments for operating	2021-2-1	-103.30	101060.91	46	Operating activities	Cash payments for	

	expenses<Operating activities						operating expenses	
35	Cash receipts from customers< Operating activities	2021-2-8	5000.00	106060.91	49	Operating activities	Cash receipts from customers	
36	Cash receipts from customers< Operating activities	2021-2-9	12821	118881.91	50	Operating activities	Cash receipts from customers	
37	Cash receipts from customers< Operating activities	2021-2-11	3500	122381.91	51	Operating activities	Cash receipts from customers	
38	Cash payments to suppliers< Operating activities	2021-2-13	-2500	119881.91	52	Operating activities	Cash payments to suppliers	
39	Cash payments to suppliers< Operating activities	2021-2-15	-15000	104881.91	53	Operating activities	Cash payments to suppliers	
40	Cash payments to suppliers< Operating activities	2021-2-17	-4000	100881.91	54	Operating activities	Cash payments to suppliers	
41	Cash receipts from customers< Operating activities	2021-2-18	360000	460881.91	55	Operating activities	Cash receipts from customers	
42	Cash payments for investment<Investing activities	2021-2-18	-356700	104181.91	56	Investing activities	Cash payments for investment	
43	Cash receipts from customers< Operating activities	2021-2-25	120000	224181.91	57	Operating activities	Cash receipts from customers	
44	Cash payments to suppliers< Operating activities	2021-2-26	-55000	169181.91	58	Operating activities	Cash payments to suppliers	
45	Cash payments for operating expenses<Operating activities	2021-2-28	-55.32	169126.59	59	Operating activities	Cash payments for operating expenses	
46	Cash payments for operating expenses<Operating activities	2021-2-28	-458.39	168668.20	60	Operating activities	Cash payments for operating expenses	
47	Cash payments for operating expenses<Operating activities	2021-2-28	-33.72	168634.48	61	Operating activities	Cash payments for operating expenses	
48	Cash payments for operating expenses<Operating activities	2021-2-28	-152.31	168482.17	62	Operating activities	Cash payments for operating expenses	
49	Cash payments for operating expenses<Operating activities	2021-2-28	-1015.98	167466.19	63	Operating activities	Cash payments for operating expenses	
50	Cash payments for operating expenses<Operating activities	2021-2-28	-117.95	167348.24	64	Operating activities	Cash payments for operating expenses	
51	Cash payments for operating expenses<Operating activities	2021-2-28	18756.00	148592.24	65	Operating activities	Cash payments for operating expenses	

52	Cash payments for operating expenses<Operating activities	2021-2-28	-293.37	148298.87	66	Operating activities	Cash payments for operating expenses	
53	Cash payments for operating expenses<Operating activities	2021-2-28	-1500.00	146798.87	67	Operating activities	Cash payments for operating expenses	

One-level on a **large** card

Financing activities (X10101) < Parent account: Cash (X101)

ID	MultiName	Amount	Ref	GeID	TransDate	Balance
1	Cash receipts from owners<Financing activities	100000		1	2021-1-2	100000
2	Cash receipts from banks<Financing activities	500000		7	2021-1-2	600000

Two-level on a **medium** card

Cash receipts from owners (X1010101) << Parent account: Cash (X101)

ID	MultiName	Amount	Ref	GeID	TransDate	Balance
1	Cash receipts from owners<Financing activities	100000		1	2021-1-2	100000

Two-level on a **medium** card

Cash receipts from banks (X1010102) << Parent account: Cash (X101)

ID	MultiName	Amount	Ref	GeID	TransDate	Balance
1	Cash receipts from banks<Financing activities	500000		7	2021-1-7	500000

One-level on a **large** card

Operating activities (X10102) < Parent account: Cash (X101)

ID	MultiName	Amount	Ref	GeID	TransDate	Balance
1	Cash payments for operating expenses<Operating activities	-193		2	2021-1-3	-193

2	Cash payments for operating expenses<Operating activities	-47	3	2021-1-3	-240
3	Cash payments to suppliers< Operating activities	-670	4	2021-1-5	-910
4	Cash receipts from customers< Operating activities	300	5	2021-1-5	-610
5	Cash receipts from customers< Operating activities	1500	6	2021-1-7	890
6	Cash payments for machinery<Operating activities	-45000	9	2021-1-8	-44110
7	Cash payments for operating expenses<Operating activities	-367	10	2021-1-8	-44477
8	Cash payments to suppliers< Operating activities	-2000	11	2021-1-9	-46477
9	Cash receipts from customers< Operating activities	3500	13	2021-1-11	-42977
10	Cash receipts from customers< Operating activities	21000	16	2021-1-17	-21977
11	Cash payments to suppliers< Operating activities	-14000	17	2021-1-21	-35977
12	Cash payments to suppliers< Operating activities	-6000	18	2021-1-21	-41977
13	Cash payments for machinery<Operating activities	-5600	22	2021-1-28	-47577
14	Cash receipts from customers< Operating activities	2558.90	24	2021-1-30	-45018.10
15	Cash receipts from customers< Operating activities	15000	25	2021-1-30	-30018.10
16	Cash receipts from customers< Operating activities	8475	26	2021-1-30	-21543.10
17	Cash payments to suppliers< Operating activities	-7500	27	2021-1-30	-29043.10
18	Cash payments for operating expenses<Operating activities	-232.76	28	2021-1-30	-29275.86
19	Cash payments for operating expenses<Operating activities	-221.30	29	2021-1-30	-29497.16
20	Cash payments for operating expenses<Operating activities	-339.52	30	2021-1-30	-29836.68
21	Cash payments for operating expenses<Operating activities	-132.26	31	2021-1-30	-29968.94
22	Cash payments for operating expenses<Operating activities	-82.33	32	2021-1-30	-30051.27
23	Cash receipts from customers< Operating activities	13000	33	2021-1-31	-17051.27
24	Cash payments to suppliers< Operating activities	-8000	34	2021-1-31	-25051.27
25	Cash payments for operating expenses<Operating activities	-419.55	35	2021-1-31	-25470.82
26	Cash payments for operating expenses<Operating activities	-18756	37	2021-1-31	-44226.82
27	Cash payments for operating expenses<Operating activities	-376.47	40	2021-1-31	-44603.29
28	Cash payments for operating expenses<Operating activities	-280.70	41	2021-1-31	-44883.99
29	Cash payments for operating expenses<Operating activities	-1500	42	2021-1-31	-46383.99
30	Cash payments for operating expenses<Operating activities	-2451.80	45	2021-2-1	-48835.79
31	Cash payments for operating expenses<Operating activities	-103.30	46	2021-2-1	-48939.09

32	Cash receipts from customers< Operating activities	5000		49	2021-2-8	-43939.09
33	Cash receipts from customers< Operating activities	12821		50	2021-2-9	-31118.09
34	Cash receipts from customers< Operating activities	3500		51	2021-2-11	-27618.09
35	Cash payments to suppliers< Operating activities	-2500		52	2021-2-13	-30118.09
36	Cash payments to suppliers< Operating activities	-15000		53	2021-2-15	-45118.09
37	Cash payments to suppliers< Operating activities	-4000		54	2021-2-17	-49118.09
38	Cash receipts from customers< Operating activities	360000		55	2021-2-18	310881.91
39	Cash receipts from customers< Operating activities	120000		57	2021-2-25	430881.91
40	Cash payments to suppliers< Operating activities	-55000		58	2021-2-26	375881.91
41	Cash payments for operating expenses<Operating activities	-55.32		59	2021-2-28	375826.59
42	Cash payments for operating expenses<Operating activities	-458.39		60	2021-2-28	375368.20
43	Cash payments for operating expenses<Operating activities	-33.72		61	2021-2-28	375334.48
44	Cash payments for operating expenses<Operating activities	-152.31		62	2021-2-28	375182.17
45	Cash payments for operating expenses<Operating activities	-1015.98		63	22021-2-28	374166.19
46	Cash payments for operating expenses<Operating activities	-117.95		64	2021-2-28	374048.24
47	Cash payments for operating expenses<Operating activities	-18756		65	2021-2-28	355292.24
48	Cash payments for operating expenses<Operating activities	-293.37		66	2021-2-28	354998.87
49	Cash payments for operating expenses<Operating activities	-1500		67	2021-2-28	353498.87

Two-level on a **medium** card

Cash payments for operating expenses (X1010201) << Parent account: Cash (X101)

ID	MultiName	Amount	Ref	GeID	TransDate	Balance
1	Cash payments for operating expenses<Operating activities	-193		2	2021-1-3	-193
2	Cash payments for operating expenses<Operating activities	-47		3	2021-1-3	-240
3	Cash payments for operating expenses<Operating activities	-367		10	2021-1-8	-607
4	Cash payments for operating expenses<Operating activities	-232.76		28	2021-1-30	-839.76
5	Cash payments for operating expenses<Operating activities	-221.30		29	2021-1-30	-1061.06
6	Cash payments for operating expenses<Operating activities	-339.52		30	2021-1-30	-1400.58
7	Cash payments for operating expenses<Operating activities	-132.26		31	2021-1-30	-1532.84

8	Cash payments for operating expenses<Operating activities	-82.33		32	2021-1-30	-1615.17
9	Cash payments for operating expenses<Operating activities	-419.55		35	2021-1-31	-2034.72
10	Cash payments for operating expenses<Operating activities	-18756		37	2021-1-31	-20790.72
11	Cash payments for operating expenses<Operating activities	-376.47		40	2021-1-31	-21167.19
12	Cash payments for operating expenses<Operating activities	-280.70		41	2021-1-31	-21447.89
13	Cash payments for operating expenses<Operating activities	-1500		42	2021-1-31	-22947.89
14	Cash payments for operating expenses<Operating activities	-2451.80		45	2021-2-1	-25399.69
15	Cash payments for operating expenses<Operating activities	-103.30		46	2021-2-1	-25502.99
16	Cash payments for operating expenses<Operating activities	-55.32		59	2021-2-28	-25558.31
17	Cash payments for operating expenses<Operating activities	-458.39		60	2021-2-28	-26016.70
18	Cash payments for operating expenses<Operating activities	-33.72		61	2021-2-28	-26050.42
19	Cash payments for operating expenses<Operating activities	-152.31		62	2021-2-28	-26202.73
20	Cash payments for operating expenses<Operating activities	-1015.98		63	2021-2-28	-27218.71
21	Cash payments for operating expenses<Operating activities	-117.95		64	2021-2-28	-27336.66
22	Cash payments for operating expenses<Operating activities	-13756		65	2021-2-28	-46092.66
23	Cash payments for operating expenses<Operating activities	-293.37		66	2021-2-28	-46386.03
24	Cash payments for operating expenses<Operating activities	-1500		67	2021-2-28	-47886.03

Two-level on a **medium** card

Cash payments to suppliers (X101_0202) << Parent account: Cash (X101)

ID	MultiName	Amount	Ref	GeID	TransDate	Balance
1	Cash payments to suppliers< Operating activities	-670		4	2021-1-5	-670
2	Cash payments to suppliers< Operating activities	-2000		11	2021-1-9	-2670
3	Cash payments to suppliers< Operating activities	-14000		17	2021-1-21	-16670
4	Cash payments to suppliers< Operating activities	-6000		18	2021-1-21	-22670
5	Cash payments to suppliers< Operating activities	-7500		27	2021-1-30	-30170
6	Cash payments to suppliers< Operating activities	-8000		34	2021-1-31	-38170
7	Cash payments to suppliers< Operating activities	-2500		52	2021-2-13	-40670
8	Cash payments to suppliers< Operating activities	-15000		53	2021-2-15	-55670

ID	MultiName	Amount	Ref	GeID	TransDate	Balance
9	Cash payments to suppliers< Operating activities	-4000		54	2021-2-17	-59670
10	Cash payments to suppliers< Operating activities	-55000		58	2021-2-26	-114670

Two-level on a **medium** card

Cash receipts from customers (X1010203) << Parent account: Cash (X101)

ID	MultiName	Amount	Ref	GeID	TransDate	Balance
1	Cash receipts from customers< Operating activities	300		5	2021-1-5	300
2	Cash receipts from customers< Operating activities	1500		6	2021-1-7	1800
3	Cash receipts from customers< Operating activities	3500		13	2021-1-11	5300
4	Cash receipts from customers< Operating activities	21000		16	2021-1-17	26300
5	Cash receipts from customers< Operating activities	2558.90		24	2021-1-30	28858.90
6	Cash receipts from customers< Operating activities	15000		25	2021-1-30	43858.90
7	Cash receipts from customers< Operating activities	8475		26	2021-1-30	52333.90
8	Cash receipts from customers< Operating activities	13000		33	2021-1-31	65333.90
9	Cash receipts from customers< Operating activities	5000		49	2021-2-8	70333.90
10	Cash receipts from customers< Operating activities	12821		50	2021-2-9	83154.90
11	Cash receipts from customers< Operating activities	3500		51	2021-2-11	86654.90
12	Cash receipts from customers< Operating activities	360000		55	2021-2-18	446654.90
13	Cash receipts from customers< Operating activities	120000		57	2021-2-25	566654.90

Two-level on a **medium** card

Cash payments for machinery (X1010204) << Parent account: Cash (X101)

ID	MultiName	Amount	Ref	GeID	TransDate	Balance
1	Cash payments for machinery< Operating activities	-45000		9	2021-1-8	-45000
2	Cash payments for machinery< Operating activities	-5600		22	2021-1-28	-50600

One-level on a **large** card

Investing activities (X10103) < Parent account: Cash (X101)

ID	MultiName	Amount	Ref	GeID	TransDate	Balance
1	Cash payments for investment<Investing activities	-450000		8	2021-1-7	-450000
2	Cash payments for investment<Investing activities	-356700		56	2021-2-18	-806700

Two-level on a **medium** card

Cash payments for investment (X1010301) << Parent account: Cash (X101)

ID	MultiName	Amount	Ref	GeID	TransDate	Balance
1	Cash payments for investment<Investing activities	-45000		8	2021-1-7	-45000
2	Cash payments for investment<Investing activities	-356700		56	2021-2-18	-806700

Table A-9 Parent account: Office supplies on a drawer

Office supplies (X102)

ID	MultiName	TransDate	Amount	Balance	GeID	SubFirst	SubSecond	SubThird
1	N	2021-1-3	193	193	2			
2	N	2021-1-31	-88	105	36			
3	N	2021-2-1	103.30	208.30	46			
4	N	2021-2-28	-101.28	107.02	65			

Table A-10 Parent account: Inventory on a drawer

Inventory (X103)

ID	MultiName	TransDate	Amount	Balance	GeID	SubFirst	SubSecond	SubThird	Unit
1	Inven111<Inven11<Inven1	2021-1-5	1650	1650	4	Inven1	Inven11	Inven111	165
2	Inven112<Inven11<Inven1	2021-1-5	900	2550	4	Inven1	Inven11	Inven112	225
3	Inven121<Inven12<Inven1	2021-1-5	520	3070	4	Inven1	Inven12	Inven121	650
4	Inven122<Inven12<Inven1	2021-1-5	330	3400	4	Inven1	Inven12	Inven122	66
5	Inven13<Inven1	2021-1-5	270	3670	4	Inven1	Inven13		9

6	Inven111<Inven11<Inven1	2021-1-5	-910	2760	5	Inven1	Inven11	Inven111	-91
7	Inven112<Inven11<Inven1	2021-1-5	-520	2240	5	Inven1	Inven11	Inven112	-130
8	Inven121<Inven12<Inven1	2021-1-5	-300	1940	5	Inven1	Inven12	Inven121	-375
9	Inven122<Inven12<Inven1	2021-1-5	-170	1770	5	Inven1	Inven12	Inven122	-34
10	Inven221<Inven22<Inven2	2021-1-9	3200	4970	11	Inven2	Inven22	Inven221	320
11	Inven222<Inven22<Inven2	2021-1-9	5000	9970	11	Inven2	Inven22	Inven221	1000
12	PPUK parts<ASD parts<Inven2	2021-1-9	4800	14770	11	Inven2	ASD parts	PPUK parts	1200
13	PPGH parts<ASD parts<Inven2	2021-1-9	3800	18570	11	Inven2	ASD parts	PPUK parts	1900
14	Inven31<Inven3	2021-1-9	5300	23870	11	Inven3	Inven31		530
15	Inven32<Inven3	2021-1-9	2900	26770	11	Inven3	Inven32		580
16	Inven331<Inven33<Inven3	2021-1-9	2700	29470	12	Inven3	Inven33	Inven331	1350
17	Inven332<Inven33<Inven3	2021-1-9	3100	32570	12	Inven3	Inven33	Inven332	620
18	HGFCVB parts<QASXC parts<Inven3	2021-1-9	4900	37470	12	Inven3	QASXC parts	HGFCVB parts	490
19	PPGHUP parts<ASDUP parts<Inven3	2021-1-9	1300	38770	12	Inven3	ASDUP parts	PPGHUP parts	130
20	Inven221<Inven22<Inven2	2021-1-11	-2900	35870	13	Inven2	Inven22	Inven221	-290
21	Inven222<Inven22<Inven2	2021-1-11	-4700	31170	13	Inven2	Inven22	Inven222	-940
22	PPUK parts<ASD parts< Inven2	2021-1-11	-2600	28570	13	Inven2	ASD parts	PPUK parts	-650
23	Inven32<Inven3	2021-1-11	-1900	26670	13	Inven3	Inven32		-380
24	HGFCVB parts<QASXC parts<Inven3	2021-1-11	-4800	21870	13	Inven3	QASXC parts	HGFCVB parts	-480
25	PPGHUP parts<ASDUP parts<Inven3	2021-1-11	-800	21070	13	Inven3	ASDUP parts	PPGHUP parts	-80
26	PPGH parts<ASD parts<Inven2	2021-1-15	-3100	17970	14	Inven2	ASD parts	PPUK parts	-1550
27	Inven31<Inven3	2021-1-15	-5000	12970	14	Inven3	Inven31		-500
28	Inven331<Inven33<Inven3	2021-1-15	-2200	10770	14	Inven3	Inven33	Inven331	-1100
29	Inven332<Inven33<Inven3	2021-1-15	-2900	7870	14	Inven3	Inven33	Inven332	-580
30	Inven411<Inven41<Inven4	2021-1-17	5100	12970	15	Inven4	Inven41	Inven411	1020
31	Inven412<Inven41<Inven4	2021-1-17	3700	16670	15	Inven4	Inven41	Inven412	1850
32	TTTCU parts<TTT parts<Inven4	2021-1-17	2300	18970	15	Inven4	TTT parts	TTTCU parts	1150
33	RRRHJK parts< Inven4	2021-1-17	1400	20370	15	Inven4	RRRHJK parts		700
34	PPUK parts<ASD parts<Inven2	2021-1-22	6500	26870	19	Inven2	ASD parts	PPUK parts	1625

35	PPGH parts<ASD parts<Inven2	2021-1-22	600C	32870	19	Inven2	ASD parts	PPGH parts	3000
36	Inven31<Inven3	2021-1-22	530C	38170	19	Inven3	Inven31		530
37	Inven32<Inven3	2021-1-22	370C	41870	19	Inven3	Inven32		740
38	PPUK parts<ASD parts<Inven2	2021-1-23	-3300	38570	20	Inven2	ASD parts	PPUK parts	-825
39	PPGH parts<ASD parts<Inven2	2021-1-23	-3900	34670	20	Inven2	ASD parts	PPGH parts	-1950
40	Inven31<Inven3	2021-1-23	-2500	32170	20	Inven3	Inven31		-250
41	Inven32<Inven3	2021-1-23	-2300	29870	20	Inven3	Inven32		-460
42	PPUK parts<ASD parts<Inven2	2021-1-25	-300⊏	26870	21	Inven2	ASD parts	PPUK parts	-750
43	PPGH parts<ASD parts<Inven2	2021-1-25	-180⊏	25070	21	Inven2	ASD parts	PPGH parts	-900
44	Inven31<Inven3	2021-1-25	-270⊏	22370	21	Inven3	Inven31		-270
45	PPUK parts<ASD parts<Inven2	2021-1-29	-220⊏	20170	23	Inven2	ASD parts	PPUK parts	-550
46	Inven32<Inven3	2021-1-29	-130C	18870	23	Inven3	Inven32		-260
47	HGFCVB parts<QASXC parts<Inven3	2021-2-3	596C●	78470	47	Inven3	QASXC parts	HGFCVB parts	5960
48	PPGHUP parts<ASDUP parts<Inven3	2021-2-3	314C0	109870	47	Inven3	ASDUP parts	PPGHUP parts	3140
49	HGFCVB parts<QASXC parts<Inven3	2021-2-4	-596C0	50270	48	Inven3	QASXC parts	HGFCVB parts	-5960
50	PPGHUP parts<ASDUP parts<Inven3	2021-2-4	-316C0	18670	48	Inven3	ASDUP parts	PPGHUP parts	-3160

One-level on a **large** card

Inven1 (X10301) < Parent account: Inventory (X103)

ID	MultiName	Amount	Unit	GeID	TransDate	Balance
1	Inven111<Inven11<Inven1	1650	165	4	2021-1-5	1650
2	Inven112<Inven11<Inven1	900	225	4	2021-1-5	2550
3	Inven121<Inven12<Inven1	520	650	4	2021-1-5	3070
4	Inven122<Inven12<Inven1	330	66	4	2021-1-5	3400
5	Inven13<Inven1	270	9	4	2021-1-5	3670
6	Inven111<Inven11<Inven1	-910	-91	5	2021-1-5	2760
7	Inven112<Inven11<Inven1	-520	-130	5	2021-1-5	2240
8	Inven121<Inven12<Inven1	-300	-375	5	2021-1-5	1940
9	Inven122<Inven12<Inven1	-170	-34	5	2021-1-5	1770

Two-level on a **medium** card

Inven11 (X1030101) << Parent account: Inventory (X103)

ID	MultiName	Amount	Unit	GeID	TransDate	Balance
1	Inven111<Inven11<Inven1	1650	165	4	2021-1-5	1650
2	Inven112<Inven11<Inven1	900	225	4	2021-1-5	2550
3	Inven111<Inven11<Inven1	-910	-91	4	2021-1-5	1640
4	Inven112<Inven11<Inven1	-520	-123	4	2021-1-5	1120

Three-level on a **small** card

Inven111 (X103010101) <<< Parent account: Inventory (X103)

ID	MultiName	Amount	Unit	GeID	TransDate	Balance
1	Inven111<Inven11<Inven1	1650	165	4	2021-1-5	1650
2	Inven111<Inven11<Inven1	-910	-91	5	2021-1-5	740

Three-level on a **small** card

Inven112 (X103010102) <<< Parent account: Inventory (X103)

ID	MultiName	Amount	Unit	GeID	TransDate	Balance
1	Inven112<Inven11<Inven1	900	225	4	2021-1-5	900
2	Inven112<Inven11<Inven1	-520	-123	5	2021-1-5	380

Two-level on a **medium** card

Inven12 (X1030102) << Parent account: Inventory (X103)

ID	MultiName	Amount	Unit	GeID	TransDate	Balance
1	Inven121<Inven12<Inven1	520	650	4	2021-1-5	520
2	Inven122<Inven12<Inven1	330	66	4	2021-1-5	850
3	Inven121<Inven12<Inven1	-300	-375	5	2021-1-5	550
4	Inven122<Inven12<Inven1	-170	-34	5	2021-1-5	380

Three-level on a **small** card

Inven121 (X103010201) <<< Parent account: Inventory (X103)

ID	MultiName	Amount	Unit	GeID	TransDate	Balance
1	Inven121<Inven12<Inven1	520	650	4	2021-1-5	520
2	Inven121<Inven12<Inven1	-300	-375	5	2021-1-5	220

Three-level on a **small** card

Inven122 (X103010202) <<< Parent account: Inventory (X103)

ID	MultiName	Amount	Unit	GeID	TransDate	Balance
1	Inven122<Inven12<Inven1	330	66	4	2021-1-5	330
2	Inven122<Inven12<Inven1	-170	-34	5	2021-1-5	160

Two-level on a **medium** card

Inven13 (X1030103) << Parent account: Inventory (X103)

ID	MultiName	Amount	Unit	GeID	TransDate	Balance
1	Inven13<Inven1	270	9	4	2021-1-5	270

One-level on a **large** card

Inven2 (X10302) < Parent account: Inventory (X103)

ID	MultiName	Amount	Unit	GeID	TransDate	Balance
1	Inven221<Inven22<Inven2	3200	320	11	2021-1-9	3200
2	Inven222<Inven22<Inven2	5000	1000	11	2021-1-9	8200
3	PPUK parts<ASD parts<Inven2	4800	1200	11	2021-1-9	13000
4	PPGH parts<ASD parts<Inven2	3800	1900	11	2021-1-9	16800
5	Inven221<Inven22<Inven2	-2900	-290	13	2021-1-11	13900
6	Inven222<Inven22<Inven2	-4700	-940	13	2021-1-11	9200
7	PPUK parts<ASD parts<Inven2	-2600	-650	13	2021-1-11	6600
8	PPGH parts<ASD parts<Inven2	-3100	-1550	14	2021-1-15	3500
9	PPUK parts<ASD parts<Inven2	6500	1625	19	2021-1-22	10000
10	PPGH parts<ASD parts<Inven2	6000	3000	19	2021-1-22	16000
11	PPUK parts<ASD parts<Inven2	-3300	-825	20	2021-1-23	12700
12	PPGH parts<ASD parts<Inven2	-3900	-1950	20	2021-1-23	8800

12	PPUK parts<ASD parts<Inven2	-3000	-750	21	2021-1-25	5800
14	PPGH parts<ASD parts<Inven2	-1800	-900	21	2021-1-25	4000
15	PPUK parts<ASD parts<Inven2	-2200	-550	23	2021-1-29	1800

Two-level on a **medium** card

Inven22 (X1030202) << Parent account: Inventory (X103)

ID	MultiName	Amount	Unit	GeID	TransDate	Balance
1	Inven221<Inven22<Inven2	3200	320	11	2021-1-9	3200
2	Inven222<Inven22< Inven2	5000	1000	11	2021-1-9	8200
3	Inven221<Inven22<Inven2	-2900	-290	13	2021-1-11	5300
4	Inven222<Inven22<Inven2	-4700	-940	13	2021-1-11	600

Three-level on a **small** card

Inven221 (X103020201) <<< Parent account: Inventory (X103)

ID	MultiName	Amount	Unit	GeID	TransDate	Balance
1	Inven221<Inven22<Inven2	3200	320	11	2021-1-9	3200
2	Inven221<Inven22<Inven2	-2900	-290	13	2021-1-11	300

Three-level on a **small** card

Inven222 (X103020202) <<< Parent account: Inventory (X103)

ID	MultiName	Amount	Unit	GeID	TransDate	Balance
1	Inven222<Inven22<Inven2	5000	1000	11	2021-1-9	5000
2	Inven222<Inven22<Inven2	-4700	-940	13	2021-1-11	300

Two-level on **medium** card

ASD parts (X1030203) << Parent account: Inventory (X103)

ID	MultiName	Amount	Unit	GeID	TransDate	Balance
1	PPUK parts<ASD parts<Inven2	4800	1200	11	2021-1-9	4800
2	PPGH parts<ASD parts<Inven2	3800	1900	11	2021-1-9	8600
3	PPUK parts<ASD parts<Inven2	-2600	-650	13	2021-1-11	6000

4	PPGH parts<ASD parts<Inven2	-3100	-1550	14	2021-1-15	2900
5	PPUK parts<ASD parts<Inven2	6500	1625	19	2021-1-22	9400
6	PPGH parts<ASD parts<Inven2	6000	3000	19	2021-1-22	15400
7	PPUK parts<ASD parts<Inven2	-3300	-825	20	2021-1-23	12100
8	PPGH parts<ASD parts<Inven2	-3900	-1950	20	2021-1-23	8200
9	PPUK parts<ASD parts<Inven2	-3000	-750	21	2021-1-25	5200
10	PPGH parts<ASD parts<Inven2	-1800	-900	21	2021-1-25	3400
11	PPUK parts<ASD parts<Inven2	-2200	-550	23	2021-1-29	1200

Three-level on a **small** card

PPUK parts (X103020301) <<< Parent account: Inventory (X103)

ID	MultiName	Amount	Unit	GeID	TransDate	Balance
1	PPUK parts<ASD parts<Inven2	4800	1200	11	2021-1-9	4800
2	PPUK parts<ASD parts<Inven2	-2600	-650	13	2021-1-11	2200
3	PPUK parts<ASD parts<Inven2	6500	1625	19	2021-1-22	8700
4	PPUK parts<ASD parts<Inven2	-3300	-825	20	2021-1-23	5400
5	PPUK parts<ASD parts<Inven2	-3000	-750	21	2021-1-25	2400
6	PPUK parts<ASD parts<Inven2	-2200	-550	23	2021-1-29	200

Three-level on a **small** card

PPGH parts (X103020302) <<< Parent account: Inventory (X103)

ID	MultiName	Amount	Unit	GeID	TransDate	Balance
1	PPGH parts<ASD parts<Inven2	3800	1900	11	2021-1-9	3800
2	PPGH parts<ASD parts<Inven2	-3100	-1550	14	2021-1-15	700
3	PPGH parts<ASD parts<Inven2	6000	3000	19	2021-1-22	6700
4	PPGH parts<ASD parts<Inven2	-3900	-1950	20	2021-1-23	2800
5	PPGH parts<ASD parts<Inven2	-1800	-900	21	2021-1-25	1000

One-level on a **large** card

Inven3 (X10303) < Parent account: Inventory (X103)

ID	MultiName	Amount	Unit	GeID	TransDate	Balance
1	Inven31<Inven3	5300	530	11	2021-1-9	5300
2	Inven32<Inven3	2900	580	11	2021-1-9	8200

3	Inven331<Inven33<Inven3	2700	1350	12	2021-1-9	10900
4	Inven332<Inven33<Inven3	3100	620	12	2021-1-9	14000
5	HGFCVB parts<QASXC parts<Inven3	4900	490	12	2021-1-9	18900
6	PPGHUP parts<ASDUP parts<Inven3	1300	130	12	2021-1-9	20200
7	Inven32<Inven3	-1900	-380	13	2021-1-11	18300
8	HGFCVB parts<QASXC parts<Inven3	-4800	-480	13	2021-1-11	13500
9	PPGHUP parts<ASDUP parts<Inven3	-800	-80	13	2021-1-11	12700
10	Inven31<Inven3	-5000	-500	14	2021-1-15	7700
11	Inven331<Inven33<Inven3	-2200	-1100	14	2021-1-15	5500
12	Inven332<Inven33< Inven3	-2900	-580	14	2021-1-15	2600
13	Inven31<Inven3	5300	530	19	2021-1-22	7900
14	Inven32<Inven3	3700	740	19	2021-1-22	11600
15	Inven31<Inven3	-2500	-250	20	2021-1-23	9100
16	Inven32<Inven3	-2300	-460	20	2021-1-23	6800
17	Inven31<Inven3	-2700	-270	21	2021-1-25	4100
18	Inven32<Inven3	-1300	-260	23	2021-1-29	2800
19	HGFCVB parts<QASXC parts<Inven3	59600	5960	47	2021-2-3	62400
20	PPGHUP parts<ASDUP parts<Inven3	31400	3140	47	2021-2-3	93800
21	HGFCVB parts<QASXC parts<Inven3	-59600	-5960	48	2021-2-4	34200
22	PPGHUP parts<ASDUP parts<Inven3	-31600	-3160	48	2021-2-4	2600

Two-level on a **medium** card

Inven31 (X1030301) << Parent account: Inventory (X103)

ID	MultiName	Amount	Unit	GeID	TransDate	Balance
1	Inven31<Inven3	5300	530	12	2021-1-9	5300
2	Inven31<Inven3	-5000	-500	14	2021-1-15	300
3	Inven31<Inven3	5300	530	19	2021-1-22	5600
4	Inven31<Inven3	-2500	-250	20	2021-1-23	3100
5	Inven31<Inven3	-2700	-270	21	2021-1-25	400

Two-level on a **medium** card

Inven32 (X1030302) << Parent account: Inventory (X103)

ID	MultiName	Amount	Unit	GeID	TransDate	Balance
1	Inven32<Inven3	2900	580	12	2021-1-9	2900

2	Inven32<Inven3	-1900	-380	13	2021-1-11	1000
3	Inven32<Inven3	3700	740	19	2021-1-22	4700
4	Inven32<Inven3	-2300	-460	20	2021-1-23	2400
5	Inven32<Inven3	-1300	-260	23	2021-1-29	1100

Two-level on a **medium** card

Inven33 (X1030303) << Parent account: Inventory (X103)

ID	MultiName	Amount	Unit	GeID	TransDate	Balance
1	Inven331<Inven33<Inven3	2700	1350	12	2021-1-9	2700
2	Inven332<Inven33<Inven3	3100	620	12	2021-1-9	5800
3	Inven331<Inven33<Inven3	-2200	-1100	14	2021-1-15	3600
4	Inven332<Inven33<Inven3	-2900	-2900	14	2021-1-15	700

Three-level on a **small** card

Inven331 (X103030301) <<< Parent account: Inventory (X103)

ID	MultiName	Amount	Unit	GeID	TransDate	Balance
1	Inven331<Inven33<Inven3	2700	1350	12	2021-1-9	2700
2	Inven331<Inven33<Inven3	-2200	-1100	14	2021-1-15	500

Three-level on a **small** card

Inven332 (X103030302) << Parent account: Inventory (X103)

ID	MultiName	Amount	Unit	GeID	TransDate	Balance
1	Inven332<Inven33<Inven3	3100	620	12	2021-1-9	3100
2	Inven332<Inven33<Inven3	-2900	-580	14	2021-1-15	200

Two-level on a **medium** card

QASXC parts (X1030304) << Parent account: Inventory (X103)

ID	MultiName	Amount	Unit	GeID	TransDate	Balance
1	HGFCVB parts<QASXC parts<Inven3	4900	490	12	2021-1-9	4900
2	HGFCVB parts<QASXC parts<Inven3	-4800	-480	13	2C21-1-11	100

3	HGFCVB parts<QASXC parts<Inven3	59600	5960	47	2021-2-3	59700
4	HGFCVB parts<QASXC parts<Inven3	-59600	5960	48	2021-2-4	100

Three-level on a **small** card

HGFCVB parts (X103030401) <<< Parent account: Inventory (X103)

ID	MultiName	Amount	Unit	GeID	TransDate	Balance
1	HGFCVB parts<QASXC parts<Inven3	4900	490	12	2021-1-9	4900
2	HGFCVB parts<QASXC parts<Inven3	-4800	-480	13	2021-1-11	100
3	HGFCVB parts<QASXC parts<Inven3	59600	5960	47	2021-2-3	59700
4	HGFCVB parts<QASXC parts<Inven3	-59600	5960	48	2021-2-4	100

Two-level on a **medium** card

ASDUP parts (X1030305) << Parent account: Inventory (X103)

ID	MultiName	Amount	Unit	GeID	TransDate	Balance
1	PPGHUP parts<ASDUP parts<Inven3	1300	130	12	2021-1-9	1300
2	PPGHUP parts<ASDUP parts<Inven3	-800	-80	13	2021-1-11	500
3	PPGHUP parts<ASDUP parts<Inven3	31400	3140	47	2021-2-3	31900
4	PPGHUP parts<ASDUP parts<Inven3	-31600	-3160	48	2021-2-4	300

Three-level on a **small** card

PPGHUP parts (X103030501) <<< Parent account: Inventory (X103)

ID	MultiName	Amount	Unit	GeID	TransDate	Balance
1	PPGHUP parts<ASDUP parts<Inven3	1300	130	12	2021-1-9	1300
2	PPGHUP parts<ASDUP parts<Inven3	-800	-80	13	2021-1-11	500
3	PPGHUP parts<ASDUP parts<Inven3	31400	3140	47	2021-2-3	31900
4	PPGHUP parts<ASDUP parts<Inven3	-31600	-3160	48	2021-2-4	300

One-level on a **large** card

Inven4 (X10304) < Parent account: Inventory (X103)

ID	MultiName	Amount	Unit	GeID	TransDate	Balance

1	Inven411<Inven41<Inven4	5100	1020	15	2021-1-17	5100
2	Inven412<Inven41<Inven4	3700	1850	15	2021-1-17	8800
3	TTTCU parts<TTT parts<Inven4	2300	1150	15	2021-1-17	11100
4	RRRHJK parts< Inven4	1400	700	15	2021-1-17	12500

Two-level on a **medium** card

Inven41 (X1030401) << Parent account: Inventory (X103)

ID	MultiName	Amount	Unit	GeID	TransDate	Balance
1	Inven411<Inven41<Inven4	5100	1020	15	2021-1-17	5100
2	Inven412<Inven41<Inven4	3700	1850	15	2021-1-17	8800

Three-level on a **small** card

Inven411 (X103040101) <<< Parent account: Inventory (X103)

ID	MultiName	Amount	Unit	GeID	TransDate	Balance
1	Inven411<Inven41<Inven4	5100	1020	15	2021-1-17	5100

Three-level on a **small** card

Inven412 (X103040102) <<< Parent account: Inventory (X103)

ID	MultiName	Amount	Unit	GeID	TransDate	Balance
1	Inven412<Inven41<Inven4	3700	1850	15	2021-1-17	3700

Two-level on a **medium** card

TTT parts (X1030402) << Parent account: Inventory (X103)

ID	MultiName	Amount	Unit	GeID	TransDate	Balance
1	TTTCU parts<TTT parts<Inven4	2300	1150	15	2021-1-17	2300

Three-level on a **small** card

TTTCU parts (X103040201) <<< Parent account: Inventory (X103)

ID	MultiName	Amount	Unit	GeID	TransDate	Balance
1	TTTCU parts<TTT parts<Inven4	2300	1150	15	2021-1-17	2300

Two-level on a **medium** card

RRRHJK parts (X1030403) << Parent account: Inventory (X103)

ID	MultiName	Amount	Unit	GeID	TransDate	Balance
1	RRRHJK parts<Inven4	1400	700	15	2021-1-17	1400

Table A-11 Parent account: HST recoverable on a drawer

HST recoverable (X104)

ID	MultiName	TransDate	Amount	Balance	GeID	SubFirst	SubSecond	SubThird
1	N	2021-1-5	477.1	477.10	4			
2	N	2021-1-9	3250	3727.10	11			
3	N	2021-1-9	1560	5287.10	12			
4	N	2021-1-17	1625	6912.10	15			
5	N	2021-1-22	2795	9707.10	19			
6	N	2021-2-1	-9707.10	0	44			
7	N	2021-2-3	11830.00	11830.00	47			

Table A-12 Parent account: Account receivable on a drawer

Account receivable (X105)

ID	MultiName	TransDate	Amount	Balance	GeID	SubFirst	SubSecond	SubThird	Ref
1	123456789	2021-1-5	2558.90	2558.90	5	123456789			
2	123456789	2021-1-7	-1500	1058.90	6	123456789			5
3	123456788	2021-1-11	29835	30893.90	13	123456788			
4	123456787	2021-1-15	24521	55414.90	14	123456787			
5	123456788	2021-1-17	-21000	34414.90	16	123456788			13
6	123456787	2021-1-23	22487	56901.90	20	123456787			
7	123456786	2021-1-25	15481	72382.90	21	123456786			
8	123456789	2021-1-29	7006	79388.90	. 23	123456789			
9	123456789	2021-1-30	-828.90	76830	24	123456789			5
10	123456789	2021-1-30	-1730	76830	24	123456789			23
11	123456787	2021-1-30	-15000	61830	25	123456787			14
12	123456786	2021-1-30	-8475	53355	26	123456786			21
13	123456787	2021-1-31	-13000	40355	33	123456787			20
14	123456788	2021-2-4	200688	241043	48	123456788			
15	123456789	2021-2-8	-5000	236043	49	123456789			23
16	123456787	2021-2-9	-9521	226522	50	123456787			14

17	123456787	2021-2-9	-3300	223222	50	123456787			20
18	123456786	2021-2-11	-3500	219722	51	123456786			21
19	123456788	2021-2-25	-120000	99722	57	123456788			43

One-level on a **large** card

123456789 (X10501) < Parent account: Account receivable (X105)

ID	MultiName	Amount	Ref	GeID	TransDate	Balance
1	123456789	2558.90		5	2021-1-5	2558.90
2	123456789	-1500	5	6	2021-1-7	1058.90
3	123456789	7006		23	2021-1-29	8064.9
4	123456789	-828.90	5	24	2021-1-30	7236
5	123456789	-1730	23	24	2021-1-30	5506
6	123456789	-5000	23	49	2021-2-8	506

One-level on a **large** card

123456788 (X10502) < Parent account: Account receivable (X105)

ID	MultiName	Amount	Ref	GeID	TransDate	Balance
1	123456788	29835		13	2021-1-11	29835
2	123456788	-21000	13	16	2021-1-17	8835
3	123456788	200688		48	2021-2-4	209523
4	123456788	-120000	48	57	2021-2-25	89523

One-level on a **large** card

123456787 (X10503) < Parent account: Account receivable (X105)

ID	MultiName	Amount	Ref	GeID	TransDate	Balance
1	123456787	24521		14	2021-1-15	24521
2	123456787	22487		20	2021-1-23	47008
3	123456787	-15000	14	25	2021-1-30	32008
4	123456787	-13000	20	33	2021-1-31	19008
5	123456787	-9521	14	50	2021-2-9	9487
6	123456787	-3300	20	50	2021-2-9	6187

One-level on a **large** card

123456786 (X10504) < Parent account: Account receivable (X105)

ID	MultiName	Amount	Ref	GeID	TransDate	Balance
1	123456786	15481		21	2021-1-25	15481
2	123456786	-8475	**21**	26	2021-1-30	7006
3	123456786	-3500	**21**	51	2021-2-11	3506

Table A-13 Parent account: Land on a drawer

Land (X106)

ID	MultiName	TransDate	Amount	Balance	GeID	SubFirst	SubSecond	SubThird
1	Land1, Downtown	2021-1-7	270000	270000	8	Land1, Downtown		
2	Land2, North York	2021-1-7	180000	450000	8	Land2, North York		
3	Land1, Downtown	2021-2-18	-270000	180000	55	Land1, Downtown		

One-level on a **large** card

Land1, Downtown (X10601) < Parent account: Land (X106)

ID	MultiName	Amount	Unit	GeID	TransDate	Balance
1	Land1, Downtown	270000	1	8	2021-1-7	270000
2	Land1, Downtown	-270000	1	55	2021-2-18	0

One-level on a **large** card

Land2, North York (X10602) < Parent account: Land (X106)

ID	MultiName	Amount	Unit	GeID	TransDate	Balance
1	Land2, North York	180000	1	8	2021-1-7	180000

Table A-14 Parent account: Truck on a drawer

Truck (X107)

ID	MultiName	TransDate	Amount	Balance	GeID	SubFirst	SubSecond	SubThird
1	Truck1	2021-1-8	45000	45000	9	Truck1		

One-level on a **large** card

Truck1 (X10701) < Parent account: Truck (X107)

ID	MultiName	Amount	Unit	GeID	TransDate	Balance
1	Truck1	45000	1	9	2021-1-8	45000

Table A-15 Parent account: Computer on a drawer

Computer (X108)

ID	MultiName	TransDate	Amount	Balance	GeID	SubFirst	SubSecond	SubThird
1	Computer1	2021-1-28	1600	1600	22	Computer1		
2	Computer server1	2021-1-28	1800	3400	22	Computer server1		
3	POS system1	2021-1-28	2200	5600	22	POS system1		

One-level on a **large** card

Computer1 (X10801) < Parent account: Computer (X108)

ID	MultiName	Amount	Unit	GeID	TransDate	Balance
1	Computer1	1600	1	22	2021-1-28	1600

One-level on a **large** card

Computer server1 (X10802) < Parent account: Computer (X108)

ID	MultiName	Amount	Unit	GeID	TransDate	Balance
1	Computer server1	1800	1	22	2021-1-28	1800

One-level on a **large** card

POS system1 (X10803) < Parent account: Computer (X108)

ID	MultiName	Amount	Unit	GeID	TransDate	Balance
1	POS system1	2200	1	22	2021-1-28	2200

Table A-16 Parent account: Accumulated amortization: truck on a drawer

Accumulated amortization: truck (X109)

ID	MultiName	TransDate	Amount	Balance	GeID	SubFirst	SubSecond	SubThird
1	Truck1-accumulated amortization	2021-1-31	-750	-750	38	Truck1-accumulated amortization		
2	Truck1-accumulated amortization	2021-2-28	-750	-1500	67	Truck1-accumulated amortization		

One-level on a **large** card

Truck1-accumulated amortization (X10901) < Parent account: Accumulated amortization: truck (X109)

ID	MultiName	Amount	Unit	GeID	TransDate	Balance
1	Truck1-accumulated amortization	-750	1	38	2021-1-31	-750
2	Truck1-accumulated amortization	-750	-1500	67	2021-2-28	-1500

Table A-17 Parent account: Accumulated amortization: computer on a drawer

Accumulated amortization: computer (X110)

ID	MultiName	TransDate	Amount	Balance	GeID	SubFirst	SubSecond	SubThird
1	Computer1-accumulated amortization	2021-1-31	-33.33	-33.33	39	Computer1-accumulated amortization		
2	Computer server1-accumulated amortization	2021-1-31	-37.50	-70.83	39	Computer server1-accumulated amortization		
3	POS system1-accumulated amortization	2021-1-31	-30.56	-101.39	39	POS system1-accumulated amortization		
4	Computer1-accumulated amortization	2021-2-28	-66.67	-168.06	68	Computer1-accumulated amortization		
5	Computer server1-accumulated amortization	2021-2-28	-75.00	-243.06	68	Computer server1-accumulated amortization		
6	POS system1-accumulated amortization	2021-2-28	-61.11	-304.17	68	POS system1-accumulated amortization		

One-level on a **large** card

Computer1-accumulated amortization (X11001) < Parent account: Accumulated amortization: computer (X110)

ID	MultiName	Amount	Unit	GeID	TransDate	Balance
1	Computer1-accumulated amortization	-33.33	1	39	2021-1-31	-33.33
2	Computer1-accumulated amortization	-66.67		63	2021-2-28	-100.00

One-level on a **large** card

Computer server1-accumulated amortization (X11002) < Parent account: Accumulated amortization: computer (X110)

ID	MultiName	Amount	Unit	GeID	TransDate	Balance
1	Computer server1-accumulated amortization	-37.5	1	39	2021-1-31	-37.50
2	Computer server1-accumulated amortization	-75.00	1	68	2021-2-28	-112.50

One-level on a **large** card

POS system1-accumulated amortization (X11003) < Parent account: Accumulated amortization: computer (X110)

ID	MultiName	Amount	Unit	GeID	TransDate	Balance
1	POS system1-accumulated amortization	-30.56	1	39	2021-1-31	-30.56
2	POS system1-accumulated amortization	-61.11	1	68	2021-2-28	-91.67

Table A-18 Parent account: Share on a drawer

Share (X111)

ID	MultiName	TransDate	Amount	Balance	GeID	SubFirst	SubSecond	SubThird
1	MicroQQ-share	2021-2-18	356700	356700	56	MicroQQ-share		

One-level on a **large** card

MicroQQ-share (X11101) < Parent account: Share (X110)

ID	MultiName	Amount	Unit	GeID	TransDate	Balance
1	MicroQQ-share	356700	1	56	2021-2-18	356700

Table A-19 Parent account: AOCI of land on a drawer

AOCI of land (X112)

ID	MultiName	TransDate	Amount	Balance	GeID	SubFirst	SubSecond	SubThird
1	AOCI-land2, North York	2021-2-18	30000	30000	56	AOCI-land2, North York		

One-level on a **large** card

AOCI-land2, North York (X11201) < Parent account: AOCI of land (X112)

ID	MultiName	Amount	Unit	GeID	TransDate	Balance
1	AOCI-land2, North York	30000	1	56	2021-2-18	30000

Table A-20 Parent account: AOCI of share on a drawer

AOCI of share (X114)

ID	MultiName	TransDate	Amount	Balance	GeID	SubFirst	SubSecond	SubThird
1	AOCI-MicroQQ	2021-2-28	-4600	-4600	74	AOCI-MicroQQ		

One-level on a **large** card

AOCI-MicroQQ (X11401) < Parent account: AOCI of share (X114)

ID	MultiName	Amount	Unit	GeID	TransDate	Balance
1	AOCI-MicroQQ	-4600	1	74	2021-2-28	-4600

In the second cabinet, there are the following tables.

Table A-21 Liabilities (X2) on the door

ID	Account Name (Mathematical Name)	Subtotal	Ref (Row)	Balance
1	Account payable (X201)	Current liabilities,203	204	72537.10
2	HST payable (X202)	Current liabilities,203	205	36797.80
3	Note payable (X203)	Current liabilities,203	207	6333.33
4	Accrued interest payable (X204)	Long term liabilities,203	252	500000
5	Tax payable	Current liabilities,203	208	48199.59

Table A-22 Parent account: Account payable on a drawer

Account payable (X201)

ID	MultiName	TransDate	Amount	Balance	GeID	SubFirst	SubSecond	SubThird	Ref
1	987654321	2021-1-5	3477.10	3477.10	4	987654321			
2	987654322	2021-1-9	26250	29727.10	11	987654322			
3	987654323	2021-1-9	13560	43287.10	12	987654323			
4	987654324	2021-1-17	14125	57412.10	15	987654324			
5	987654322	2021-1-21	-14000	43412.10	17	987654322			**11**
6	987654323	2021-1-21	-6000	37412.10	18	987654323			**12**
7	987654322	2021-1-22	24295	61707.10	19	987654322			
8	987654322	2021-1-30	-7500	5420410	27	987654322			**11**
9	987654324	2021-1-31	-8000	46207.10	34	987654324			**15**
10	987654323	2021-2-3	102830	149037.10	47	987654323			
11	987654321	2021-2-13	-2500	146537.10	52	987654321			**4**
12	987654322	2021-2-15	-15000	131537.10	53	987654322			**19**
13	987654323	2021-2-17	-4000	127537.10	54	987654323			**12**
14	987654323	2021-2-26	-55000	72537.10	58	987654323			**47**

One-level on a **large** card

987654321 (X20101) < Parent account: Account payable (X201)

ID	MultiName	Amount	Ref	GeID	TransDate	Balance
1	987654321	3477.10		4	2021-1-5	3477.10
2	987654321	-2500	**4**	52	2021-2-13	977.10

One-level on a **large** card

987654322 (X20102) < Parent account: Account payable (X201)

ID	MultiName	Amount	Ref	GeID	TransDate	Balance
1	987654322	26250		11	2021-1-9	26250
2	987654322	-14000	**11**	18	2021-1-21	12250
3	987654322	24295		19	2021-1-22	36545
4	987654322	-7500	**11**	27	2021-1-30	29045
5	987654322	-15000	**19**	53	2021-2-15	14045

One-level on a **large** card

987654323 (X20103) < Parent account: Account payable (X201)

ID	MultiName	Amount	Ref	GeID	TransDate	Balance
1	987654323	13560		12	2021-1-9	13560
2	987654323	-6000	**12**	18	2021-1-21	7560
3	987654323	102830		47	2021-2-3	110390
4	987654323	-4000	**12**	54	2021-2-17	106390
5	987654323	-55000	**47**	58	2021-2-26	51390

One-level on a **large** card

987654324 (X20104) < Parent account: Account payable (X201)

ID	MultiName	Amount	Ref	GeID	TransDate	Balance
1	987654324	14125		15	2021-1-17	14125
2	987654324	-8000	**15**	34	2021-1-31	6125

Table A-23 Parent account: HST payable on a drawer

HST payable (X202)

ID	MultiName	TransDate	Amount	Balance	GeID	SubFirst	SubSecond	SubThird
1	N	2021-1-5	328.90	328.90	5			
2	N	2021-1-11	3835	4163.90	13			
3	N	2021-1-15	2821	6984.90	14			
4	N	2021-1-23	2587	9571.90	20			
5	N	2021-1-25	1781	11352.90	21			
6	N	2021-1-29	806	12158.90	23			
7	N	2021-2-1	-9707.10	2451.8	44			
8	N	2021-2-1	-2451.80	0	45			
9	N	2021-2-4	23088.00	23088.00	48			

Table A-24 Parent account: Note payable on a drawer

Note payable (X203)

ID	MultiName	TransDate	Amount	Balance	GeID	SubFirst	SubSecond	SubThird
1	N	2021-1-7	500000	500000	7			

Table A-25 Parent account: Accrued interest payable on a drawer

Accrued interest payable (X204)

ID	MultiName	TransDate	Amount	Balance	GeID	SubFirst	SubSecond	SubThird
1	Note1-TD bank	2021-1-31	3000	3000	43	Note1-TD bank		
2	Note1-TD bank	2021-2-28	3333.33	6333.33	71	Note1-TD bank		

One-level on a **large** card

Note1-TD bank (X20401) < Parent account: Accrued interest payable (X204)

ID	MultiName	Amount	Ref	GeID	TransDate	Balance
1	Note1-TD bank	3000		43	2021-1-31	3000
2	Note1-TD bank	3333.33		71	2021-2-28	6333.33

In the third cabinet, there are the following tables.

Table A-26 Parent account: Tax payable on a drawer

Tax payable (X205)

ID	MultiName	TransDate	Amount	Balance	GeID	SubFirst	SubSecond	SubThird
1	N	2021-2-28	48199.59	48199.59	43			

Table A-27 Shareholders' Equity (X3) on the door

ID	Account Name (Mathematical Name)	Subtotal	Ref (Row)	Balance
1	Share capital (X301)	Owners' Capital,303	304	100000

Table A-28 Parent account: Share capital on a drawer

Share capital (X301)

ID	MultiName	TransDate	Amount	Balance	GeID	SubFirst	SubSecond	SubThird
1	Capital-Ping Wang	2021-1-2	40000	40000	1	Capital-Ping Wang		
2	Capital-Hua Li	2021-1-2	30000	70000	1	Capital-Hua Li		

3	Capital-Mike Newsome	2021-1-2	30000	100000	1	Capital-Mike Newsome		

One-level on a **large** card

Capital-Ping Wang (X30101) < Parent account: Share capital (X301)

ID	MultiName	Amount	Unit	GeID	TransDate	Balance
1	Capital-Ping Wang	40000	1	1	2021-1-2	40000

One-level on a **large** card

Capital- Hua Li (X30102) < Parent account: Share capital (X301)

ID	MultiName	Amount	Unit	GeID	TransDate	Balance
1	Capital-Hua Li	30000	1	1	2021-1-2	30000

One-level on a **large** card

Capital-Mike Newsome (X30103) < Parent account: Share capital (X301)

ID	MultiName	Amount	Unit	GeID	TransDate	Balance
1	Capital- Mike Newsome	30000	1	1	2021-1-2	30000

In the fourth cabinet, there are following tables.

Table A-29 Revenue (X4) on the door

ID	Account Name (Mathematical Name)	Subtotal	Ref (Row)	Balance
1	Sales (X401)	Owners' Capital,303	404	271130.00
2	Investment income	Other income,475	476	90000.00
3	Unrealized holding gain or loss	Other comprehensive income,713	715	25400.00

Table A-30 Parent accounts: Sales on a drawer

Sales (X401)

ID	MultiName	TransDate	Amount	Balance	GeID	SubFirst	SubSecond	SubThird
1	Xiao Zhou-sales	2021-1-5	2530	2530	5	Xiao Zhou-sales		

2	Xiao Zhou-sales	2021-1-11	29500	32030	13	Xiao Zhou-sales		
3	ZhenDao Yuan-sales	2021-1-15	21700	53730	14	ZhenDao Yuan-sales		
4	Yi Liu-sales	2021-1-23	19900	73630	20	Yi Liu-sales		
5	ZhenDao Yuan-sales	2021-1-25	13700	87330	21	ZhenDao Yuan-sales		
6	Jun Wang-sales	2021-1-29	6200	93530	23	Jun Wang-sales		
7	Jun Wang-sales	2021-2-4	177600	271130	48	Jun Wang-sales		

One-level on a **large** card

Xiao Zhou-sales (X40101) < Parent account Sales (X401)

ID	MultiName	Amount	Unit	GeID	TransDate	Balance
1	Xiao Zhou-sales	2530	1	5	2021-1-5	2530
2	Xiao Zhou-sales	29500	1	13	2021-1-11	32030

One-level on a **large** card

ZhenDao Yuan-sales (X40102) < Parent account: Sales (X401)

ID	MultiName	Amount	Unit	GeID	TransDate	Balance
1	Xiao Zhou-sales	21700	1	14	2021-1-15	21700
2	Xiao Zhou-sales	13700	1	21	2021-1-25	35400

One-level on a **large** card

Yi Liu-sales (X40103) < Parent account: Sales (X401)

ID	MultiName	Amount	Unit	GeID	TransDate	Balance
1	Yi Liu-sales	19900	1	20	2021-1-23	19900

One-level on a **large** card

Jun Wang-sales (X40104) < Parent account: Sales (X401)

ID	MultiName	Amount	Unit	GeID	TransDate	Balance
1	Jun Wang-sales	6200	1	23	2021-1-29	6200
2	Jun Wang-sales	177600	1	48	2021-2-4	183800

Table A-31 Parent accounts: Investment income on a drawer

Investment income (X402)

ID	MultiName	TransDate	Amount	Balance	GeID	SubFirst	SubSecond	SubThird
1	N	2021-2-18	90000	90000	55			

Table A-32 Parent accounts: Unrealized holding gain or loss on a drawer

Unrealized holding gain or loss (X403)

ID	MultiName	TransDate	Amount	Balance	GeID	SubFirst	SubSecond	SubThird
1	Unrealized holding gain or loss-land	2021-2-28	30000	30000	73	Unrealized holding gain or loss-land		
2	Unrealized holding gain or loss-share	2021-2-28	-4600	25400	74	Unrealized holding gain or loss-share		

One-level on a **large** card

Unrealized holding gain or loss-land (X40301) < Parent account: Unrealized holding gain or loss (X403)

ID	MultiName	Amount	Unit	GeID	TransDate	Balance
1	Unrealized holding gain or loss-land	30000	1	73	2021-2-28	30000

One-level on a **large** card

Unrealized holding gain or loss-share (X40302) < Parent account: Unrealized holding gain or loss (X403)

ID	MultiName	Amount	Unit	GeID	TransDate	Balance
1	Unrealized holding gain or loss-share	-4600	1	74	2021-2-28	-4600

In the fifth cabinet, there are following tables.

Table A-33 Expenses (X5) on the door

ID	Account Name (Mathematical Name)	Subtotal	Ref (Row)	Balance
1	Administrative expenses (X501)	Operating and administrative expenses,453	454	-4815.21
2	Cost of sales (X502)	Cost,431	432	-147000.00
3	Salary expenses (X503)	Operating and administrative expenses,453	459	-37512.00

4	Amortization expenses (X504)	Operating and administrative expenses,453	458	-1804.17
5	Office rent expenses (X505)	Operating and administrative expenses,453	459	-3000.0
6	Interest expenses (X506)	Operating and administrative expenses,453	461	-6333.3
7	Tax expenses	Tax,600	601	-48199.59

Table A-34 Parent accounts: Administrative expenses on a drawer

Administrative expenses (X501)

ID	MultiName	TransDate	Amount	Balance	GeID	SubFirst	SubSecond	SubThird
1	Hua Li-taxi<Purchase department-taxi<Taxi expenses	2021-1-3	-47	-47	3	Taxi expenses	Purchase Department-taxi	Hua Li-taxi
2	Ping Wang-open company<Office department-open company<Other expenses	2021-1-8	-367	-414	10	Other expenses	Office department-open company	Ping Wang-open company
3	Dan Zhu-taxi< Purchase department-taxi<Taxi expenses	2021-1-30	-178	-592	28	Taxi expenses	Purchase department-taxi	Dan Zhu-taxi
4	Dan Zhu-mobile< Purchase department-mobile <Mobile expenses	2021-1-30	-54.76	-646.76	28	Mobile expenses	Purchase department-mobile	Dan Zhu-mobile
5	Hua Li-taxi<Purchase department-taxi<Taxi expenses	2021-1-30	-135.12	-781.88	29	Taxi expenses	Purchase department-taxi	Hua Li-taxi
6	Hua Li-other< Purchase department-other<Other expenses	2021-1-30	-86.18	-868.06	29	Other expenses	Purchase department-other	Hua Li-other
7	Xiao Zhou-taxi<Sales department-taxi<Taxi expenses	2021-1-30	-243	-1111.06	30	Taxi expenses	Sales department-taxi	Xiao Zhou-taxi
8	Xiao Zhou-other< Sales department-other<Other expenses	2021-1-30	-96.52	-1207.58	30	Other expenses	Purchase department-other	Xiao Zhou-other
9	Jun Wang-other< Sales department-other<Other expenses	2021-1-30	-132.26	-1339.84	31	Other expenses	Purchase department-other	Jun Wang-other
10	Zhendao Yuan-other<Sales department-other <Other expenses	2021-1-30	-82.33	-1422.17	32	Other expenses	Sales department-other	Zhendao Yuan-other
11	Yi Liu-taxi<Sales department-taxi<Taxi expenses	2021-1-30	-347.70	1769.87	35	Taxi expenses	Sales department-taxi	Yi Liu-taxi
12	Yi Liu-other<Sales department-other< Other expenses	2021-1-31	-71.85	-1841.72	35	Other expenses	Sales department-other	Yi Liu-other
13	Office supplies expenses	2021-1-31	-88	-1929.72	36	Office supplies expenses		

ID	MultiName							
14	Mike Newsome-taxi<Office department-taxi<Taxi expenses	2021-1-31	-298.69	-2228.41	40	Taxi expenses	Office department-taxi	Mike Newsome-taxi
15	Mike Newsome-other<Office department-other<Other expenses	2021-1-31	-77.78	-2306.19	40	Other expenses	Office department-other	Mike Newsome-other
16	Utility expenses	2021-1-31	-280.70	-2586.89	41	Utility expenses		
17	Dan Zhu-other<Purchase department-other<Other expenses	2021-2-28	-55.32	-2642.21	59	Other expenses	Purchase department-other	Dan Zhu-other
18	Hua Li-taxi<Purchase department-taxi<Taxi expenses	2021-2-28	-336.41	-2978.62	60	Taxi expenses	Purchase department-taxi	Hua Li-taxi
19	Hua Li-other<Purchase department-other<Other expenses	2021-2-28	-121.98	-3100.60	60	Other expenses	Purchase department-other	Hua Li-other
20	Xiao Zhou-other<Sales department-other<Other expenses	2021-2-28	-33.72	-3134.32	61	Other expenses	Purchase department-other	Xiao Zhou-other
21	Jun Wang-taxi<Sales department-taxi<Taxi expenses	2021-2-28	-152.31	-3286.63	62	Taxi expenses	Sales department-taxi	Jun Wang-taxi
22	Zhendao Yuan-other<Sales department-other<Other expenses	2021-2-28	-1015.98	-4302.61	63	Other expenses	Zhendao Yuan-other<Sales department-other	Zhendao Yuan-other
23	Yi Liu-taxi<Sales department-taxi<Taxi expenses	2021-2-28	-99.80	-4402.41	64	Taxi expenses	Sales department-taxi	Yi Liu-taxi
24	Yi Liu-other<Sales department-other<Other expenses	2021-2-28	-18.15	-4420.56	64	Other expenses	Sales department-other	Yi Liu-other
25	Office supplies expenses	2021-2-28	-101.28	4521.84	65	Office supplies expenses		
26	Utility expenses	2021-2-28	-293.37	-4815.21	70	Utility expenses		

One-level on a **large** card

Taxi expenses (X50101) < Parent account: Administrative expenses (X501)

ID	MultiName	Amount	Unit	GeID	TransDate	Balance
1	Hua Li-taxi<Purchase department-taxi<Taxi expenses	-47	1	3	2021-1-3	-47
2	Dan Zhu-taxi<Purchase department-taxi<Taxi expenses	-178	1	28	2021-1-30	-225
3	Hua Li-taxi<Purchase department-taxi<Taxi expenses	-135.12	1	29	2021-1-30	-360.12
4	Xiao Zhou-taxi<Sales department-taxi<Taxi expenses	-243	1	30	2021-1-30	-603.12
5	Yi Liu-taxi<Sales department-taxi<Taxi expenses	-347.70	1	35	2021-1-31	-950.82

6	Mike Newsome-taxi<Office department-taxi<Taxi expenses	-298.69	1	40	2021-1-31	-1249.51
7	Hua Li-taxi<Purchase department-taxi<Taxi expenses	-336.41	1	60	2021-2-28	-1585.92
8	Jun Wang-taxi<Sales department-taxi<Taxi expenses	-152.31	1	62	2021-2-28	-1738.23
9	Yi Liu-taxi<Sales department-taxi<Taxi expenses	-99.80	1	64	2021-2-28	-1838.03

Two-level on a **medium** card

Purchase department-taxi (X5010101) << Administrative expenses (X501)

ID	MultiName	Amount	Unit	GeID	TransDate	Balance
1	Hua Li-taxi<Purchase department-taxi<Taxi expenses	-47	1	3	2021-1-3	-47
2	Dan Zhu-taxi<Purchase department-taxi<Taxi expenses	-178	1	28	2021-1-30	-225
3	Hua Li-taxi<Purchase department-taxi<Taxi expenses	-135.12	1	29	2021-1-30	-360.12
4	Hua Li-taxi<Purchase department-taxi<Taxi expenses	-336.41	1	60	2021-2-28	-696.53

Three-level on a **small** card

Hua Li-taxi (X501010101) <<< Administrative expenses (X501)

ID	MultiName	Amount	Unit	GeID	TransDate	Balance
1	Hua Li-taxi<Purchase department-taxi<Taxi expenses	-47	1	3	2021-1-3	-47
2	Hua Li-taxi<Purchase department-taxi<Taxi expenses	-135.12	1	29	2021-1-30	-182.12
3	Hua Li-taxi<Purchase department-taxi<Taxi expenses	-336.41	1	60	2021-2-28	-518.53

Three-level on a **small** card

Dan Zhu-taxi (X501010102) <<< Administrative expenses (X501)

ID	MultiName	Amount	Unit	GeID	TransDate	Balance
1	Dan Zhu-taxi<Purchase department-taxi<Taxi expenses	-178	1	28	2021-1-30	-178.00

Two-level on a **medium** card

Sales department-taxi (X5010102) << Administrative expenses (X501)

ID	MultiName	Amount	Unit	GeID	TransDate	Balance
1	Xiao Zhou-taxi<Sales department-taxi<Taxi expenses	-243	1	30	2021-1-30	-243
2	Yi Liu-taxi<Sales department-taxi<Taxi expenses	-347.70	1	35	2021-1-31	-590.70
3	Jun Wang-taxi<Sales department-taxi<Taxi expenses	-152.31	1	62	2021-2-28	-743.01
4	Yi Liu-taxi<Sales department-taxi<Taxi expenses	-99.80	1	64	2021-2-28	-842.81

Three-level on a **small** card

Xiao Zhou-taxi (X501010201) <<< Administrative expenses (X501)

ID	MultiName	Amount	Unit	GeID	TransDate	Balance
1	Xiao Zhou-taxi<Sales department-taxi<Taxi expenses	-243	1	30	2021-1-30	-243

Three-level on a **small** card

Yi Liu-taxi (X501010202) <<< Administrative expenses (X501)

ID	MultiName	Amount	Unit	GeID	TransDate	Balance
1	Yi Liu-taxi<Sales department-taxi<Taxi expenses	-347.70	1	35	2021-1-31	-347.70
2	Yi Liu-taxi<Sales department-taxi<Taxi expenses	-99.80	1	64	2021-2-28	-447.50

Three-level on a **small** card

Jun Wang-taxi (X501010203) <<< Administrative expenses (X501)

ID	MultiName	Amount	Unit	GeID	TransDate	Balance
1	Jun Wang-taxi<Sales department-taxi<Taxi expenses	-152.31	1	62	2021-2-28	-152.31

Two-level on a **medium** card

Office department-taxi (X5010103) << Administrative expenses (X501)

ID	MultiName	Amount	Unit	GeID	TransDate	Balance
1	Mike Newsome-taxi<Office department-taxi<Taxi expenses	-298.69	1	40	2021-1-31	-298.69

Three-level on a **small** card

Mike Newsome-taxi (X501010301) <<< Administrative expenses (X501)

ID	MultiName	Amount	Unit	GeID	TransDate	Balance
1	Mike Newsome-taxi<Office department-taxi<Taxi expenses	-298.69	1	40	2021-1-31	-298.69

One-level on a **large** card

Other expenses (X50102) < Parent account Administrative expenses (X501)

ID	MultiName	Amount	Unit	GeID	TransDate	Balance
1	Ping Wang-open company<Office department-open company<Other expenses	-367	1	10	2021-1-8	-367
2	Hua Li-other<Purchase department-other<Other expenses	-86.18	1	29	2021-1-30	-453.18
3	Xiao Zhou-other<Sales department-other<Other expenses	-96.52	1	30	2021-1-30	-549.70
4	Jun Wang-other<Sales department-other<Other expenses	-132.26	1	31	2021-1-30	-681.96
5	Zhendao Yuan-other<Sales department-other<Other expenses	-82.33	1	32	2021-1-30	-764.29
6	Yi Liu-other<Sales department-other<Other expenses	-71.85	1	35	2021-1-31	-836.14
7	Mike Newsome-other<Office department-other<Other expenses	-77.78	1	40	2021-1-31	-913.92
8	Dan Zhu-other<Purchase department-other<Other expenses	-55.32	1	59	2021-2-28	-969.24
9	Hua Li-other<Purchase department-other<Other expenses	-121.98	1	60	2021-2-28	-1091.22
10	Xiao Zhou-other<Sales department-other<Other expenses	-33.72	1	61	2021-2-28	-1124.94
11	Zhendao Yuan-other<Sales department-other<Other expenses	-1015.98	1	62	2021-2-28	-2140.92
12	Yi Liu-other<Sales department-other<Other expenses	-18.15	1	63	2021-2-28	-2159.07

Two-level on a **medium** card

Office department-open company (X501C201) << Administrative expenses (X501)

ID	MultiName	Amount	Unit	GeID	TransDate	Balance
1	Ping Wang-open company<Office department-open company<Other expenses	-367	1	10	2021-1-8	-367

Three-level on a **small** card

Ping Wang-open company (X501020101) <<< Administrative expenses (X501)

ID	MultiName	Amount	Unit	GeID	TransDate	Balance
1	Ping Wang-open company<Office department-open company<Other expenses	-367	1	10	2021-1-8	-367

Two-level on a **medium** card

Purchase department-other (X5010202) << Administrative expenses (X501)

ID	MultiName	Amount	Unit	GeID	TransDate	Balance
1	Hua Li-other<Purchase department-other<Other expenses	-86.18	1	29	2021-1-30	-86.18
2	Dan Zhu-other<Purchase department-other<Other expenses	-55.32	1	59	2021-2-28	-141.50
3	Hua Li-other<Purchase department-other<Other expenses	-121.98	1	60	2021-2-28	-263.48

Three-level on a **small** card

Hua Li-other (X501020201) <<< Administrative expenses (X501)

ID	MultiName	Amount	Unit	GeID	TransDate	Balance
1	Hua Li-other<Purchase department-other<Other expenses	-86.18	1	29	2021-1-30	-86.18
2	Hua Li-other<Purchase department-other<Other expenses	-121.98	1	60	2021-2-28	-208.16

Three-level on a **small** card

Dan Zhu-other (X501020202) <<< Administrative expenses (X501)

ID	MultiName	Amount	Unit	GeID	TransDate	Balance
1	Dan Zhu-other<Purchase department-other<Other expenses	-55.32	1	59	2021-2-28	-55.32

Two-level on a **medium** card

Sales department-other (X5010203) << Administrative expenses (X501)

ID	MultiName	Amount	Unit	GeID	TransDate	Balance
1	Xiao Zhou-other<Sales department-other<Other expenses	-96.52	1	30	2021-1-30	-96.53

2	Jun Wang-other<Sales department-other<Other expenses	-132.26	1	31	2021-1-30	-228.78
3	Zhendao Yuan-other<Sales department-other<Other expenses	-82.33	1	32	2021-1-30	-311.11
4	Yi Liu-other<Sales department-other<Other expenses	-71.85	1	35	2021-1-31	-382.96
5	Xiao Zhou-other<Sales department-other<Other expenses	-33.72	1	61	2021-2-28	-416.68
6	Zhendao Yuan-other<Sales department-other<Other expenses	-1015.98	1	63	2021-2-28	-1432.66
7	Yi Liu-other<Sales department-other<Other expenses	-18.15	1	64	2021-2-28	-1450.81

Three-level on a **small** card

Xiao Zhou-other (X501020301) <<< Administrative expenses (X501)

ID	MultiName	Amount	Unit	GeID	TransDate	Balance
1	Xiao Zhou-other<Sales department-other<Other expenses	-96.52	1	30	2021-1-30	-96.52
2	Xiao Zhou-other<Sales department-other<Other expenses	-33.72	1	61	2021-2-28	-130.24

Three-level on a **small** card

Jun Wang-other (X501020302) <<< Administrative expenses (X501)

ID	MultiName	Amount	Unit	GeID	TransDate	Balance
1	Jun Wang-other<Sales department-other<Other expenses	-132.26	1	31	2021-1-30	-132.26

Three-level on a **small** card

Zhendao Yuan-other (X5010203C3) <<< Administrative expenses (X501)

ID	MultiName	Amount	Unit	GeID	TransDate	Balance
1	Zhendao Yuan-other<Sales department-other<Other expenses	-82.33	1	32	2021-1-30	-82.23
2	Zhendao Yuan-other<Sales department-other<Other expenses	-1015.98	1	63	2021-2-28	-1098.21

Three-level on a **small** card

Yi Liu-other (X501020304) <<< Administrative expenses (X501)

ID	MultiName	Amount	Unit	GeID	TransDate	Balance
1	Yi Liu-other<Sales department-other<Other expenses	-71.85	1	35	2021-1-31	-71.85
2	Yi Liu-other<Sales department-other<Other expenses	-18.15	1	64	2021-2-28	-90.00

Two-level on a **medium** card

Office department-other (X5010204) << Administrative expenses (X501)

ID	MultiName	Amount	Unit	GeID	TransDate	Balance
1	Mike Newsome-other<Office department-other<Other expenses	-77.78	1	40	2021-1-31	-77.78

Three-level on a **small** card

Mike Newsome-other (X501020401) <<< Administrative expenses (X501)

ID	MultiName	Amount	Unit	GeID	TransDate	Balance
1	Mike Newsome-other<Office department-other<Other expenses	-77.78	1	40	2021-1-31	-77.78

One-level on a **large** card

Mobile expenses (X50103) < Parent account: Administrative expenses (X501)

ID	MultiName	Amount	Unit	GeID	TransDate	Balance
1	Dan Zhu-mobile<Purchase department-mobile<Mobile expenses	-54.76	1	28	2021-1-30	-54.76

Two-level on a **medium** card

Purchase department-mobile (X5010301) << Administrative expenses (X501)

ID	MultiName	Amount	Unit	GeID	TransDate	Balance
1	Dan Zhu-mobile<Purchase department-mobile<Mobile expenses	-54.76	1	28	2021-1-30	-54.76

Three-level on a **small** card

Dan Zhu-mobile (X501030101) <<< Administrative expenses (X501)

ID	MultiName	Amount	Unit	GeID	TransDate	Balance
1	Dan Zhu-mobile<Purchase department-mobile<Mobile expenses	-54.76	1	28	2021-1-30	-54.76

One-level on a **large** card

Office supplies expenses (X50104) < Parent account: Administrative expenses (X501)

ID	MultiName	Amount	Unit	GeID	TransDate	Balance
1	Office supplies expenses	-88.00	1	36	2021-1-31	-88.00
2	Office supplies expenses	-101.28	1	65	2021-2-28	-189.28

One-level on a **large** card

Utility expenses (X50105) < Parent account: Administrative expenses (X501)

ID	MultiName	Amount	Unit	GeID	TransDate	Balance
1	Utility expenses	-280.70	1	41	2021-1-31	-280.70
2	Utility expenses	-293.37	1	69	2021-2-28	-574.07

Table A-35 Parent accounts: Cost of sales on a drawer

Cost of sales (X502)

ID	MultiName	TransDate	Amount	Balance	GeID	SubFirst	SubSecond	SubThird
1	N	2021-1-5	-1900	-1900	5			
2	N	2021-1-11	-17700	-19600	13			
3	N	2021-1-15	-13200	-32800	14			
4	N	2021-1-23	-12000	-44800	20			
5	N	2021-1-25	-7500	-52300	21			
6	N	2021-1-29	-3500	-55800	23			
7	N	2021-2-4	-91200	-147000	48			

Table A-36 Parent accounts: Salary expenses on a drawer

Salary expenses (X503)

ID	MultiName	TransDate	Amount	Balance	GeID	SubFirst	SubSecond	SubThird
1	N	2021-1-31	-18756	-18756	37			
2	N	2021-2-28	-18756	-37512	66			

Table A-37 Parent accounts: Amortization expenses on a drawer

Amortization expenses (X504)

ID	MultiName	TransDate	Amount	Balance	GeID	SubFirst	SubSecond	SubThird
1	Truck1-amortization	2021-1-31	-750	-750	38	Truck1-amortization		
2	Computer1-amortization<Computer-amortization	2021-1-31	-33.33	-783.33	39	Computer-amortization	Computer1-amortization	
3	Computer server1-amortization<Computer-amortization	2021-1-31	-37.50	-820.83	39	Computer-amortization	Computer server1-amortization	
4	POS system1-amortization< Computer-amortization	2021-1-31	-30.56	-851.39	39	Computer-amortization	POS system1-amortization	
5	Truck1-amortization	2021-2-28	-750	-1601.39	67	Truck1-amortization		
6	Computer1-amortization<Computer-amortization	2021-2-28	-66.67	-1668.08	68	Computer-amortization	Computer1-amortization	
7	Computer server1-amortization<Computer-amortization	2021-2-28	-75	-1743.06	68	Computer-amortization	Computer server1-amortization	
8	POS system1-amortization< Computer-amortization	2021-2-28	-61.11	-1804.17	68	Computer-amortization	POS system1-amortization	

One-level on a **large** card

Truck1-amortization (X50401) < Parent account: Amortization expenses (X504)

ID	MultiName	Amount	Unit	GeID	TransDate	Balance
1	Truck1-amortization	-750	1	38	2021-1-31	-750
2	Truck1-amortization	-750	1	67	2021-2-28	-1500

One-level on a **large** card

Computer-amortization (X50402) < Parent account: Amortization expenses (X504)

ID	MultiName	Amount	Unit	GeID	TransDate	Balance
1	Computer1-amortization<Computer-amortization	-33.33	1	39	2021-1-31	-33.33
2	Computer server1-amortization<Computer-amortization	-37.50	1	39	2021-1-31	-70.83
3	POS system1-amortization< Computer-amortization	-30.56	1	39	2021-1-31	-101.39
4	Computer1-amortization<Computer-amortization	-66.67	1	68	2021-2-28	-168.06
5	Computer server1-amortization<Computer-amortization	-75.00	1	68	2021-2-28	-243.06
6	POS system1-amortization< Computer-amortization	-61.11	1	68	2021-2-28	-304.17

Two-level on a **medium** card

Computer1-amortization (X5040201) << Amortization expenses (X504)

ID	MultiName	Amount	Unit	GeID	TransDate	Balance
1	Computer1-amortization<Computer-amortization	-33.33	1	39	2021-1-31	-33.33
2	Computer1-amortization<Computer-amortization	-66.67	1	68	2021-2-28	-100.00

Two-level on a **medium** card

Computer server1-amortization (X5040202) << Amortization expenses (X504)

ID	MultiName	Amount	Unit	GeID	TransDate	Balance
1	Computer server1-amortization<Computer-amortization	-37.50	1	39	2021-1-31	-37.50
2	Computer server1-amortization<Computer-amortization	-75	1	68	2021-2-28	-112.50

Two-level on a **medium** card

POS system1-amortization (X5040203) << Amortization expenses (X504)

ID	MultiName	Amount	Unit	GeID	TransDate	Balance
1	POS system1-amortization< Computer-amortization	-30.56	1	39	2021-1-31	-30.56
2	POS system1-amortization< Computer-amortization	-61.11	1	68	2021-2-28	-91.67

Table A-38 Parent accounts: Office rent expenses on a drawer

Office rent expenses (X505)

ID	MultiName	TransDate	Amount	Balance	GeID	SubFirst	SubSecond	SubThird
1	N	2021-1-31	-1500	-1500	42			
2	N	2021-2-28	-1500	-3000	70			

Table A-39 Parent accounts: Interest expenses on a drawer

Interest expenses (X506)

ID	MultiName	TransDate	Amount	Balance	GeID	SubFirst	SubSecond	SubThird
1	N	2021-1-31	-3000	-3000	43			
2	N	2021-2-28	-3333.33	-6333.33	71			

Table A-40 Parent accounts: Tax expenses on a drawer

Tax expenses (X507)

ID	MultiName	TransDate	Amount	Balance	GeID	SubFirst	SubSecond	SubThird
1	N	2021-2-28	-48199.59	-48199.59	72			

Appendixes B

In the sixth cabinet, there are the following tables.

Table B-1 General equation

GeID	TransDate	General Equation	Left Amount	Right Amount	Explanation	Enter Date
1	2021-1-2	Cash(1): 10000 = Share capital(3): 4000 + Capital(3): 3000 + Capital(3): 3000	100000	100000	Ping Wang, Hua Li and Mike Newsome decide to open a RR trade business	2021-1-4
2	2021-1-3	Cash(1): -193 + Office supplies(1): 193 = 0	0	0	Purchase of Office supplies	2021-1-4
3	2021-1-3	Cash(1): -47 = Administrative expenses (5): -47	-47	-47	Cash payments for Hua Li's taxi fee expense	2021-1-4
4	2021-1-5	Cash(1): -670 + Inventory(1): 3670 + HST recoverable(1): 477.10 = Account payable(2): 3477.10	3477.10	3477.10	RR purchases $3,670 inventory by $670 cash and other on credit from A1 company (phone number: 987654321)	2021-1-6
5	2021-1-5	Cash(1): 300 + Inventory(1): -1900 + Account receivable(1): 2558.90 = HST payable(2): 328.90 + Sales(4): 2530 + Cost of sales (5): -1900	958.90	958.90	RR sells $1,900 inventory to B1 Company (phone number: 123456789) for sales of $2,530 and receives $300 cash	2021-1-6
6	2021-1-7	Cash(1): 1500 + Account receivable(1): -1500 = 0	0	0	RR Company receives $1,500 cash from B1 Company (phone number: 123456789) with the General ID 5	2021-1-8
7	2021-1-7	Cash (1): 500000 = Note payable (2): 500000	500000	500000	RR Company raises funds of $500,000 cash with interest rate 8% (paying interest at the end of each year) and two years from TD bank on January 7, 2014.	2021-1-8
8	2021-1-7	Cash (1): -450000 + Land (1): 450000 = 0	0	0	RR Company purchases two lands (Land1, Downtown for $270,000; Land2, North York for $180,000) for $450,000 cash as available for sale	2021-1-8
9	2021-1-8	Cash (1): -45000 + Truck (1): 45000 = 0	0	0	RR Company purchases a truck for $45,000 cash	2021-1-9
10	2021-1-8	Cash (1): -367 = Administrative expenses (5): -367	-367	-367	RR Company pays $367 cash to Ping Wang (Office department) for opening company expenses	2021-1-9
11	2021-1-9	Cash(1): -2000 + Inventory(1): 25000 + HST recoverable(1): 3250 = Account payable(2): 26250	26250	26250	RR Company purchases $25,000 inventory for $2,000 cash and $23,000 on credit from C1 Company (phone number: 987654322).	2021-1-10
12	2021-1-9	Inventory(1): 12000 + HST recoverable(1): 1560 = Account payable(2): 13560	13560	13560	RR Company purchases $12,000 inventory on credit from D1 Company (phone number: 987654323)	2021-1-10
13	2021-1-11	Cash(1): 3500 + Inventory(1): -17700 + Account receivable(1):	15635	15635	Xiao Zhou sales $17,700 inventory for $3,500 cash	2021-1-12

		29835 = HST payable(2): 3835 + Sales(4): 29500 + Cost of sales (5): -17700			and $26,000 on credit to E1 Company (phone number: 123456788)	
14	2021-1-15	Inventory(1): -13200 + Account receivable(1): 24521 = HST payable(2): 2821 + Sales(4): 21700 + Cost of sales (5): -13200	11321	11321	ZhenDao Yuan sales $13,200 inventory for $21,700 on credit to F1 Company (phone number: 123456787)	2021-1-16
15	2021-1-17	Inventory(1): 12500 + HST recoverable(1): 1625 = Account payable(2): 14125	14125	14125	RR Company purchases $12,500 inventory on credit from G1 Company (phone number: 987654324)	2021-1-18
16	2021-1-17	Cash(1): 21000 + Account receivable: -21000 = 0	0	0	Receive $21,000 cash from E1 Company (phone number: 123456788) with the General ID 13	2021-1-18
17	2021-1-21	Cash (1) -14000 = Account payable(2): -14000	-14000	-14000	Pay $14,000 cash to C1 Company (phone number: 987654322) with the General ID 11	2021-1-22
18	2021-1-21	Cash (1) -6000 = Account payable(2): -6000	-6000	-6000	Pay $6,000 cash to D1 Company (phone number: 987654323) with the General ID 12	2021-1-22
19	2021-1-22	Inventory(1): 21500 + HST recoverable(1): 2795 = Account payable(2): 24295	24295	24295	RR Company purchases $21,500 inventory on credit from C1 Company (phone number: 987654322)	2021-1-23
20	2021-1-23	Inventory(1): -12000 + Account receivable(1): 22487 = HST payable(2): 2587 + Sales(4): 19900 + Cost of sales (5): -12000	10487	10487	Yi Liu sales $12,000 inventory for $19,900 on credit to F1 Company (phone number: 123456787)	2021-1-24
21	2021-1-25	Inventory(1): -7500 + Account receivable(1): 15481 = HST payable(2): 1781 + Sales(4): 13700 + Cost of sales (5): -7500	7981	7981	ZhenDao Yuan sales $7,500 inventory for $13,700 on credit to H1 Company (phone number: 123456786)	2021-1-26
22	2021-1-28	Cash(1): -5600 + Computer(1): 1600 + Computer(1): 1800 + Computer(1): 2200 = 0	0	0	Purchase $5,600 computers equipment for $5,600 cash	2021-1-29
23	2021-1-29	Inventory(1): -3500 + Account receivable(1): 7006 = HST payable(2): 806 + Sales(4): 6200 + Cost of sales (5): -3500	3506	3506	Jun Wang sales $3,500 inventory for $6,200 on credit to B1 Company (phone number: 123456789)	2021-1-30
24	2021-1-30	Cash(1): 2558.90 + Account receivable(1): -828.90 + Account receivable(1): -1730 = 0	0	0	Receive $2558.90 cash from B1 Company (phone number: 123456789) with the General ID 5 ($828.9) and General ID 23 ($1730)	2021-1-30
25	2021-1-30	Cash(1): 15000 + Account receivable(1): -15000 = 0	0	0	Receive $15,000 cash from F1 Company (phone number: 123456787) with the General ID 14	2021-1-31
26	2021-1-30	Cash(1): 8475 + Account receivable(1): -8475 = 0	0	0	Receive $8,475 cash from H1 Company (phone number: 123456786) with the General ID 21	2021-1-31
27	2021-1-30	Cash (1) -7500 = Account payable(2): -7500	-7500	-7500	Pay $7,500 cash to C1Company (phone number: 987654322) with the General ID 11	2021-1-31

28	2021-1-30	Cash (1): -232.76 = Administrative expenses(5): -178 + Administrative expenses (5): -54.76	-232.76	-232.76	Pay $232.76 cash to Dan Zhu (Purchase department) for the taxi expenses $178 and the mobile expenses$54.76	2021-1-31
29	2021-1-30	Cash (1): -221.30 = Administrative expenses(5): -135.12 + Administrative expenses (5): -86.18	-221.30	-221.30	Pay $221.30 cash to Hua Li (Purchase department) for the taxi expenses $135.12 and the other expenses $86.18	2021-1-31
30	2021-1-30	Cash (1): -339.52 = Administrative expenses(5) -243 + Administrative expenses (5): -96.52	-339.52	-339.52	RR Company pays $339.52 cash to Xiao Zhou (Sales department) for the taxi expenses $243 and the other expenses $96.52	2021-1-31
31	2021-1-30	Cash (1): -132.26 = Administrative expenses(5): -132.26	-132.26	-132.26	RR Company pays $132.26 cash to Jun Wang (Sales department) for the other expenses	2021-1-31
32	2021-1-30	Cash (1): -82.33 = Administrative expenses(5): -82.33	-82.33	-82.33	RR Company pays $82.33 cash to Zhendao Yuan (Sales department) for the other expenses	2021-1-31
33	2021-1-31	Cash(1): 13000 – Account receivable(1): -13000 = 0	0	0	RR Company receives $13,000 cash from F1Company (phone number: 123456787) with the General ID 20	2021-1-31
34	2021-1-31	Cash (1) -8000 = Account payable(2): -8000	-8000	-8000	RR Company pays $8,000 cash to G1Company (phone number: 987654324) with the General ID 15	2021-1-31
35	2021-1-31	Cash (1): -419.55 = Administrative expenses (5): -347.70 + Administrative expenses (5): -71.85	-419.55	-419.55	RR Company pays $419.55 cash to Yi Liu (Sales department) for the taxi expenses $347.7 and the mobile expenses$71.85	2021-1-31
36	2021-1-31	Office supplies(1): -88 = Administrative expenses(5): -88	-88	-88	RR Company records the Office supplies expenses $88	2021-1-31
37	2021-1-31	Cash (1): -18756 = Salary expenses (5): -18756	-18756	-18756	RR Company pays $18,756 cash for all salary of January, 2014	2021-1-31
38	2021-1-31	Accumulated amortization: Truck(1): -750 = Amortization expenses(5): -750	-750	-750	Record truck's amortization expenses $750 one month (5 years, straight line, and full first month)	2021-1-31
39	2021-1-31	Accumulated amortization: Computer(1): -33.33 + Accumulated amortization: Computer(1): -37.5 + Accumulated amortization: Computer(1): -30.56 = -Amortization expenses(5): 33.33 - Amortization expenses(5): 37.5 - Amortization expenses(5): 30.56	-101.39	-101.39	RR Company records the computers' amortization expenses $101.39	2021-1-31
40	2021-1-31	Cash (1): -376.47 = Administrative expenses (5): -298.69 + Administrative expenses(5): -77.78	-376.47	-376.47	Pay $376.47 cash to Mike Newsome (Office department) for taxi expenses $298.69 and the mobile expenses$77.78	2021-1-31

41	2021-1-31	Cash (1): -280.70 = Administrative expenses(5): -280.70	-280.70	-280.70	RR Company pays $280.70 cash for the utility expenses	2021-1-31
42	2021-1-31	Cash (1): -1500 = Office rent expenses (5): -1500	-1500	-1500	RR Company pays $1500 cash for the office rent expenses	2021-1-31
43	2021-1-31	0 = Accrued interest payable (2): 3000 + Interest expenses (5): -3000	0	0	Record the note payable's interest expenses $3,000 and the accrued interest payable (500,000*8%/12*27/30)	2021-1-31
44	2021-2-1	HST recoverable (1) -9707.10 = HST payable(2): -9707.10	-9707.10	-9707.10	RR Company records the new balance of the HST payable	2021-2-1
45	2021-2-1	Cash (1) -2451.80 = Account payable(2): -2451.80	-2451.80	-2451.80	RR Company pays the cash of the new balance of the HST payable	2021-2-1
46	2021-2-1	Cash (1): -103.3 + Office supplies (1): 103.3 = 0	0	0	RR Company purchases the Office supplies for cash $103.3	2021-2-2
47	2021-2-3	Inventory(1): 91000 + HST recoverable (1) 11830 = Account payable(2): 102830	102830	102830	RR Company purchases $91,000 inventory on credit from D1 Company (phone number: 987654323)	2021-2-10
48	2021-2-4	Inventory(1): -91200 + Account receivable(1): 200688 = HST payable(2): 23088 + Sales(4): 177600 + Cost of sales (5): -91200	109488	109488	Jun Wang sales $91,200 inventory to E1 Company (phone number: 123456788) on credit $177,600	2021-2-10
49	2021-2-8	Cash(1): 5000 + Account receivable(1): -5000 = 0	0	0	RR Company receives $5,000 cash from B1 Company (phone number: 123456789) with the General ID 23	2021-2-10
50	2021-2-9	Cash(1): 12821 + Account receivable(1): -9521 + Account receivable(1): -3300 = 0	0	0	RR Company receives $12,821 cash from F1 Company (phone number: 123456787) with the General ID 14 ($9521) and the General ID 20 ($3300)	2021-2-10
51	2021-2-11	Cash(1): 3500 + Account receivable(1): -3500 = 0	0	0	RR Company receives $3,500 cash from H1 Company (phone number: 123456786) with the General ID 21	2021-2-20
52	2021-2-13	Cash (1) -2500 = Account payable(2): -2500	-2500	-2500	RR Company pays $2,500 cash to A1 Company (phone number: 987654321) with the General ID 4	2021-2-20
53	2021-2-15	Cash (1) -15000 = Account payable(2): -15000	-15000	-15000	RR Company pays $15,000 cash to C1 Company (phone number: 987654322) with the General ID 19	2021-2-20
54	2021-2-17	Cash (1) -4000 = Account payable(2): -4000	-4000	-4000	RR Company pays $4,000 cash to D1 Company (phone number: 987654323) with the General ID 12	2021-2-20

55	2021-2-18	Cash (1): 360000 + Land(1): -270000 = Investment income(4): 90000	90000	90000	RR Company sells land1 (downtown) for $360,000 cash	2021-2-20
56	2021-2-18	Cash(1): -356700 + Share(1) 356700 = 0	0	0	RR Company purchases 10,000 the MicroQQ Company shares for $35.67 each share. Total amount is $356,700	2021-2-20
57	2021-2-25	Cash(1): 120000 + Account receivable(1): -120000 = 0	0	0	RR Company receives $120,000 cash from E1 Company (phone number: 123456788) with the General ID 48	2021-2-28
58	2021-2-26	Cash (1) -55000 = Account payable(2): -55000	-55000	-55000	RR Company pays $55,000 cash to D1 Company (phone number: 987654323) with the General ID 47	2021-2-28
59	2021-2-28	Cash (1): -55.32 = Administrative expenses(5): -55.32	-55.32	-55.32	RR Company pays $55.32 cash to Dan Zhu (Purchase department) for the other expenses	2021-2-28
60	2021-2-28	Cash (1): -458.39 = Administrative expenses(5): -336.41 + Administrative expenses(5): -121.98	-458.39	-458.39	RR Company pays $458.39 cash to Hua Li (Purchase department) for the taxi expenses $336.41 and the other expenses $121.98	2021-2-28
61	2021-2-28	Cash (1): -33.72 = Administrative expenses(5): -33.72	-33.72	-33.72	RR Company pays $33.72 cash to Xiao Zhou (Sales department) for the other expenses	2021-2-28
62	2021-2-28	Cash (1): -152.31 = Administrative expenses(5): -152.31	-152.31	-152.31	RR Company pays $152.31 cash to Jun Wang (Sales department) for the taxi expenses	2021-2-28
63	2021-2-28	Cash (1): -1015.98 = Administrative expenses(5): -1015.98	-1015.98	-1015.98	RR Company pays $1,015.98 cash to Zhendao Yuan (Sales department) for the other expenses	2021-2-28
64	2021-2-28	Cash (1): -117.95 = Administrative expenses(5): -117.95	-117.95	-117.95	RR Company pays $117.95 cash to Yi Liu (Sales department) for the taxi expenses $99.8 and the other expenses $18.15	2021-2-28
65	2021-2-28	Office supplies (1): -101.28 = Office supplies expenses(5): -101.28	-101.28	-101.28	RR Company records the Office supplies expenses $101.28	2021-2-28
66	2021-2-28	Cash (1): -18756 = Salary expenses(5): -18756	-18756	-18756	RR Company pays $18,756 cash for all salary of February, 2014	2021-2-28
67	2021-2-28	Accumulated amortization: Truck(1): -750 = Amortization expenses(5): -750	-750	-750	Record truck's amortization expenses $750 one month (5 years, straight line, and full first month)	2021-2-28
68	2021-2-28	Accumulated amortization: Computer(1): -66.67 + Accumulated amortization: Computer(1): -75 + Accumulated amortization: Computer(1): -61.11 = - Amortization expenses(5): 66.67 –	-202.78	-202.78	RR Company records the computers' amortization expenses $101.39	2021-2-28

		Amortization expenses(5): 75 − Amortization expenses(5): 61.11				
69	021-2-28	Cash (1): -293.37 = Utility expenses(5): -293.37	-293.37	-293.37	RR Company pays $293.37 cash for the utility expenses	2021-2-28
70	2021-2-28	Cash (1): -1500 = Office rent expenses(5): -1500	-1500	-1500	RR Company pays $1,500 cash for the office rent expenses	2021-2-28
71	2021-2-28	0 = Accrued interest payable (2): 3333.33 + Interest expenses (5): -3333.33	0	0	RR Company records the note payable's interest expenses $3,333.33 and the accrued interest payable (500,000*8%/12)	2021-2-28
72	2021-2-28	0 = Tax payable (2): 48199.59 + Tax expenses (5): -48199.59	0	0	RR Company records the tax expenses $48,199.59 and the tax payable $48,199.59	2021-2-28
73	2021-2-28	Accumulated other comprehensive income of land (1): 30000 = Unrealized holding gain or loss (4): 30000	30000	30000	RR Company records the land's unrealized holding gain or loss	2021-2-28
74	2021-2-28	Accumulated other comprehensive income: share (1): -4600 = Unrealized holding gain or loss (4): -4600	-4600	-4600	RR Company records the share's unrealized holding gain or loss	2021-2-28
75	2021-3-1	HST recoverable (1) -11830 = HST payable(2): -11830	-11830	-11830	RR Company records the new balance of the HST payable	2021-3-1
76	2021-3-1	Cash (1) -11258 = Account payable(2): -11258	-11258	-11258	RR Company pays the cash of the new balance of the HST payable	2021-3-1
77	2021-3-2	Cash (1) -123.87 + Office supplies (1): -123.87 = 0	0	0	RR Company purchases the Office supplies for cash $123.87	2021-3-2
78	2021-3-3	Inventory(1): 85,360 + HST recoverable (1) 11096.80 = Account payable(2): 96456.80	96456.80	96456.80	RR Company purchases the $85,360 inventory on credit from G1 Company (phone number: 987654324)	2021-3-3
79	2021-3-4	Inventory(1): -85200 + Account receivable(1): 174924 = HST payable(2): 20124 + Sales(4): 154800 + Cost of sales (5): -85200	89724	89724	Yi Liu sales $85,200 inventory to F1 Company (phone number: 123456787) on credit $154,800	2021-3-4
80	2021-3-10	Cash(1): 52000 + Account receivable(1): -52000 = 0	0	0	RR Company receives $52,000 cash from E1 Company (phone number: 123456788) with the General ID 48	2021-3-10
81	2021-3-12	Cash(1): 506 + Account receivable(1): -230 + Account receivable(1): -276 = 0	0	0	RR Company receives $506 cash from B1 Company (phone number: 123456789) with the General ID 5 ($230) and the General ID 23 ($276)	2021-3-12
82	2021-3-13	Cash(1): 2200 + Account receivable(1): -2200 = 0	0	0	RR Company receives $2,200 cash from H1 Company (phone number: 123456786) with the General ID 21	2021-3-13
83	2021-3-14	Cash (1) -977.10 = Account payable(2): -977.10	-977.10	-977.10	RR Company pays $977.10 cash to A1 Company (phone	2021-3-14

					number: 987654321) with the General ID 4	
84	2021-3-15	Cash (1) -4500 = Account payable(2): -4500	-4500	-4500	RR Company pays $4,500 cash to C1 Company (phone number: 987654322) with the General ID 11	2021-3-15
85	2021-3-17	Cash (1) -30000 = Account payable(2): -30000	-30000	-30000	RR Company pays $30,000 cash to D1 Company (phone number: 987654323) with the General ID 47	2021-3-17
86	2021-3-28	Cash (1): -153.72 = Administrative expenses(5) - 153.72	-153.72	-153.72	RR Company pays $153.72 cash to Mike Newsome (Office department) for the other expenses	2021-3-28
87	2021-3-29	Cash(1): 120000 + Account receivable(1): -120000 = 0	0	0	RR Company receives $120,000 cash from F1 Company (phone number: 123456787) with the General ID 79	2021-3-29
88	2021-3-29	Cash (1) -82360 = Account payable(2): -82360	-82360	-82360	RR Company pays $82,360 cash to G1 Company (phone number: 987654324) with the General ID 78	2021-3-29
89	2021-3-29	Cash (1): -171.63 = Administrative expenses(5): -101.33 + Admin strative expenses(5): -70.30	-171.63	-171.63	RR Company pays $171.63 cash to Hua Li (Purchase department) for taxi expenses $101.33 and the other expenses $70.30	2021-3-29
90	2021-3-29	Cash (1): -52.17 = Administrative expenses(5): -52.17	-52.17	-52.17	RR Company pays $52.17 cash to Xiao Zhou (Sales department) the other expenses	2021-3-29
91	2021-3-29	Cash (1): -129.34 = Administrative expenses(5): -129.34	-129.34	-129.34	RR Company pays $129.34 cash to Jun Wang (Sales department) for the taxi expenses	2021-3-29
92	2021-3-29	Cash (1): -111.93 = Administrative expenses(5): -111.93	-111.93	-111.93	RR Company pays $111.93 cash to Zhendao Yuan (Sales department) for the other expenses	2021-3-29
93	2021-3-30	Cash (1): -1210.91 = Administrative expenses(5): -1132.56 + Administrative expenses(5): -78.35	-1210.91	-1210.91	RR Company pays $1,210.91 cash to Yi Liu (Sales department) for the taxi expenses $1132.56 and the other expenses $78.35	2021-3-30
94	2021-3-30	Cash (1): -201.99 = Administrative expenses(5): -201.99	-201.99	-201.99	RR Company pays $201.99 cash to Ping Wang (Office department) for the other expenses	2021-3-30
95	2021-3-30	Cash (1): -48199.59 = Tax payable (2): -48199.59	-48199.59	-48199.59	RR Company pays $48,199.59 cash to the Canada Revenue Agency	2021-3-30
96	2021-3-31	Office supplies (1): -101.28 = Office supplies expenses(5): -101.28	-101.28	-101.28	RR Company records the Office supplies expenses $101.28	2021-3-31
97	2021-3-31	Cash (1): -23790 = Salary expenses(5): -23790	-23790	-23790	RR Company pays $23,790 cash for all salary of March, 2014	2021-3-31

98	2021-3-31	Accumulated amortization: Truck(1): -750 = Amortization expenses(5): -750	-750	-750	RR Company records the truck's amortization expenses $750 one month (5 years, straight line, and third month)	2021-3-31
99	2021-3-31	Accumulated amortization: Computer(1): -66.67 + Accumulated amortization: Computer(1): -75 + Accumulated amortization: Computer(1): -61.11 = - Amortization expenses(5): 66.67 – Amortization expenses(5): 75 – Amortization expenses(5): 61.11	-202.78	-202.78	RR Company records the computers' amortization expenses ($202.78)	2021-3-31
100	2021-3-31	Cash (1): -323.14 = Utility expenses(5): -323.14	-323.14	-323.14	RR Company pays $323.14 cash for the utility expenses	2021-3-31
101	2021-3-31	Cash (1): -1500 = Office rent expenses(5): -1500	-1500	-1500	RR Company pays $1,500 cash for the office rent expenses	2021-3-31
102	2021-3-31	0 = Accrued interest payable (2): 3333.33 + Interest expenses (5): -3333.33	0	0	RR Company records the note payable's interest expenses $3,333.33 and the accrued interest payable (500,000*8%/12)	2021-3-31
103	2021-3-31	Cash (1): -20000 = Share capital (3): -8000 + Share capital (3): -6000 + Share capital (3): -6000	-20000	-20000	RR Company decides to return $20,000 to the owners	2021-3-31
104	2021-3-31	0 = Tax payable (2): 11270.33 + Tax expenses (5): -11270.33	0	0	RR Company records the tax expenses $11270.33 and the tax payable $11270.33	2021-3-31
105	2021-3-31	Accumulated other comprehensive income of land (1): 25000 = Unrealized holding gain or loss (4): 25000	25000	25000	RR Company records the land's unrealized holding gain or loss	2021-3-31
106	2021-3-31	Accumulated other comprehensive income: share (1): 45700 = Unrealized holding gain or loss (4): 45700	45700	45700	RR Company records the share's unrealized holding gain or loss	2021-3-31
Total Amount			907080.94	907080.94		

Table B-2 Reference

ID	Account Name (Subtotal Name)	Row	GeID	Balance
1	**Current assets**	**103**	**1**	**226437.89**
2	Cash	104	1	96441.48
3	Office supplies	106	2	129.61
4	Inventory	108	4	18830.00
5	HST recoverable	109	4	11096.80
6	Account receivable	110	5	99940.00
7	**Long term investments**	**141**	**8**	**562100.00**
8	Land	143	8	180000.00

9	AOCI of land	144	73	55000.00
10	Shares	145	56	356700.00
11	AOCI of share	146	74	41100.00
12	**Equipment**	**171**	**9**	**47843.05**
13	Truck	173	8	45000.00
14	Accumulated amortization: truck	174	38	-2250.00
15	Computers	175	22	5600.00
16	Accumulated amortization: computer	176	39	-506.95
17	**Current liabilities**	**203**	**4**	**92217.79**
18	Account payable	204	4	51156.80
19	HST payable	205	5	20124.00
20	Accrued interest payable	207	43	9666.66
21	Tax payable	209	75	11270.33
22	**Long term liabilities**	**251**	**7**	**500000.00**
23	Note payable	252	7	500000.00
24	**Owners' capital**	**303**	**1**	**80000.00**
25	Share capital	304	1	80000.00
26	**Revenues**	**403**	**5**	**154500.00**
27	Sales	404	5	154500.00
28	**Cost**	**431**	**5**	**-85200.00**
29	Cost of sales	432	5	-85200.00
30	**Operating and administrative expenses**	**453**	**3**	**-32032.22**
31	Administrative expenses	454	3	-2456.11
32	Salary expenses	456	37	-23790.00
33	Amortization expenses	458	38	-952.78
34	Office rent expenses	459	42	-1500.00
35	Interest expenses	461	43	-3333.33
36	**Other income**	**475**	**4**	**0.00**
37	Investment income	476	4	0.00
38	**Tax**	**600**	**5**	**-11270.33**
39	Tax expenses	602	5	-11270.33
40	**Other comprehensive income**	**713**	**4**	**70700.00**
41	Unrealized holding gain or loss	715	4	70700.00

Table B-3 Subtotal Name

ID	Subtotal Name	Row	GeID	Class
1	Current assets,103	103	1	1
2	Long term investments,141	141	8	1
3	Equipment	171	9	1

4	Current liabilities,203	203	4	2
5	Long term liabilities,251	251	7	2
6	Owners' capital,303	303	1	3
7	Revenues,403	403	5	4
8	Cost,431	431	5	5
9	Operating and administrative expenses,453	453	3	5
10	Other income,475	475	55	4
11	Tax,600	600	75	5
12	Other comprehensive income,713	713	73	4

Table B-4 Multi-subaccounts

ID	Multi-subaccount Name	Parent Account	GeID	Class
1	Cash receipts from owners<Financing activities	Cash	1	1
2	Capital-Ping Wang	Share capital	1	3
3	Capital-Hua Li	Share capital	1	3
4	Capital-Mike Newsome	Share capital	1	3
5	Cash payments for operating expenses<Operating activities	Cash	2	1
6	N	Office supplies	2	1
7	Hua Li-taxi<Purchase department-taxi<Taxi expenses	Administrative expenses	3	5
8	Cash payments to suppliers<Operating activities	Cash	4	1
9	Inven111<Inven11<Inven1	Inventory	4	1
10	Inven112<Inven11<Inven1	Inventory	4	1
11	Inven121<Inven12<Inven1	Inventory	4	1
12	Inven122<Inven12<Inven1	Inventory	4	1
13	Inven13<Inven1	Inventory	4	1
14	987654321	Account payable	4	2
15	Cash receipts from customers<Operating activities	Cash	5	1
16	123456789	Account receivable	5	1
17	Xiao Zhou-sales	Sales	5	4
18	N	Cost of sales	5	5
19	Cash receipts from banks<Financing activities	Cash	7	1
20	N	Note payable	7	2
21	Cash payments for investment<Operating activities	Cash	8	1
22	Land1, Downtown	Land	8	1
23	Land2, North York	Land	8	1
24	Cash payments for machinery<Operating activities	Cash	9	1
25	Truck1	Truck	9	1
26	Ping Wang-open fees<Office department-open fees<Other expenses	Administrative expenses	10	5

27	Inven221<Inven22<Inven2	Inventory	11	1
28	Inven222<Inven22<Inven2	Inventory	11	1
29	PPUK parts<ASD parts<Inven2	Inventory	11	1
30	PPGH parts<ASD parts<Inven2	Inventory	11	1
31	Inven31<Inven3	Inventory	11	1
32	Inven32<Inven3	Inventory	11	1
33	987654322	Account payable	11	2
34	Inven331<Inven33<Inven3	Inventory	12	1
35	Inven332<Inven33<Inven3	Inventory	12	1
36	HGFCVB parts<QASXC parts<Inven3	Inventory	12	1
37	PPGHUP parts<ASDUP parts<Inven3	Inventory	12	1
38	987654323	Account payable	12	2
39	123456788	Account receivable	13	1
40	123456787	Account receivable	14	1
41	ZhenDao Yuan-sales	Sales	14	4
42	Inven411<Inven41<Inven4	Inventory	15	1
43	Inven412<Inven41<Inven4	Inventory	15	1
44	TTTCU parts<TTT parts<Inven4	Inventory	15	1
45	RRRHJK parts<Inven4	Inventory	15	1
46	987654324	Account payable	15	2
47	Yi Liu-sales	Sales	20	4
48	123456786	Account receivable	21	1
49	Computer1	Computers	22	1
50	Computer server1	Computers	22	1
51	POS system1	Computers	22	1
52	Jun Wang-sales	Sales	23	4
53	Dan Zhu-taxi<Purchase department-taxi<Taxi expenses	Administrative expenses	28	5
54	Dan Zhu-mobile<Purchase department-mobile<Mobile expenses	Administrative expenses	28	5
55	Hua Li-other<Purchase department-other<Other expenses	Administrative expenses	29	5
56	Xiao Zhou-taxi<Sales department-taxi<Taxi expenses	Administrative expenses	30	5
57	Xiao Zhou-other<Sales department-other<Other expenses	Administrative expenses	30	5
58	Jun Wang-other<Sales department-other<Other expenses	Administrative expenses	31	5
59	Zhendao Yuan-other<Sales department-other<Other expenses	Administrative expenses	32	5
60	Yi Liu-taxi<Sales department-tax<Taxi expenses	Administrative expenses	35	5
61	Yi Liu-other<Sales department-other<Other expenses	Administrative expenses	35	5
62	Office supplies expenses	Administrative expenses	36	5
63	N	Salary expenses	37	5
64	Truck1-accumulated amortization	Accumulated amortization: truck	38	1
65	Truck1-amortization	Amortization expenses	38	5
66	Computer1-accumulated amortization	Accumulated amortization: Computer	39	1

67	Computer server1-accumulated amortization	Accumulated amortization: Computer	39	1
68	POS system1-accumulated amortization	Accumulated amortization: computer	39	1
69	Computer1-amortization<Computer-amortization	Amortization expenses	39	5
70	Computer server1-amortization<Computer-amortization	Amortization expenses	39	5
71	POS system1-amortization<Computer-amortization	Amortization expenses	39	5
72	Mike Newsome-taxi<Office department-taxi<Taxi expenses	Accumulated amortization: Computer	40	1
73	Mike Newsome-other<Office department-other<Other expenses	Accumulated amortization: computer	40	1
74	Utility expenses	Administrative expenses	41	5
75	N	Office supplies expenses	42	5
76	Note1-TD bank	Accrued interest payable	43	2
77	MicroQQ-share	Share	56	1
78	Dan Zhu-other<Purchase department-other<Other expenses	Administrative expenses	59	5
79	Jun Wang-taxi<Sales department-taxi<Taxi expenses	Administrative expenses	62	5
80	AOCI-land2, North York	AOCI of land	73	1
81	Unrealized holding gain or loss-land	Unrealized holding gain or loss	73	4
82	AOCI-microQQ	AOCI of share	74	1
83	Unrealized holding gain or loss-share	Unrealized holding gain or loss	74	4
84	N	Tax expenses	75	5
85	Ping Wang-other<Office department-other<Other expenses	Administrative expenses	94	5

Table B-5 Suppliers information

Suppliers

ID	Supplier Phone	Supplier Name	Address	E-mail	Postal Code	City	State	Country
1	987654321	A1	A2	A3	A4	A5	A6	A7
2	987654322	C1	C2	C3	C4	C5	C6	C7
3	987654323	D1	D2	D3	D4	D5	D6	D7
4	987654324	G1	G2	G3	G4	G5	G6	G7

Supplier A1: Account payable (X201)

ID	MultiName	Amount	Balance	Ref	GeID	TransDate
1	987654321	3477.10	3477.10		4	2021-1-5
2	987654321	-2500.00	977.10	4	52	2021-2-13
3	987654321	-977.10	0	4	83	2021-3-14

Supplier C1: Account payable (X201)

ID	MultiName	Amount	Balance	Ref	GeID	TransDate
1	987654322	26250	26250		11	2021-1-9
2	987654322	-14000	12250	11	17	2021-1-21
3	987654322	24295	36545		19	2021-1-22
4	987654322	-7500	29045	11	27	2021-1-30
5	987654322	-15000	14045	19	53	2021-2-15
6	987654322	-4500	9545	11	84	2021-3-15

Supplier D1: Account payable (X201)

ID	MultiName	Amount	Balance	Ref	GeID	TransDate
1	987654323	13560	13560		12	2021-1-9
2	987654323	-6000	7560	12	18	2021-1-21
3	987654323	102830	110390		47	2021-2-3
4	987654323	-4000	106390	12	54	2021-2-17
5	987654323	-55000	51390	47	58	2021-2-26
6	987654323	-30000	21390	47	85	2021-3-17

Supplier G1: Account payable (X201)

ID	MultiName	Amount	Balance	Ref	GeID	TransDate
1	987654324	14125	14125		15	2021-1-17
2	987654324	-8000	6125	15	34	2021-1-31
3	987654324	96456.80	102581.80		78	2021-3-3
4	987654324	-82360.00	20221.80	78	88	2021-3-29

Table B-6 Customers information

Customers

ID	Customer Phone	Customer Name	Address	E-mail	Postal Code	City	State	Country
1	123456789	B1	B2	B3	B4	B5	B6	B7
2	123456788	E1	E2	E3	E4	E5	E6	E7
3	123456787	F1	F2	F3	F4	F5	F6	F7
4	123456786	H1	H2	H3	H4	H5	H6	H7

Customer B1: Account receivable (X105)

ID	MultiName	Amount	Balance	Ref	GeID	TransDate
1	123456789	2558.90	2558.90		5	2021-1-5
2	123456789	-1500	1058.90	5	6	2021-1-7
3	123456789	7006	8064.90		23	2021-1-29
4	123456789	-828.90	7236	5	24	2021-1-30
5	123456789	-1730	5506	23	24	2021-1-30
6	123456789	-5000	506	23	49	2021-2-8
7	123456789	-230	276	5	81	2021-3-12
8	123456789	-276	0	23	81	2021-3-12

Customer E1: Account receivable (X105)

ID	MultiName	Amount	Balance	Ref	GeID	TransDate
1	123456788	29835	29835		13	2021-1-11
2	123456788	-21000	8835	13	16	2021-1-17
3	123456788	200688	109523		48	2021-2-4
4	123456788	-120000	89523	48	57	2021-2-25
5	123456788	-52000	37523	48	80	2021-3-10

Customer F1: Account receivable (X105)

ID	MultiName	Amount	Balance	Ref	GeID	TransDate
1	123456787	24521	24521		14	2021-1-15
2	123456787	22487	47008		20	2021-1-23
3	123456787	-15000	32008	14	25	2021-1-30
4	123456787	-13000	19008	20	33	2021-1-31
5	123456787	-9521	9487	14	50	2021-2-9
6	123456787	-3300	6187	20	50	2021-2-9
7	123456787	174924	181111		79	2021-3-4
8	123456787	-120000	61111	79	84	2021-3-29

Customer H1: Account receivable (X105)

ID	MultiName	Amount	Balance	Ref	GeID	TransDate
1	123456786	15481	15481		21	2021-1-25
2	123456786	-8475	7006	21	26	2021-1-30
3	123456786	-3500	3506	21	51	2021-2-11
4	123456786	-2200	1306	21	82	2021-3-13

In the first cabinet, there are the following tables.

Table B-7 Assets (X1) on the door

ID	Account Name (Mathematical Name)	Subtotal	Ref (Row)	Balance
1	Cash (X101)	Current assets,103	104	96441.48
2	Office supplies (X102)	Current assets,103	106	129.61
3	Inventory (X103)	Current assets,103	108	18830.00
4	HST recoverable (X104)	Current assets,103	109	11096.80
5	Account receivable (X105)	Current assets,103	110	99940.00
6	Land (X106)	Long term investments,141	143	180000.00
7	Truck (X107)	Equipment, 171	172	45000.00
8	Accumulated amortization: truck1 (X109)	Equipment, 171	173	-2250.00
9	Computer (X108)	Equipment, 171	174	5600.00
10	Accumulated amortization: Computer (X110)	Equipment, 171	175	-506.95
11	AOCI of land (X111)	Long term investments,141	144	30000.00
12	Shares (X112)	Long term investments,141	145	356700.00
13	AOCI of share (X113)	Long term investments,141	146	-4600.00

Table B-8 Parent account: Cash on a drawer

Cash (X101)

ID	MultiName	TransDate	Amount	Balance	GeID	SubFirst	SubSecond	SubThird
1	Cash receipts from owners<Financing activities	2021-1-2	100000	100000	1	Financing activities	Cash receipts from owners	
2	Cash payments for operating expenses<Operating activities	2021-1-3	-193	99807	2	Operating activities	Cash payments for operating expenses	
3	Cash payments for operating expenses<Operating activities	2021-1-3	-47	99760	3	Operating activities	Cash payments for operating expenses	
4	Cash payments to suppliers< Operating activities	2021-1-5	-670	99090	4	Operating activities	Cash payments to suppliers	
5	Cash receipts from customers< Operating activities	2021-1-5	300	99390	5	Operating activities	Cash receipts from customers	
6	Cash receipts from customers< Operating activities	2021-1-7	1500	100890	6	Operating activities	Cash receipts from customers	
7	Cash receipts from banks< Financing activities	2021-1-7	500000	600890	7	Cash receipts from banks	Financing activities	

8	Cash payments for investment<Investing activities	2021-1-7	-450000	150890	8	Cash payments for investment	Investing activities	
9	Cash payments for machinery<Operating activities	2021-1-8	-45000	105890	9	Cash payments for machinery	Operating activities	
10	Cash payments for operating expenses<Operating activities	2021-1-8	-367	105523	10	Cash payments for operating expenses	Operating activities	
11	Cash payments to suppliers< Operating activities	2021-1-9	-2000	103523	11	Operating activities	Cash payments to suppliers	
12	Cash receipts from customers< Operating activities	2021-1-11	3500	107023	13	Operating activities	Cash receipts from customers	
13	Cash receipts from customers< Operating activities	2021-1-17	21000	128023	16	Operating activities	Cash receipts from customers	
14	Cash payments to suppliers< Operating activities	2021-1-21	-14000	114023	17	Operating activities	Cash payments to suppliers	
15	Cash payments to suppliers< Operating activities	2021-1-21	-6000	108023	18	Operating activities	Cash payments to suppliers	
16	Cash payments for machinery<Operating activities	2021-1-28	-5600	102423	22	Operating activities	Cash payments for machinery	
17	Cash receipts from customers< Operating activities	2021-1-30	2558.90	104981.90	24	Operating activities	Cash receipts from customers	
18	Cash receipts from customers< Operating activities	2021-1-30	15000	119981.90	25	Operating activities	Cash receipts from customers	
19	Cash receipts from customers< Operating activities	2021-1-30	8475	128456.90	26	Operating activities	Cash receipts from customers	
20	Cash payments to suppliers<Operating activities	2021-1-30	-7500	120956.9	27	Operating activities	Cash payments to suppliers	
21	Cash payments for operating expenses<Operating activities	2021-1-30	-232.76	120724.14	28	Operating activities	Cash payments for operating expenses	
22	Cash payments for operating expenses<Operating activities	2021-1-30	-221.30	120502.84	29	Operating activities	Cash payments for operating expenses	
23	Cash payments for operating expenses<Operating activities	2021-1-30	-339.52	120163.32	30	Operating activities	Cash payments for operating expenses	
24	Cash payments for operating expenses<Operating activities	2021-1-30	-132.26	120031.06	31	Operating activities	Cash payments for operating expenses	
25	Cash payments for operating expenses<Operating activities	2021-1-30	-82.33	119948.73	32	Operating activities	Cash payments for operating expenses	

26	Cash receipts from customers< Operating activities	2021-1-31	13000	132948.73	33	Operating activities	Cash receipts from customers	
27	Cash payments to suppliers<Operating activities	2021-1-31	-8000	124948.73	34	Operating activities	Cash payments to suppliers	
28	Cash payments for operating expenses<Operating activities	2021-1-31	-419.55	124529.18	35	Operating activities	Cash payments for operating expenses	
29	Cash payments for operating expenses<Operating activities	2021-1-31	-18756	105773.18	37	Operating activities	Cash payments for operating expenses	
30	Cash payments for operating expenses<Operating activities	2021-1-31	-376.47	105396.71	40	Operating activities	Cash payments for operating expenses	
31	Cash payments for operating expenses<Operating activities	2021-1-31	-280.70	105116.01	41	Operating activities	Cash payments for operating expenses	
32	Cash payments for operating expenses<Operating activities	2021-1-31	-1500.00	103616.01	42	Operating activities	Cash payments for operating expenses	
33	Cash payments for operating expenses<Operating activities	2021-2-1	-2451.80	101164.21	45	Operating activities	Cash payments for operating expenses	
34	Cash payments for operating expenses<Operating activities	2021-2-1	-103.30	101060.91	46	Operating activities	Cash payments for operating expenses	
35	Cash receipts from customers< Operating activities	2021-2-8	5000.00	106060.91	49	Operating activities	Cash receipts from customers	
36	Cash receipts from customers< Operating activities	2021-2-9	12821	118881.91	50	Operating activities	Cash receipts from customers	
37	Cash receipts from customers< Operating activities	2021-2-11	3500	122381.91	51	Operating activities	Cash receipts from customers	
38	Cash payments to suppliers< Operating activities	2021-2-13	-2500	119881.91	52	Operating activities	Cash payments to suppliers	
39	Cash payments to suppliers< Operating activities	2021-2-15	-15000	104881.91	53	Operating activities	Cash payments to suppliers	
40	Cash payments to suppliers< Operating activities	2021-2-17	-4000	100881.91	54	Operating activities	Cash payments to suppliers	
41	Cash receipts from customers< Operating activities	2021-2-18	360000	460881.91	55	Operating activities	Cash receipts from customers	
42	Cash payments for investment<Investing activities	2021-2-18	-356700	104181.91	56	Investing activities	Cash payments for investment	
43	Cash receipts from customers< Operating activities	2021-2-25	120000	224181.91	57	Operating activities	Cash receipts from customers	

44	Cash payments to suppliers< Operating activities	2021-2-26	-55000	169181.91	58	Operating activities	Cash payments to suppliers
45	Cash payments for operating expenses<Operating activities	2021-2-28	-55.32	169126.59	59	Operating activities	Cash payments for operating expenses
46	Cash payments for operating expenses<Operating activities	2021-2-28	-458.39	168668.20	60	Operating activities	Cash payments for operating expenses
47	Cash payments for operating expenses<Operating activities	2021-2-28	-33.72	168634.48	61	Operating activities	Cash payments for operating expenses
48	Cash payments for operating expenses<Operating activities	2021-2-28	-152.31	168482.17	62	Operating activities	Cash payments for operating expenses
49	Cash payments for operating expenses<Operating activities	2021-2-28	-1015.98	167466.19	63	Operating activities	Cash payments for operating expenses
50	Cash payments for operating expenses<Operating activities	2021-2-28	-117.95	167348.24	64	Operating activities	Cash payments for operating expenses
51	Cash payments for operating expenses<Operating activities	2021-2-28	-18756.00	148592.24	65	Operating activities	Cash payments for operating expenses
52	Cash payments for operating expenses<Operating activities	2021-2-28	-293.37	148298.87	66	Operating activities	Cash payments for operating expenses
53	Cash payments for operating expenses<Operating activities	2021-2-28	-1500.00	146798.87	67	Operating activities	Cash payments for operating expenses
54	Cash payments for operating expenses<Operating activities	2021-3-1	-11258	135540.87	76	Operating activities	Cash payments for operating expenses
55	Cash payments for operating expenses<Operating activities	2021-3-2	-123.87	135417.00	77	Operating activities	Cash payments for operating expenses
56	Cash receipts from customers< Operating activities	2021-3-10	52000	187417.00	80	Operating activities	Cash receipts from customers
57	Cash receipts from customers< Operating activities	2021-3-12	506	187923.00	81	Operating activities	Cash receipts from customers
58	Cash receipts from customers< Operating activities	2021-3-13	2200	190123.00	82	Operating activities	Cash receipts from customers
59	Cash payments to suppliers<Operating activities	2021-3-14	-977.10	189145.90	83	Operating activities	Cash payments to suppliers

60	Cash payments to suppliers<Operating activities	2021-3-15	-4500	184645.90	84	Operating activities	Cash payments to suppliers	
61	Cash payments to suppliers<Operating activities	2021-3-17	-30000	154645.90	85	Operating activities	Cash payments to suppliers	
62	Cash payments for operating expenses<Operating activities	2021-3-28	-153.72	154492.18	86	Operating activities	Cash payments for operating expenses	
63	Cash receipts from customers< Operating activities	2021-3-29	120000	274492.18	87	Operating activities	Cash receipts from customers	
64	Cash payments to suppliers<Operating activities	2021-3-29	-82360	192132.18	88	Operating activities	Cash payments to suppliers	
65	Cash payments for operating expenses<Operating activities	2021-3-29	-171.63	191960.55	89	Operating activities	Cash payments for operating expenses	
66	Cash payments for operating expenses<Operating activities	2021-3-29	-52.17	191908.38	90	Operating activities	Cash payments for operating expenses	
67	Cash payments for operating expenses<Operating activities	2021-3-29	-129.34	191779.04	91	Operating activities	Cash payments for operating expenses	
68	Cash payments for operating expenses<Operating activities	2021-3-29	-111.93	191667.11	92	Operating activities	Cash payments for operating expenses	
69	Cash payments for operating expenses<Operating activities	2021-3-30	-1210.91	190456.20	93	Operating activities	Cash payments for operating expenses	
70	Cash payments for operating expenses<Operating activities	2021-3-30	-201.99	190254.21	94	Operating activities	Cash payments for operating expenses	
71	Cash payments for operating expenses<Operating activities	2021-3-31	-23790	166464.21	96	Operating activities	Cash payments for operating expenses	
72	Cash payments for operating expenses<Operating activities	2021-3-31	-323.14	166141.07	99	Operating activities	Cash payments for operating expenses	
73	Cash payments for operating expenses<Operating activities	2021-3-31	-1500	164641.07	100	Operating activities	Cash payments for operating expenses	
74	Cash payments for operating expenses<Operating activities	2021-3-31	-48199.59	116441.48	103	Operating activities	Cash payments for operating expenses	
75	Cash receipts from owners<Financing activities	2021-3-31	-20000	96441.48	104	Financing activities	Cash receipts from owners	

One-level on a **large** card

Financing activities (X10101) < Parent account: Cash (X101)

ID	MultiName	Amount	Ref	GeID	TransDate	Balance
1	Cash receipts from owners<Financing activities	100000		1	2021-1-2	100000
2	Cash receipts from banks<Financing activities	500000		7	2021-1-2	600000
3	Cash receipts from owners<Financing activities	-20000		104	2021-3-31	580000

Two-level on a **medium** card

Cash receipts from owners (X1010101) << Parent account: Cash (X101)

ID	MultiName	Amount	Ref	GeID	TransDate	Balance
1	Cash receipts from owners<Financing activities	100000		1	2021-1-2	100000
2	Cash receipts from owners<Financing activities	-20000		104	2021-3-31	80000

Two-level on a **medium** card

Cash receipts from banks (X1010102) << Parent account: Cash (X101)

ID	MultiName	Amount	Ref	GeID	TransDate	Balance
1	Cash receipts from banks<Financing activities	500000		7	2021-1-7	500000

One-level on a **large** card

Operating activities (X10102) < Parent account: Cash (X101)

ID	MultiName	Amount	Ref	GeID	TransDate	Balance
1	Cash payments for operating expenses<Operating activities	-193		2	2021-1-3	-193
2	Cash payments for operating expenses<Operating activities	-47		3	2021-1-3	-240
3	Cash payments to suppliers< Operating activities	-670		4	2021-1-5	-910
4	Cash receipts from customers< Operating activities	300		5	2021-1-5	-610
5	Cash receipts from customers< Operating activities	1500		6	2021-1-7	890

6	Cash payments for machinery<Operating activities	-45000		9	2021-1-8	-44110
7	Cash payments for operating expenses<Operating activities	-367		10	2021-1-8	-44477
8	Cash payments to suppliers< Operating activities	-2000		11	2021-1-9	-46477
9	Cash receipts from customers< Operating activities	3500		13	2021-1-11	-42977
10	Cash receipts from customers< Operating activities	21000		16	2021-1-17	-21977
11	Cash payments to suppliers< Operating activities	-14000		17	2021-1-21	-35977
12	Cash payments to suppliers< Operating activities	-6000		18	2021-1-21	-41977
13	Cash payments for machinery<Operating activities	-5600		22	2021-1-28	-47577
14	Cash receipts from customers< Operating activities	2558.90		24	2021-1-30	-45018.10
15	Cash receipts from customers< Operating activities	15000		25	2021-1-30	-30018.10
16	Cash receipts from customers< Operating activities	8475		26	2021-1-30	-21543.10
17	Cash payments to suppliers< Operating activities	-7500		27	2021-1-30	-29043.10
18	Cash payments for operating expenses<Operating activities	-232.76		28	2021-1-30	-29275.86
19	Cash payments for operating expenses<Operating activities	-221.30		29	2021-1-30	-29497.16
20	Cash payments for operating expenses<Operating activities	-339.52		30	2021-1-30	-29836.68
21	Cash payments for operating expenses<Operating activities	-132.26		31	2021-1-30	-29968.94
22	Cash payments for operating expenses<Operating activities	-82.33		32	2021-1-30	-30051.27
23	Cash receipts from customers< Operating activities	13000		33	2021-1-31	-17051.27
24	Cash payments to suppliers< Operating activities	-8000		34	2021-1-31	-25051.27
25	Cash payments for operating expenses<Operating activities	-419.55		35	2021-1-31	-25470.82
26	Cash payments for operating expenses<Operating activities	-18756		37	2021-1-31	-44226.82
27	Cash payments for operating expenses<Operating activities	-376.47		40	2021-1-31	-44603.29
28	Cash payments for operating expenses<Operating activities	-280.70		41	2021-1-31	-44883.99
29	Cash payments for operating expenses<Operating activities	-1500		42	2021-1-31	-46383.99
30	Cash payments for operating expenses<Operating activities	-2451.80		45	2021-2-1	-48835.79
31	Cash payments for operating expenses<Operating activities	-103.30		46	2021-2-1	-48939.09
32	Cash receipts from customers< Operating activities	5000		49	2021-2-8	-43939.09
33	Cash receipts from customers< Operating activities	12821		50	2021-2-9	-31118.09
34	Cash receipts from customers< Operating activities	3500		51	2021-2-11	-27618.09
35	Cash payments to suppliers< Operating activities	-2500		52	2021-2-13	-30118.09

36	Cash payments to suppliers<Operating activities	-15000		53	2021-2-15	-45118.09
37	Cash payments to suppliers<Operating activities	-4000		54	2021-2-17	-49118.09
38	Cash receipts from customers<Operating activities	360000		55	2021-2-18	310881.91
39	Cash receipts from customers<Operating activities	120000		57	2021-2-25	430881.91
40	Cash payments to suppliers<Operating activities	-55000		58	2021-2-26	375881.91
41	Cash payments for operating expenses<Operating activities	-55.32		59	2021-2-28	375826.59
42	Cash payments for operating expenses<Operating activities	-458.39		60	2021-2-28	375368.20
43	Cash payments for operating expenses<Operating activities	-33.72		61	2021-2-28	375334.48
44	Cash payments for operating expenses<Operating activities	-152.31		62	2021-2-28	375182.17
45	Cash payments for operating expenses<Operating activities	-1015.98		63	228021-2-28	374166.19
46	Cash payments for operating expenses<Operating activities	-117.95		64	2021-2-28	374048.24
47	Cash payments for operating expenses<Operating activities	-18756		65	2021-2-28	355292.24
48	Cash payments for operating expenses<Operating activities	-293.37		66	2021-2-28	354998.87
49	Cash payments for operating expenses<Operating activities	-1500		67	2021-2-28	353498.87
50	Cash payments for operating expenses<Operating activities	-11258		76	2021-3-1	342240.87
51	Cash payments for operating expenses<Operating activities	-123.87		77	2021-3-2	342117.00
52	Cash payments for operating expenses<Operating activities	52000		80	2021-3-10	394117.00
53	Cash payments for operating expenses<Operating activities	506		81	2021-3-12	394623.00
54	Cash payments for operating expenses<Operating activities	2200		82	2021-3-13	396823.00
55	Cash payments for operating expenses<Operating activities	-977.10		83	2021-3-14	395845.90
56	Cash payments for operating expenses<Operating activities	-4500		84	2021-3-15	391345.90
57	Cash payments for operating expenses<Operating activities	-30000		85	2021-3-17	361345.90
58	Cash payments for operating expenses<Operating activities	-153.72		86	2021-3-28	361192.18
59	Cash payments for operating expenses<Operating activities	120000		87	2021-3-29	481192.18
60	Cash payments for operating expenses<Operating activities	-82360		88	2021-3-29	398832.18
61	Cash payments for operating expenses<Operating activities	-171.63		89	2021-3-29	398660.55
62	Cash payments for operating expenses<Operating activities	-52.17		90	2021-3-29	398608.38
63	Cash payments for operating expenses<Operating activities	-129.34		91	2021-3-29	398479.04
64	Cash payments for operating expenses<Operating activities	-111.93		92	2021-3-29	398367.11
65	Cash payments for operating expenses<Operating activities	-1210.91		93	2021-3-30	397156.20

66	Cash payments for operating expenses<Operating activities	-201.99		94	2021-3-30	396954.21
67	Cash payments for operating expenses<Operating activities	-43199.59		95	2021-3-30	348754.62
68	Cash payments for operating expenses<Operating activities	-23790		97	2021-3-31	324964.62
69	Cash payments for operating expenses<Operating activities	-323.14		100	2021-3-31	324641.48
70	Cash payments for operating expenses<Operating activities	-1500		101	2021-3-31	323141.48

Two-level on a **medium** card

Cash payments for operating expenses (X1010201) << Parent account: Cash (X101)

ID	MultiName	Amount	Ref	GeID	TransDate	Balance
1	Cash payments for operating expenses<Operating activities	-193		2	2021-1-3	-193
2	Cash payments for operating expenses<Operating activities	-47		3	2021-1-3	-240
3	Cash payments for operating expenses<Operating activities	-367		10	2021-1-8	-607
4	Cash payments for operating expenses<Operating activities	-232.76		28	2021-1-30	-839.76
5	Cash payments for operating expenses<Operating activities	-221.30		29	2021-1-30	-1061.06
6	Cash payments for operating expenses<Operating activities	-339.52		30	2021-1-30	-1400.58
7	Cash payments for operating expenses<Operating activities	-132.26		31	2021-1-30	-1532.84
8	Cash payments for operating expenses<Operating activities	-82.33		32	2021-1-30	-1615.17
9	Cash payments for operating expenses<Operating activities	-419.55		35	2021-1-31	-2034.72
10	Cash payments for operating expenses<Operating activities	-18756		37	2021-1-31	-20790.72
11	Cash payments for operating expenses<Operating activities	-376.47		40	2021-1-31	-21167.19
12	Cash payments for operating expenses<Operating activities	-280.70		41	2021-1-31	-21447.89
13	Cash payments for operating expenses<Operating activities	-1500		42	2021-1-31	-22947.89
14	Cash payments for operating expenses<Operating activities	-2451.80		45	2021-2-1	-25399.69
15	Cash payments for operating expenses<Operating activities	-103.30		46	2021-2-1	-25502.99
16	Cash payments for operating expenses<Operating activities	-55.32		59	2021-2-28	-25558.31
17	Cash payments for operating expenses<Operating activities	-458.39		60	2021-2-28	-26016.70
18	Cash payments for operating expenses<Operating activities	-33.72		61	2021-2-28	-26050.42
19	Cash payments for operating expenses<Operating activities	-152.31		62	2021-2-28	-26202.73
20	Cash payments for operating expenses<Operating activities	-1015.98		63	2021-2-28	-27218.71

21	Cash payments for operating expenses<Operating activities	-117.95		64	2021-2-28	-27336.66
22	Cash payments for operating expenses<Operating activities	-18756		65	2021-2-28	-46092.66
23	Cash payments for operating expenses<Operating activities	-293.37		66	2021-2-28	-46386.03
24	Cash payments for operating expenses<Operating activities	-1500		67	2021-2-28	-47886.03
25	Cash payments for operating expenses<Operating activities	-11258		76	2021-3-1	-59144.03
26	Cash payments for operating expenses<Operating activities	-123.87		77	2021-3-2	-59267.90
27	Cash payments for operating expenses<Operating activities	-153.72		86	2021-3-28	-59421.62
28	Cash payments for operating expenses<Operating activities	-171.63		89	2021-3-29	-59593.25
29	Cash payments for operating expenses<Operating activities	-52.17		90	2021-3-29	-59645.42
30	Cash payments for operating expenses<Operating activities	-129.34		91	2021-3-29	-59774.76
31	Cash payments for operating expenses<Operating activities	-111.93		92	2021-3-29	-59886.69
32	Cash payments for operating expenses<Operating activities	-1210.91		93	2021-3-30	-61097.60
33	Cash payments for operating expenses<Operating activities	-201.99		94	2021-3-30	-61299.59
34	Cash payments for operating expenses<Operating activities	-48199.59		95	2021-3-30	-109499.18
35	Cash payments for operating expenses<Operating activities	-23790		97	2021-3-31	-133289.18
36	Cash payments for operating expenses<Operating activities	-323.14		100	2021-3-31	-133612.32
37	Cash payments for operating expenses<Operating activities	-1500		101	2021-3-31	-135112.32

Two-level on a **medium** card

Cash payments to suppliers (X1010202) << Parent account: Cash (X101)

ID	MultiName	Amount	Ref	GeID	TransDate	Balance
1	Cash payments to suppliers< Operating activities	-670		4	2021-1-5	-670
2	Cash payments to suppliers< Operating activities	-2000		11	2021-1-9	-2670
3	Cash payments to suppliers< Operating activities	-14000		17	2021-1-21	-16670
4	Cash payments to suppliers< Operating activities	-6000		18	2021-1-21	-22670
5	Cash payments to suppliers< Operating activities	-7500		27	2021-1-30	-30170
6	Cash payments to suppliers< Operating activities	-8000		34	2021-1-31	-38170
7	Cash payments to suppliers< Operating activities	-2500		52	2021-2-13	-40670
8	Cash payments to suppliers< Operating activities	-15000		53	2021-2-15	-55670

9	Cash payments to suppliers Operating activities	-4000		54	2021-2-17	-59670
10	Cash payments to suppliers Operating activities	-55000		58	2021-2-26	-114670
11	Cash payments to suppliers Operating activities	-977.10		83	2021-3-14	-115647.10
12	Cash payments to suppliers Operating activities	-4500		84	2021-3-15	-120147.10
13	Cash payments to suppliers Operating activities	-30000		85	2021-3-17	-150147.10
14	Cash payments to suppliers Operating activities	-32360		88	2021-3-29	-232507.10

Two-level on a **medium** card

Cash receipts from customers (X1010203) << Parent account: Cash (X101)

ID	MultiName	Amount	Ref	GeID	TransDate	Balance
1	Cash receipts from customers< Operating activities	300		5	2021-1-5	300
2	Cash receipts from customers< Operating activities	1500		6	2021-1-7	1800
3	Cash receipts from customers< Operating activities	3500		13	2021-1-11	5300
4	Cash receipts from customers< Operating activities	21000		16	2021-1-17	26300
5	Cash receipts from customers< Operating activities	2558.90		24	2021-1-30	28858.90
6	Cash receipts from customers< Operating activities	15000		25	2021-1-30	43858.90
7	Cash receipts from customers< Operating activities	8475		26	2021-1-30	52333.90
8	Cash receipts from customers< Operating activities	13000		33	2021-1-31	65333.90
9	Cash receipts from customers< Operating activities	5000		49	2021-2-8	70333.90
10	Cash receipts from customers< Operating activities	12821		50	2021-2-9	83154.90
11	Cash receipts from customers< Operating activities	3500		51	2021-2-11	86654.90
12	Cash receipts from customers< Operating activities	360000		55	2021-2-18	446654.90
13	Cash receipts from customers< Operating activities	120000		57	2021-2-25	566654.90
14	Cash receipts from customers< Operating activities	52000		80	2021-3-10	618654.90
15	Cash receipts from customers< Operating activities	506		81	2021-3-12	619160.90
16	Cash receipts from customers< Operating activities	2200		82	2021-3-13	621360.90
17	Cash receipts from customers< Operating activities	120000		87	2021-3-29	741360.90

Two-level on a **medium** card

Cash payments for machinery (X1010204) << Parent account: Cash (X101)

ID	MultiName	Amount	Ref	GeID	TransDate	Balance
1	Cash payments for machinery< Operating activities	-45000		9	2021-1-8	-45000
2	Cash payments for machinery< Operating activities	-5600		22	2021-1-28	-50600

One-level on a **large** card

Investing activities (X10103) < Parent account: Cash (X101)

ID	MultiName	Amount	Ref	GeID	TransDate	Balance
1	Cash payments for investment<Investing activities	-450000		8	2021-1-7	-450000
2	Cash payments for investment<Investing activities	-356700		56	2021-2-18	-806700

Two-level on a **medium** card

Cash payments for investment (X1010301) << Parent account: Cash (X101)

ID	MultiName	Amount	Ref	GeID	TransDate	Balance
1	Cash payments for investment<Investing activities	-45000		8	2021-1-7	-45000
2	Cash payments for investment<Investing activities	-356700		56	2021-2-18	-806700

Table B-9 Parent account: Office supplies on a drawer

Office supplies (X102)

ID	MultiName	TransDate	Amount	Balance	GeID	SubFirst	SubSecond	SubThird
1	N	2021-1-3	193	193	2			
2	N	2021-1-31	-88	105	36			
3	N	2021-2-1	103.30	208.30	46			
4	N	2021-2-28	-101.28	107.02	65			
5	N	2021-3-2	123.87	230.89	77			
6	N	2021-3-31	-101.28	129.61	96			

Table B-10 Parent account: Inventory on a drawer

Inventory (X103)

ID	MultiName	TransDate	Amount	Balance	GeID	SubFirst	SubSecond	SubThird	Unit
1	Inven111<Inven11<Inven1	2021-1-5	1650	1650	4	Inven1	Inven11	Inven111	165
2	Inven112<Inven11<Inven1	2021-1-5	900	2550	4	Inven1	Inven11	Inven112	225
3	Inven121<Inven12<Inven1	2021-1-5	520	3070	4	Inven1	Inven12	Inven121	650
4	Inven122<Inven12<Inven1	2021-1-5	330	3400	4	Inven1	Inven12	Inven122	66
5	Inven13<Inven1	2021-1-5	270	3670	4	Inven1	Inven13		9
6	Inven111<Inven11<Inven1	2021-1-5	-910	2760	5	Inven1	Inven11	Inven111	-91
7	Inven112<Inven11<Inven1	2021-1-5	-520	2240	5	Inven1	Inven11	Inven112	-130
8	Inven121<Inven12<Inven1	2021-1-5	-300	1940	5	Inven1	Inven12	Inven121	-375
9	Inven122<Inven12<Inven1	2021-1-5	-170	1770	5	Inven1	Inven12	Inven122	-34
10	Inven221<Inven22<Inven2	2021-1-9	3200	4970	11	Inven2	Inven22	Inven221	320
11	Inven222<Inven22<Inven2	2021-1-9	5000	9970	11	Inven2	Inven22	Inven221	1000
12	PPUK parts<ASD parts<Inven2	2021-1-9	4800	14770	11	Inven2	ASD parts	PPUK parts	1200
13	PPGH parts<ASD parts<Inven2	2021-1-9	3800	18570	11	Inven2	ASD parts	PPUK parts	1900
14	Inven31<Inven3	2021-1-9	5300	23870	11	Inven3	Inven31		530
15	Inven32<Inven3	2021-1-9	2900	26770	11	Inven3	Inven32		580
16	Inven331<Inven33<Inven3	2021-1-9	2700	29470	12	Inven3	Inven33	Inven331	1350
17	Inven332<Inven33<Inven3	2021-1-9	3100	32570	12	Inven3	Inven33	Inven332	620
18	HGFCVB parts<QASXC parts<Inven3	2021-1-9	4900	37470	12	Inven3	QASXC parts	HGFCVB parts	490
19	PPGHUP parts<ASDUP parts<Inven3	2021-1-9	1300	38770	12	Inven3	ASDUP parts	PPGHUP parts	130
20	Inven221<Inven22<Inven2	2021-1-11	-2900	35870	13	Inven2	Inven22	Inven221	-290
21	Inven222<Inven22<Inven2	2021-1-11	-4700	31170	13	Inven2	Inven22	Inven222	-940
22	PPUK parts<ASD parts< Inven2	2021-1-11	-2600	28570	13	Inven2	ASD parts	PPUK parts	-650
23	Inven32<Inven3	2021-1-11	-1900	26670	13	Inven3	Inven32		-380
24	HGFCVB parts<QASXC parts<Inven3	2021-1-11	-4800	21870	13	Inven3	QASXC parts	HGFCVB parts	-480
25	PPGHUP parts<ASDUP parts<Inven3	2021-1-11	-800	21070	13	Inven3	ASDUP parts	PPGHUP parts	-80
26	PPGH parts<ASD parts<Inven2	2021-1-15	-3100	17970	14	Inven2	ASD parts	PPUK parts	-1550

27	Inven31<Inven3	2021-1-15	-5000	12970	14	Inven3	Inven31		-500
28	Inven331<Inven33<Inven3	2021-1-15	-2200	10770	14	Inven3	Inven33	Inven331	-1100
29	Inven332<Inven33<Inven3	2021-1-15	-2900	7870	14	Inven3	Inven33	Inven332	-580
30	Inven411<Inven41<Inven4	2021-1-17	5100	12970	15	Inven4	Inven41	Inven411	1020
31	Inven412<Inven41<Inven4	2021-1-17	3700	16670	15	Inven4	Inven41	Inven412	1850
32	TTTCU parts<TTT parts<Inven4	2021-1-17	2300	18970	15	Inven4	TTT parts	TTTCU parts	1150
33	RRRHJK parts< Inven4	2021-1-17	1400	20370	15	Inven4	RRRHJK parts		700
34	PPUK parts<ASD parts<Inven2	2021-1-22	6500	26870	19	Inven2	ASD parts	PPUK parts	1625
35	PPGH parts<ASD parts<Inven2	2021-1-22	6000	32870	19	Inven2	ASD parts	PPGH parts	3000
36	Inven31<Inven3	2021-1-22	5300	38170	19	Inven3	Inven31		530
37	Inven32<Inven3	2021-1-22	3700	41870	19	Inven3	Inven32		740
38	PPUK parts<ASD parts<Inven2	2021-1-23	-3300	38570	20	Inven2	ASD parts	PPUK parts	-825
39	PPGH parts<ASD parts<Inven2	2021-1-23	-3900	34670	20	Inven2	ASD parts	PPGH parts	-1950
40	Inven31<Inven3	2021-1-23	-2500	32170	20	Inven3	Inven31		-250
41	Inven32<Inven3	2021-1-23	-2300	29870	20	Inven3	Inven32		-460
42	PPUK parts<ASD parts<Inven2	2021-1-25	-3000	26870	21	Inven2	ASD parts	PPUK parts	-750
43	PPGH parts<ASD parts<Inven2	2021-1-25	-1800	25070	21	Inven2	ASD parts	PPGH parts	-900
44	Inven31<Inven3	2021-1-25	-2700	22370	21	Inven3	Inven31		-270
45	PPUK parts<ASD parts<Inven2	2021-1-29	-2200	20170	23	Inven2	ASD parts	PPUK parts	-550
46	Inven32<Inven3	2021-1-29	-1300	18870	23	Inven3	Inven32		-260
47	HGFCVB parts<QASXC parts<Inven3	2021-2-3	59600	78470	47	Inven3	QASXC parts	HGFCVB parts	5960
48	PPGHUP parts<ASDUP parts<Inven3	2021-2-3	31400	109870	47	Inven3	ASDUP parts	PPGHUP parts	3140
49	HGFCVB parts<QASXC parts<Inven3	2021-2-4	-59600	50270	48	Inven3	QASXC parts	HGFCVB parts	-5960
50	PPGHUP parts<ASDUP parts<Inven3	2021-2-4	-31600	18670	48	Inven3	ASDUP parts	PPGHUP parts	-3160
51	TTTCU parts<TTT parts<Inven4	2021-3-3	66210	84880	78	Inven4	TTT parts	TTTCU parts	33105
52	RRRHJK parts< Inven4	2021-3-3	19150	104030	78	Inven4	RRRHJK parts		9575
53	TTTCU parts<TTT parts<Inven4	2021-3-4	-66070	37960	79	Inven4	TTT parts	TTTCU parts	-33035
54	RRRHJK parts< Inven4	2021-3-4	-19130	18830	79	Inven4	RRRHJK parts		-9565

One-level on a **large** card

Inven1 (X10301) < Parent account: Inventory (X103)

ID	MultiName	Amount	Unit	GeID	TransDate	Balance
1	Inven111<Inven11<Inven1	1650	165	4	2021-1-5	1650
2	Inven112<Inven11<Inven1	900	225	4	2021-1-5	2550
3	Inven121<Inven12<Inven1	520	650	4	2021-1-5	3070
4	Inven122<Inven12<Inven1	330	66	4	2021-1-5	3400
5	Inven13<Inven1	270	9	4	2021-1-5	3670
6	Inven111<Inven11<Inven1	-910	-91	5	2021-1-5	2760
7	Inven112<Inven11<Inven1	-520	-130	5	2021-1-5	2240
8	Inven121<Inven12<Inven1	-300	-375	5	2021-1-5	1940
9	Inven122<Inven12<Inven1	-170	-34	5	2021-1-5	1770

Two-level on a **medium** card

Inven11 (X1030101) << Parent account: Inventory (X103)

ID	MultiName	Amount	Unit	GeID	TransDate	Balance
1	Inven111<Inven11<Inven1	1650	165	4	2021-1-5	1650
2	Inven112<Inven11<Inven1	900	225	4	2021-1-5	2550
3	Inven111<Inven11<Inven1	-910	-91	4	2021-1-5	1640
4	Inven112<Inven11<Inven1	-520	-123	4	2021-1-5	1120

Three-level on a **small** card

Inven111 (X103010101) <<< Parent account: Inventory (X103)

ID	MultiName	Amount	Unit	GeID	TransDate	Balance
1	Inven111<Inven11<Inven1	1650	165	4	2021-1-5	1650
2	Inven111<Inven11<Inven1	-910	-91	5	2021-1-5	740

Three-level on a **small** card

Inven112 (X103010102) <<< Parent acccunt: Inventory (X103)

ID	MultiName	Amount	Unit	GeID	TransDate	Balance
1	Inven112<Inven11<Inven1	900	225	4	2021-1-5	900
2	Inven112<Inven11<Inven1	-520	-123	5	2021-1-5	380

Two-level on a **medium** card

Inven12 (X1030102) << Parent account: Inventory (X103)

ID	MultiName	Amount	Unit	GeID	TransDate	Balance
1	Inven121<Inven12<Inven1	520	650	4	2021-1-5	520
2	Inven122<Inven12<Inven1	330	66	4	2021-1-5	850
3	Inven121<Inven12<Inven1	-300	-375	5	2021-1-5	550
4	Inven122<Inven12<Inven1	-170	-34	5	2021-1-5	380

Three-level on a **small** card

Inven121 (X103010201) <<< Parent account: Inventory (X103)

ID	MultiName	Amount	Unit	GeID	TransDate	Balance
1	Inven121<Inven12<Inven1	520	650	4	2021-1-5	520
2	Inven121<Inven12<Inven1	-300	-375	5	2021-1-5	220

Three-level on a **small** card

Inven122 (X103010202) <<< Parent account: Inventory (X103)

ID	MultiName	Amount	Unit	GeID	TransDate	Balance
1	Inven122<Inven12<Inven1	330	66	4	2021-1-5	330
2	Inven122<Inven12<Inven1	-170	-34	5	2021-1-5	160

Two-level on a **medium** card

Inven13 (X1030103) << Parent account: Inventory (X103)

ID	MultiName	Amount	Unit	GeID	TransDate	Balance
1	Inven13<Inven1	270	9	4	2021-1-5	270

One-level on a **large** card

Inven2 (X10302) < Parent account: Inventory (X103)

ID	MultiName	Amount	Unit	GeID	TransDate	Balance
1	Inven221<Inven22<Inven2	3200	320	11	2021-1-9	3200
2	Inven222<Inven22<Inven2	5000	1000	11	2021-1-9	8200

3	PPUK parts<ASD parts<Inven2	4800	1200	11	2021-1-9	13000
4	PPGH parts<ASD parts<Inven2	3800	1900	11	2021-1-9	16800
5	Inven221<Inven22<Inven2	-2900	-290	13	2021-1-11	13900
6	Inven222<Inven22<Inven2	-4700	-940	13	2021-1-11	9200
7	PPUK parts<ASD parts<Inven2	-2600	-650	13	2021-1-11	6600
8	PPGH parts<ASD parts<Inven2	-3100	-1550	14	2021-1-15	3500
9	PPUK parts<ASD parts<Inven2	6500	1625	19	2021-1-22	10000
10	PPGH parts<ASD parts<Inven2	6000	3000	19	2021-1-22	16000
11	PPUK parts<ASD parts<Inven2	-3300	-825	20	2021-1-23	12700
12	PPGH parts<ASD parts<Inven2	-3900	-1950	20	2021-1-23	8800
12	PPUK parts<ASD parts<Inven2	-3000	-750	21	2021-1-25	5800
14	PPGH parts<ASD parts<Inven2	-1800	-900	21	2021-1-25	4000
15	PPUK parts<ASD parts<Inven2	-2200	-550	23	2021-1-29	1800

Two-level on a **medium** card

Inven22 (X1030202) << Parent account: Inventory (X103)

ID	MultiName	Amount	Unit	GeID	TransDate	Balance
1	Inven221<Inven22<Inven2	3200	320	11	2021-1-9	3200
2	Inven222<Inven22< Inven2	5000	1000	11	2021-1-9	8200
3	Inven221<Inven22<Inven2	-2900	-290	13	2021-1-11	5300
4	Inven222<Inven22<Inven2	-4700	-940	13	2021-1-11	600

Three-level on a **small** card

Inven221 (X103020201) <<< Parent account: Inventory (X103)

ID	MultiName	Amount	Unit	GeID	TransDate	Balance
1	Inven221<Inven22<Inven2	3200	320	11	2021-1-9	3200
2	Inven221<Inven22<Inven2	-2900	-290	13	2021-1-11	300

Three-level on a **small** card

Inven222 (X103020202) <<< Parent account: Inventory (X103)

ID	MultiName	Amount	Unit	GeID	TransDate	Balance
1	Inven222<Inven22<Inven2	5000	1000	11	2021-1-9	5000

2	Inven222<Inven22<Inven2	-4700	-940	13	2021-1-11	300

Two-level on **medium** card

ASD parts (X1030203) << Parent account: Inventory (X103)

ID	MultiName	Amount	Unit	GeID	TransDate	Balance
1	PPUK parts<ASD parts<Inven2	4800	1200	11	2021-1-9	4800
2	PPGH parts<ASD parts<Inven2	3800	1900	11	2021-1-9	8600
3	PPUK parts<ASD parts<Inven2	-2600	-650	13	2021-1-11	6000
4	PPGH parts<ASD parts<Inven2	-3100	-1550	14	2021-1-15	2900
5	PPUK parts<ASD parts<Inven2	6500	1625	19	2021-1-22	9400
6	PPGH parts<ASD parts<Inven2	6000	3000	19	2021-1-22	15400
7	PPUK parts<ASD parts<Inven2	-3300	-825	20	2021-1-23	12100
8	PPGH parts<ASD parts<Inven2	-3900	-1950	20	2021-1-23	8200
9	PPUK parts<ASD parts<Inven2	-3000	-750	21	2021-1-25	5200
10	PPGH parts<ASD parts<Inven2	-1800	-900	21	2021-1-25	3400
11	PPUK parts<ASD parts<Inven2	-2200	-550	23	2021-1-29	1200

Three-level on a **small** card

PPUK parts (X103020301) <<< Parent account: Inventory (X103)

ID	MultiName	Amount	Unit	GeID	TransDate	Balance
1	PPUK parts<ASD parts<Inven2	4800	1200	11	2021-1-9	4800
2	PPUK parts<ASD parts<Inven2	-2600	-650	13	2021-1-11	2200
3	PPUK parts<ASD parts<Inven2	6500	1625	19	2021-1-22	8700
4	PPUK parts<ASD parts<Inven2	-3300	-825	20	2021-1-23	5400
5	PPUK parts<ASD parts<Inven2	-3000	-750	21	2021-1-25	2400
6	PPUK parts<ASD parts<Inven2	-2200	-550	23	2021-1-29	200

Three-level on a **small** card

PPGH parts (X103020302) <<< Parent account: Inventory (X103)

ID	MultiName	Amount	Unit	GeID	TransDate	Balance
1	PPGH parts<ASD parts<Inven2	3800	1900	11	2021-1-9	3800
2	PPGH parts<ASD parts<Inven2	-3100	-1550	14	2021-1-15	700
3	PPGH parts<ASD parts<Inven2	6000	3000	19	2021-1-22	6700

4	PPGH parts<ASD parts<Inven2	-3900	-1950	20	2021-1-23	2800
5	PPGH parts<ASD parts<Inven2	-1800	-900	21	2021-1-25	1000

One-level on a **large** card

Inven3 (X10303) < Parent account: Inventory (X103)

ID	MultiName	Amount	Unit	GeID	TransDate	Balance
1	Inven31<Inven3	5300	530	11	2021-1-9	5300
2	Inven32<Inven3	2900	580	11	2021-1-9	8200
3	Inven331<Inven33<Inven3	2700	1350	12	2021-1-9	10900
4	Inven332<Inven33<Inven3	3100	620	12	2021-1-9	14000
5	HGFCVB parts<QASXC parts<Inven3	4900	490	12	2021-1-9	18900
6	PPGHUP parts<ASDUP parts<Inven3	1300	130	12	2021-1-9	20200
7	Inven32<Inven3	-1900	-380	13	2021-1-11	18300
8	HGFCVB parts<QASXC parts<Inven3	-4800	-480	13	2021-1-11	13500
9	PPGHUP parts<ASDUP parts<Inven3	-800	-80	13	2021-1-11	12700
10	Inven31<Inven3	-5000	-500	14	2021-1-15	7700
11	Inven331<Inven33<Inven3	-2200	-1100	14	2021-1-15	5500
12	Inven332<Inven33< Inven3	-2900	-580	14	2021-1-15	2600
13	Inven31<Inven3	5300	530	19	2021-1-22	7900
14	Inven32<Inven3	3700	740	19	2021-1-22	11600
15	Inven31<Inven3	-2500	-250	20	2021-1-23	9100
16	Inven32<Inven3	-2300	-460	20	2021-1-23	6800
17	Inven31<Inven3	-2700	-270	21	2021-1-25	4100
18	Inven32<Inven3	-1300	-260	23	2021-1-29	2800
19	HGFCVB parts<QASXC parts<Inven3	59600	5960	47	2021-2-3	62400
20	PPGHUP parts<ASDUP parts<Inven3	31400	3140	47	2021-2-3	93800
21	HGFCVB parts<QASXC parts<Inven3	-59600	-5960	48	2021-2-4	34200
22	PPGHUP parts<ASDUP parts<Inven3	-31600	-3160	48	2021-2-4	2600

Two-level on a **medium** card

Inven31 (X1030301) << Parent account: Inventory (X103)

ID	MultiName	Amount	Unit	GeID	TransDate	Balance
1	Inven31<Inven3	5300	530	12	2021-1-9	5300
2	Inven31<Inven3	-5000	-500	14	2021-1-15	300
3	Inven31<Inven3	5300	530	19	2021-1-22	5600

ID		Amount	Unit	GeID	TransDate	Balance
4	Inven31<Inven3	-2500	-250	20	2021-1-23	3100
5	Inven31<Inven3	-2700	-270	21	2021-1-25	400

Two-level on a **medium** card

Inven32 (X1030302) << Parent account: Inventory (X103)

ID	MultiName	Amount	Unit	GeID	TransDate	Balance
1	Inven32<Inven3	2900	580	12	2021-1-9	2900
2	Inven32<Inven3	-1900	-380	13	2021-1-11	1000
3	Inven32<Inven3	3700	740	19	2021-1-22	4700
4	Inven32<Inven3	-2300	-460	20	2021-1-23	2400
5	Inven32<Inven3	-1300	-260	23	2021-1-29	1100

Two-level on a **medium** card

Inven33 (X1030303) << Parent account: Inventory (X103)

ID	MultiName	Amount	Unit	GeID	TransDate	Balance
1	Inven331<Inven33<Inven3	2700	1350	12	2021-1-9	2700
2	Inven332<Inven33<Inven3	3100	620	12	2021-1-9	5800
3	Inven331<Inven33<Inven3	-2200	-1100	14	2021-1-15	3600
4	Inven332<Inven33<Inven3	-2900	-2900	14	2021-1-15	700

Three-level on a **small** card

Inven331 (X103030301) <<< Parent account: Inventory (X103)

ID	MultiName	Amount	Unit	GeID	TransDate	Balance
1	Inven331<Inven33<Inven3	2700	1350	12	2021-1-9	2700
2	Inven331<Inven33<Inven3	-2200	-1100	14	2021-1-15	500

Three-level on a **small** card

Inven332 (X103030302) << Parent account: Inventory (X103)

ID	MultiName	Amount	Unit	GeID	TransDate	Balance
1	Inven332<Inven33<Inven3	3100	620	12	2021-1-9	3100
2	Inven332<Inven33<Inven3	-2900	-580	14	2021-1-15	200

Two-level on a **medium** card

QASXC parts (X1030304) << Parent account: Inventory (X103)

ID	MultiName	Amount	Unit	GeID	TransDate	Balance
1	HGFCVB parts<QASXC parts<Inven3	4900	490	12	2021-1-9	4900
2	HGFCVB parts<QASXC parts<Inven3	-4800	-480	13	2021-1-11	100
3	HGFCVB parts<QASXC parts<Inven3	59600	5960	47	2021-2-3	59700
4	HGFCVB parts<QASXC parts<Inven3	-59600	5960	48	2021-2-4	100

Three-level on a **small** card

HGFCVB parts (X103030401) <<< Parent account: Inventory (X103)

ID	MultiName	Amount	Unit	GeID	TransDate	Balance
1	HGFCVB parts<QASXC parts<Inven3	4900	490	12	2021-1-9	4900
2	HGFCVB parts<QASXC parts<Inven3	-4800	-480	13	2021-1-11	100
3	HGFCVB parts<QASXC parts<Inven3	59600	5960	47	2021-2-3	59700
4	HGFCVB parts<QASXC parts<Inven3	-59600	5960	48	2021-2-4	100

Two-level on a **medium** card

ASDUP parts (X1030305) << Parent account: Inventory (X103)

ID	MultiName	Amount	Unit	GeID	TransDate	Balance
1	PPGHUP parts<ASDUP parts<Inven3	1300	130	12	2021-1-9	1300
2	PPGHUP parts<ASDUP parts<Inven3	-800	-80	13	2021-1-11	500
3	PPGHUP parts<ASDUP parts<Inven3	31400	3140	47	2021-2-3	31900
4	PPGHUP parts<ASDUP parts<Inven3	-31600	-3160	48	2021-2-4	300

Three-level on a **small** card

PPGHUP parts (X103030501) <<< Parent account: Inventory (X103)

ID	MultiName	Amount	Unit	GeID	TransDate	Balance
1	PPGHUP parts<ASDUP parts<Inven3	1300	130	12	2021-1-9	1300
2	PPGHUP parts<ASDUP parts<Inven3	-800	-80	13	2021-1-11	500
3	PPGHUP parts<ASDUP parts<Inven3	31400	3140	47	2021-2-3	31900
4	PPGHUP parts<ASDUP parts<Inven3	-31600	-3160	48	2021-2-4	300

One-level on a **large** card

Inven4 (X10304) < Parent account: Inventory (X103)

ID	MultiName	Amount	Unit	GeID	TransDate	Balance
1	Inven411<Inven41<Inven4	5100	1020	15	2021-1-17	5100
2	Inven412<Inven41<Inven4	3700	1850	15	2021-1-17	8800
3	TTTCU parts<TTT parts<Inven4	2300	1150	15	2021-1-17	11100
4	RRRHJK parts< Inven4	1400	700	15	2021-1-17	12500
5	TTTCU parts<TTT parts<Inven4	66210	33105	78	2021-3-3	78710
6	RRRHJK parts< Inven4	19150	9575	78	2021-3-3	97860
7	TTTCU parts<TTT parts<Inven4	-66070	-33035	79	2021-3-4	31790
8	RRRHJK parts< Inven4	-19130	-9565	79	2021-3-4	12660

Two-level on a **medium** card

Inven41 (X1030401) << Parent account: Inventory (X103)

ID	MultiName	Amount	Unit	GeID	TransDate	Balance
1	Inven411<Inven41<Inven4	5100	1020	15	2021-1-17	5100
2	Inven412<Inven41<Inven4	3700	1850	15	2021-1-17	8800

Three-level on a **small** card

Inven411 (X103040101) <<< Parent account: Inventory (X103)

ID	MultiName	Amount	Unit	GeID	TransDate	Balance
1	Inven411<Inven41<Inven4	5100	1020	15	2021-1-17	5100

Three-level on a **small** card

Inven412 (X103040102) <<< Parent account: Inventory (X103)

ID	MultiName	Amount	Unit	GeID	TransDate	Balance
1	Inven412<Inven41<Inven4	3700	1850	15	2021-1-17	3700

Two-level on a **medium** card

TTT parts (X1030402) << Parent account: Inventory (X103)

ID	MultiName	Amount	Unit	GeID	TransDate	Balance
1	TTTCU parts<TTT parts<Inven4	2300	1150	15	2021-1-17	2300
2	TTTCU parts<TTT parts<Inven4	66210	33105	78	2021-3-3	68510
3	TTTCU parts<TTT parts<Inven4	-66070	-33025	79	2021-3-4	2440

Three-level on a **small** card

TTTCU parts (X103040201) <<< Parent account: Inventory (X103)

ID	MultiName	Amount	Unit	GeID	TransDate	Balance
1	TTTCU parts<TTT parts<Inven4	2300	1150	15	2021-1-17	2300
2	TTTCU parts<TTT parts<Inven4	66210	33105	78	2021-3-3	68510
3	TTTCU parts<TTT parts<Inven4	-66070	-33025	79	2021-3-4	2440

Two-level on a **medium** card

RRRHJK parts (X1030403) << Parent account: Inventory (X103)

ID	MultiName	Amount	Unit	GeID	TransDate	Balance
1	RRRHJK parts<Inven4	1400	700	15	2021-1-17	1400
2	RRRHJK parts<Inven4	19150	9575	78	2021-3-3	20550
3	RRRHJK parts<Inven4	-19130	-9565	79	2021-3-4	1420

Table B-11 Parent account: HST recoverable on a drawer

HST recoverable (X104)

ID	MultiName	TransDate	Amount	Balance	GeID	SubFirst	SubSecond	SubThird
1	N	2021-1-5	477.1	477.10	4			
2	N	2021-1-9	3250	3727.10	11			
3	N	2021-1-9	1560	5287.10	12			
4	N	2021-1-17	1625	6912.10	15			
5	N	2021-1-22	2795	9707.10	19			
6	N	2021-2-1	-9707.10	0	44			
7	N	2021-2-3	11830.00	11830.00	47			
8	N	2021-3-1	-11830.00	0	75			

9	N		2021-3-3	11096.80	11096.80	78				

Table B-12 Parent account: Account receivable on a drawer

Account receivable (X105)

ID	MultiName	TransDate	Amount	Balance	GeID	SubFirst	SubSecond	SubThird	Ref
1	123456789	2021-1-5	2558.90	2558.90	5	123456789			
2	123456789	2021-1-7	-1500	1058.90	6	123456789			5
3	123456788	2021-1-11	29835	30893.90	13	123456788			
4	123456787	2021-1-15	24521	55414.90	14	123456787			
5	123456788	2021-1-17	-21000	34414.90	16	123456788			13
6	123456787	2021-1-23	22487	56901.90	20	123456787			
7	123456786	2021-1-25	15481	72382.90	21	123456786			
8	123456789	2021-1-29	7006	79388.90	23	123456789			
9	123456789	2021-1-30	-828.90	76830	24	123456789			5
10	123456789	2021-1-30	-1730	76830	24	123456789			23
11	123456787	2021-1-30	-15000	61830	25	123456787			14
12	123456786	2021-1-30	-8475	53355	26	123456786			21
13	123456787	2021-1-31	-13000	40355	33	123456787			20
14	123456788	2021-2-4	200688	241043	48	123456788			
15	123456789	2021-2-8	-5000	236043	49	123456789			23
16	123456787	2021-2-9	-9521	226522	50	123456787			14
17	123456787	2021-2-9	-3300	223222	50	123456787			20
18	123456786	2021-2-11	-3500	219722	51	123456786			21
19	123456788	2021-2-25	-120000	99722	57	123456788			48
20	123456787	2021-3-4	174924	274646	79	123456787			
21	123456788	2021-3-10	-52000	222646	80	123456788			48
22	123456789	2021-3-12	-230	222416	81	123456789			5
23	123456789	2021-3-12	-276	222140	81	123456789			23
24	123456786	2021-3-13	-2200	219940	82	123456786			21
25	123456787	2021-3-29	-120000	99940	87	123456787			79

One-level on a **large** card

123456789 (X10501) < Parent account: Account receivable (X105)

ID	MultiName	Amount	Ref	GeID	TransDate	Balance
1	123456789	2558.90		5	2021-1-5	2558.90

2	123456789	-1500	**5**	6	2021-1-7	1058.90
3	123456789	7006		23	2021-1-29	8064.9
4	123456789	-828.90	**5**	24	2021-1-30	7236
5	123456789	-1730	**23**	24	2021-1-30	5506
6	123456789	-5000	**23**	49	2021-2-8	506
7	123456789	-230	**5**	81	2021-3-12	276
8	123456789	-276	**23**	81	2021-3-12	0

One-level on a **large** card

123456788 (X10502) < Parent account: Account receivable (X105)

ID	MultiName	Amount	Ref	GeID	TransDate	Balance
1	123456788	29835		13	2021-1-11	29835
2	123456788	-21000	**13**	16	2021-1-17	8835
3	123456788	200688		48	2021-2-4	209523
4	123456788	-120000	**48**	57	2021-2-25	89523
5	123456788	-52000	**48**	80	2021-3-10	37523

One-level on a **large** card

123456787 (X10503) < Parent account: Account receivable (X105)

ID	MultiName	Amount	Ref	GeID	TransDate	Balance
1	123456787	24521		14	2021-1-15	24521
2	123456787	22487		20	2021-1-23	47008
3	123456787	-15000	**14**	25	2021-1-30	32008
4	123456787	-13000	**20**	33	2021-1-31	19008
5	123456787	-9521	**14**	50	2021-2-9	9487
6	123456787	-3300	**20**	50	2021-2-9	6187
7	123456787	174924		79	2021-3-4	181111
8	123456787	-120000	**79**	87	2021-3-29	61111

One-level on a **large** card

123456786 (X10504) < Parent account: Account receivable (X105)

ID	MultiName	Amount	Ref	GeID	TransDate	Balance
1	123456786	15481		21	2021-1-25	15481
2	123456786	-8475	**21**	26	2021-1-30	7006

3	123456786		-3500	**21**	51	2021-2-11	3506
4	123456786		-2200	**21**	82	2021-3-13	1306

Table B-13 Parent account: Land on a drawer

Land (X106)

ID	MultiName	TransDate	Amount	Balance	GeID	SubFirst	SubSecond	SubThird
1	Land1, Downtown	2021-1-7	270000	270000	8	Land1, Downtown		
2	Land2, North York	2021-1-7	180000	450000	8	Land2, North York		
3	Land1, Downtown	2021-2-18	-270000	180000	55	Land1, Downtown		

One-level on a **large** card

Land1, Downtown (X10601) < Parent account: Land (X106)

ID	MultiName	Amount	Unit	GeID	TransDate	Balance
1	Land1, Downtown	270000	1	8	2021-1-7	270000
2	Land1, Downtown	-270000	1	55	2021-2-18	0

One-level on a **large** card

Land2, North York (X10602) < Parent account: Land (X106)

ID	MultiName	Amount	Unit	GeID	TransDate	Balance
1	Land2, North York	180000	1	8	2021-1-7	180000

Table B-14 Parent account: Truck on a drawer

Truck (X107)

ID	MultiName	TransDate	Amount	Balance	GeID	SubFirst	SubSecond	SubThird
1	Truck1	2021-1-8	45000	45000	9	Truck1		

One-level on a **large** card

Truck1 (X10701) < Parent account: Truck (X107)

ID	MultiName	Amount	Unit	GeID	TransDate	Balance
1	Truck1	45000	1	9	2021-1-8	45000

Table B-15 Parent account: Computer on a drawer

Computer (X108)

ID	MultiName	TransDate	Amount	Balance	GeID	SubFirst	SubSecond	SubThird
1	Computer1	2021-1-28	1600	1600	22	Computer1		
2	Computer server1	2021-1-28	1800	3400	22	Computer server1		
3	POS system1	2021-1-28	2200	5600	22	POS system1		

One-level on a **large** card

Computer1 (X10801) < Parent account: Computer (X108)

ID	MultiName	Amount	Unit	GeID	TransDate	Balance
1	Computer1	1600	1	22	2021-1-28	1600

One-level on a **large** card

Computer server1 (X10802) < Parent account: Computer (X108)

ID	MultiName	Amount	Unit	GeID	TransDate	Balance
1	Computer server1	1800	1	22	2021-1-28	1800

One-level on a **large** card

POS system1 (X10803) < Parent account: Computer (X108)

ID	MultiName	Amount	Unit	GeID	TransDate	Balance
1	POS system1	2200	1	22	2021-1-28	2200

Table B-16 Parent account: Accumulated amortization: truck on a drawer

Accumulated amortization: truck (X109)

ID	MultiName	TransDate	Amount	Balance	GeID	SubFirst	SubSecond	SubThird
1	Truck1-accumulated amortization	2021-1-31	-750	-750	38	Truck1-accumulated amortization		
2	Truck1-accumulated amortization	2021-2-28	-750	-1500	67	Truck1-accumulated amortization		

| 3 | Truck1-accumulated amortization | 2021-3-31 | -750 | -2250 | 98 | Truck1-accumulated amortization | | |

One-level on a **large** card

Truck1-accumulated amortization (X10901) < Parent account: Accumulated amortization: truck (X109)

ID	MultiName	Amount	Unit	GeID	TransDate	Balance
1	Truck1-accumulated amortization	-750	1	38	2021-1-31	-750
2	Truck1-accumulated amortization	-750	-1500	67	2021-2-28	-1500
3	Truck1-accumulated amortization	-750	-2250	98	2021-3-31	-2250

Table B-17 Parent account: Accumulated amortization: computer on a drawer

Accumulated amortization: computer (X110)

ID	MultiName	TransDate	Amount	Balance	GeID	SubFirst	SubSecond	SubThird
1	Computer1-accumulated amortization	2021-1-31	-33.33	-33.33	39	Computer1-accumulated amortization		
2	Computer server1-accumulated amortization	2021-1-31	-37.50	-70.83	39	Computer server1-accumulated amortization		
3	POS system1-accumulated amortization	2021-1-31	-30.56	-101.39	39	POS system1-accumulated amortization		
4	Computer1-accumulated amortization	2021-2-28	-66.67	-168.06	68	Computer1-accumulated amortization		
5	Computer server1-accumulated amortization	2021-2-28	-75.00	-243.06	68	Computer server1-accumulated amortization		
6	POS system1-accumulated amortization	2021-2-28	-61.11	-304.17	68	POS system1-accumulated amortization		
7	Computer1-accumulated amortization	2021-3-31	-66.67	-370.84	99	Computer1-accumulated amortization		
8	Computer server1-accumulated amortization	2021-3-31	-75.00	-445.84	99	Computer server1-accumulated amortization		
9	POS system1-accumulated amortization	2021-3-31	-61.11	-506.95	99	POS system1-accumulated amortization		

One-level on a **large** card

Computer1-accumulated amortization (X11001) < Parent account: Accumulated amortization: computer (X110)

ID	MultiName	Amount	Unit	GeID	TransDate	Balance
1	Computer1-accumulated amortization	-33.33	1	39	2021-1-31	-33.33
2	Computer1-accumulated amortization	-66.67	1	68	2021-2-28	-100.00
3	Computer1-accumulated amortization	-66.67	1	99	2021-3-31	-166.67

One-level on a **large** card

Computer server1-accumulated amortization (X11002) < Parent account: Accumulated amortization: computer (X110)

ID	MultiName	Amount	Unit	GeID	TransDate	Balance
1	Computer server1-accumulated amortization	-37.5	1	39	2021-1-31	-37.50
2	Computer server1-accumulated amortization	-75.00	1	68	2021-2-28	-112.50
3	Computer server1-accumulated amortization	-75.00	1	99	2021-3-31	-187.50

One-level on a **large** card

POS system1-accumulated amortization (X11003) < Parent account: Accumulated amortization: computer (X110)

ID	MultiName	Amount	Unit	GeID	TransDate	Balance
1	POS system1-accumulated amortization	-30.56	1	39	2021-1-31	-30.56
2	POS system1-accumulated amortization	-61.11	1	68	2021-2-28	-91.67
3	POS system1-accumulated amortization	-61.11	1	99	2021-3-31	-152.78

Table B-18 Parent account: Share on a drawer

Share (X111)

ID	MultiName	TransDate	Amount	Balance	GeID	SubFirst	SubSecond	SubThird
1	MicroQQ-share	2021-2-18	355700	356700	56	MicroQQ-share		

One-level on a **large** card

MicroQQ-share (X11101) < Parent account: Share (X110)

ID	MultiName	Amount	Unit	GeID	TransDate	Balance
1	MicroQQ-share	356700	1	56	2021-2-18	356700

Table B-19 Parent account: AOCI of land on a drawer

AOCI of land (X112)

ID	MultiName	TransDate	Amount	Balance	GeID	SubFirst	SubSecond	SubThird
1	AOCI-land2, North York	2021-2-18	30000	30000	56	AOCI-land2, North York		
2	AOCI-land2, North York	2021-3-31	25000	55000	104	AOCI-land2, North York		

One-level on a **large** card

AOCI-land2, North York (X11201) < Parent account: AOCI of land (X112)

ID	MultiName	Amount	Unit	GeID	TransDate	Balance
1	AOCI-land2, North York	30000	1	56	2021-2-18	30000
2	AOCI-land2, North York	25000	1	104	2021-3-31	55000

Table B-20 Parent account: AOCI of share on a drawer

AOCI of share (X114)

ID	MultiName	TransDate	Amount	Balance	GeID	SubFirst	SubSecond	SubThird
1	AOCI-MicroQQ	2021-2-28	-4600	-4600	74	AOCI-MicroQQ		
2	AOCI-MicroQQ	2021-3-31	45700	41100	105	AOCI-MicroQQ		

One-level on a **large** card

AOCI-MicroQQ (X11401) < Parent account: AOCI of share (X114)

ID	MultiName	Amount	Unit	GeID	TransDate	Balance
1	AOCI-MicroQQ	-4600	1	74	2021-2-28	-4600
2	AOCI-MicroQQ	45700	1	105	2021-3-31	41100

In the second cabinet, there are the following tables.

Table B-21 Liabilities (X2) on the door

ID	Account Name (Mathematical Name)	Subtotal	Ref (Row)	Balance
1	Account payable (X201)	Current liabilities,203	204	72537.10
2	HST payable (X202)	Current liabilities,203	205	36797.80
3	Note payable (X203)	Current liabilities,203	207	6333.33
4	Accrued interest payable (X204)	Long term liabilities,203	252	500000
5	Tax payable	Current liabilities,203	208	48199.59

Table B-22 Parent account: Account payable on a drawer

Account payable (X201)

ID	MultiName	TransDate	Amount	Balance	GeID	SubFirst	SubSecond	SubThird	Ref
1	987654321	2021-1-5	3477.10	3477.10	4	987654321			
2	987654322	2021-1-9	26250	29727.10	11	987654322			
3	987654323	2021-1-9	13560	43287.10	12	987654323			
4	987654324	2021-1-17	14125	57412.10	15	987654324			
5	987654322	2021-1-21	-14000	43412.10	17	987654322			11
6	987654323	2021-1-21	-6000	37412.10	18	987654323			12
7	987654322	2021-1-22	24295	61707.10	19	987654322			
8	987654322	2021-1-30	-7500	5420410	27	987654322			11
9	987654324	2021-1-31	-8000	46207.10	34	987654324			15
10	987654323	2021-2-3	102830	149037.10	47	987654323			
11	987654321	2021-2-13	-2500	146537.10	52	987654321			4
12	987654322	2021-2-15	-15000	131537.10	53	987654322			19
13	987654323	2021-2-17	-4000	127537.10	54	987654323			12
14	987654323	2021-2-26	-55000	72537.10	58	987654323			47
15	987654324	2021-3-3	96456.80	168993.90	78	987654324			
16	987654321	2021-3-14	-977.10	168016.80	83	987654321			4
17	987654322	2021-3-15	-4500	163516.80	84	987654322			11
18	987654323	2021-3-17	-30000	133516.80	85	987654323			47
19	987654324	2021-3-29	-82360	51156.80	88	987654324			78

One-level on a **large** card

987654321 (X20101) < Parent account: Account payable (X201)

ID	MultiName	Amount	Ref	GeID	TransDate	Balance
1	987654321	3477.10		4	2021-1-5	3477.10
2	987654321	-2500	4	52	2021-2-13	977.10
3	987654321	-977.10	4	83	2021-3-3	0

One-level on a **large** card

987654322 (X20102) < Parent account: Account payable (X201)

ID	MultiName	Amount	Ref	GeID	TransDate	Balance
1	987654322	26250		11	2021-1-9	26250
2	987654322	-14000	11	18	2021-1-21	12250
3	987654322	24295		19	2021-1-22	36545
4	987654322	-7500	11	27	2021-1-30	29045
5	987654322	-15000	19	53	2021-2-15	14045
6	987654322	-4500	11	84	2021-3-15	9545

One-level on a **large** card

987654323 (X20103) < Parent account: Account payable (X201)

ID	MultiName	Amount	Ref	GeID	TransDate	Balance
1	987654323	13560		12	2021-1-9	13560
2	987654323	-6000	12	18	2021-1-21	7560
3	987654323	102830		47	2021-2-3	110390
4	987654323	-4000	12	54	2021-2-17	106390
5	987654323	-55000	47	58	2021-2-26	51390
6	987654323	-30000	47	85	2021-3-17	21390

One-level on a **large** card

987654324 (X20104) < Parent account: Account payable (X201)

ID	MultiName	Amount	Ref	GeID	TransDate	Balance
1	987654324	14125		15	2021-1-17	14125
2	987654324	-8000	15	34	2021-1-31	6125

3	987654324	96456.80		78	2021-3-3	102581.80
4	987654324	-82360.00	**78**	88	2021-3-29	20221.80

Table B-23 Parent account: HST payable on a drawer

HST payable (X202)

ID	MultiName	TransDate	Amount	Balance	GeID	SubFirst	SubSecond	SubThird
1	N	2021-1-5	328.90	328.90	5			
2	N	2021-1-11	3835	4163.90	13			
3	N	2021-1-15	2821	6984.90	14			
4	N	2021-1-23	2587	9571.90	20			
5	N	2021-1-25	1781	11352.90	21			
6	N	2021-1-29	806	12158.90	23			
7	N	2021-2-1	-9707.10	2451.8	44			
8	N	2021-2-1	-2451.80	0	45			
9	N	2021-2-4	23088	23088	48			
10	N	2021-3-1	-11830	11258	75			
11	N	2021-3-1	-11258	0	76			
12	N	2021-3-4	20124	20124	79			

Table B-24 Parent account: Note payable on a drawer

Note payable (X203)

ID	MultiName	TransDate	Amount	Balance	GeID	SubFirst	SubSecond	SubThird
1	N	2021-1-7	500000	500000	7			

Table B-25 Parent account: Accrued interest payable on a drawer

Accrued interest payable (X204)

ID	MultiName	TransDate	Amount	Balance	GeID	SubFirst	SubSecond	SubThird
1	Note1-TD bank	2021-1-31	3000	3000	43	Note1-TD bank		
2	Note1-TD bank	2021-2-28	3333.33	6333.33	71	Note1-TD bank		
3	Note1-TD bank	2021-3-31	3333.33	9666.66	102	Note1-TD bank		

One-level on a **large** card

Note1-TD bank (X20401) < Parent account: Accrued interest payable (X204)

ID	MultiName	Amount	Ref	GeID	TransDate	Balance
1	Note1-TD bank	3000		43	2021-1-31	3000
2	Note1-TD bank	3333.33		71	2021-2-28	6333.33
3	Note1-TD bank	3333.33		102	2021-3-31	9666.66

Table B-26 Parent account: Tax payable on a drawer

Tax payable (X205)

ID	MultiName	TransDate	Amount	Balance	GeID	SubFirst	SubSecond	SubThird
1	N	2021-2-28	48199.59	48199.59	43			
2	N	2021-3-30	-48199.59	0	95			
3	N							

In the third cabinet, there are the following tables.

Table B-27 Shareholders' Equity (X3) on the door

ID	Account Name (Mathematical Name)	Subtotal	Ref (Row)	Balance
1	Share capital (X301)	Owners' Capital,303	304	80000.00
2	Retained earnings	Owners' Capital,303	304	112,465.70
3	Accumulated other comprehensive income	Owners' Capital,303	304	25,400.00

In this table, the amounts (balances) of the Retained earnings and the Accumulated other comprehensive income are from the Table 2-39. The two amounts are not entered in by transactions and are only gotten by calculating.

Table B-28 Parent account: Share capital on a drawer

Share capital (X301)

ID	MultiName	TransDate	Amount	Balance	GeID	SubFirst	SubSecond	SubThird
1	Capital-Ping Wang	2021-1-2	40000	40000	1	Capital-Ping Wang		

2	Capital-Hua Li	2021-1-2	30000	70000	1	Capital-Hua Li		
3	Capital-Mike Newsome	2021-1-2	30000	100000	1	Capital-Mike Newsome		
4	Capital-Ping Wang	2021-3-31	-8000	92000	103	Capital-Ping Wang		
5	Capital-Hua Li	2021-3-31	-6000	86000	103	Capital-Hua Li		
6	Capital-Mike Newsome	2021-3-31	-6000	80000	103	Capital-Mike Newsome		

One-level on a **large** card

Capital-Ping Wang (X30101) < Parent account: Share capital (X301)

ID	MultiName	Amount	Unit	GeID	TransDate	Balance
1	Capital-Ping Wang	40000	1	1	2021-1-2	40000
2	Capital-Ping Wang	-8000	1	103	2021-3-31	32000

One-level on a **large** card

Capital- Hua Li (X30102) < Parent account: Share capital (X301)

ID	MultiName	Amount	Unit	GeID	TransDate	Balance
1	Capital-Hua Li	30000	1	1	2021-1-2	30000
2	Capital-Hua Li	-6000	1	103	2021-3-31	24000

One-level on a **large** card

Capital-Mike Newsome (X30103) < Parent account: Share capital (X301)

ID	MultiName	Amount	Unit	GeID	TransDate	Balance
1	Capital- Mike Newsome	30000	1	1	2021-1-2	30000
2	Capital- Mike Newsome	-6000	1	103	2021-3-31	24000

In the fourth cabinet, there are following tables.

Table B-29 Revenue (X4) on the door

ID	Account Name (Mathematical Name)	Subtotal	Ref (Row)	Balance
1	Sales (X401)	Owners' Capital,303	404	154800
2	Investment income	Other income,475	476	0
3	Unrealized holding gain or loss	Other comprehensive income,713	715	0

Table B-30 Parent accounts: Sales on a drawer

Sales (X401)

ID	MultiName	TransDate	Amount	Balance	GeID	SubFirst	SubSecond	SubThird
1	Yi Liu-sales	2021-3-4	154800	154800	79	Yi Liu-sales		

One-level on a **large** card

Xiao Zhou-sales (X40101) < Parent account: Sales (X401)

ID	MultiName	Amount	Unit	GeID	TransDate	Balance

One-level on a **large** card

ZhenDao Yuan-sales (X40102) < Parent account: Sales (X401)

ID	MultiName	Amount	Unit	GeID	TransDate	Balance

One-level on a **large** card

Yi Liu-sales (X40103) < Parent account: Sales (X401)

ID	MultiName	Amount	Unit	GeID	TransDate	Balance
1	Yi Liu-sales	154800	1	79	2021-3-4	154800

One-level on a **large** card

Jun Wang-sales (X40104) < Parent account: Sales (X401)

ID	MultiName	Amount	Unit	GeID	TransDate	Balance

Table B-31 Parent accounts: Investment income on a drawer

Investment income (X402)

ID	MultiName	TransDate	Amount	Balance	GeID	SubFirst	SubSecond	SubThird

Table B-32 Parent accounts: Unrealized holding gain or loss on a drawer

Unrealized holding gain or loss (X403)

ID	MultiName	TransDate	Amount	Balance	GeID	SubFirst	SubSecond	SubThird
1	Unrealized holding gain or loss-land	2021-3-31	25000	25000	105	Unrealized holding gain or loss-land		
2	Unrealized holding gain or loss-share	2021-3-31	45700	70700	106	Unrealized holding gain or loss-share		

One-level on a **large** card

Unrealized holding gain or loss-land (X40301) < Parent account: Unrealized holding gain or loss (X403)

ID	MultiName	Amount	Unit	GeID	TransDate	Balance
1	Unrealized holding gain or loss-land	25000	1	105	2021-3-31	25000

One-level on a **large** card

Unrealized holding gain or loss-share (X40302) < Parent account: Unrealized holding gain or loss (X403)

ID	MultiName	Amount	Unit	GeID	TransDate	Balance
1	Unrealized holding gain or loss-share	45700	1	106	2021-3-31	45700

In the fifth cabinet, there are following tables.

Table B-33 Expenses (X5) on the door

ID	Account Name (Mathematical Name)	Subtotal	Ref (Row)	Balance
1	Administrative expenses (X501)	Operating and administrative expenses,453	454	-2456.11
2	Cost of sales (X502)	Cost,431	432	-85200.00
3	Salary expenses (X503)	Operating and administrative expenses,453	459	-23790.00
4	Amortization expenses (X504)	Operating and administrative expenses,453	458	-952.78
5	Office rent expenses (X505)	Operating and administrative expenses,453	459	-1500.00
6	Interest expenses (X506)	Operating and administrative expenses,453	461	-3333.3
7	Tax expenses	Tax,600	601	-11270.33

Table B-34 Parent accounts: Administrative expenses on a drawer

Administrative expenses (X501)

ID	MultiName	TransDate	Amount	Balance	GeID	SubFirst	SubSecond	SubThird
1	Mike Newsome-other<Office department-other<Other expenses	2021-3-28	-153.72	-153.72	86	Other expenses	Office department-other	Mike Newsome-other
2	Hua Li-taxi<Purchase department-taxi<Taxi expenses	2021-3-29	-101.33	-255.05	87	Taxi expenses	Purchase Department-taxi	Hua Li-taxi
3	Hua Li-other< Purchase department-other<Other expenses	2021-3-29	-70.30	-325.35	89	Other expenses	Purchase department-other	Hua Li-other
4	Xiao Zhou-other< Sales department-other<Other expenses	2021-3-29	-52.17	-377.52	90	Other expenses	Purchase department-other	Xiao Zhou-other
5	Jun Wang-taxi<Sales department-taxi<Taxi expenses	2021-3-29	-129.34	-506.86	91	Taxi expenses	Sales department-taxi	Jun Wang-taxi
6	Zhendao Yuan-other<Sales department-other <Other expenses	2021-3-29	-111.93	-618.79	92	Other expenses	Sales department-other	Zhendao Yuan-other
7	Yi Liu-other<Sales department-other< Other expenses	2021-3-30	-78.35	-697.14	93	Other expenses	Sales department-other	Yi Liu-other
8	Yi Liu-taxi<Sales department-taxi<Taxi expenses	2021-3-30	-1132.56	-1829.70	93	Taxi expenses	Sales department-taxi	Yi Liu-taxi
9	Ping Wang-other<Office department-other<Other expenses	2021-3-30	-201.99	-2031.69	94	Other expenses	Office department-other	Ping Wang-other
10	Office supplies expenses	2021-3-31	-101.28	-2132.97	96	Office supplies expenses		
11	Utility expenses	2021-3-31	-323.14	-2456.11	100	Utility expenses		

One-level on a **large** card

Taxi expenses (X50101) < Parent account: Administrative expenses (X501)

ID	MultiName	Amount	Unit	GeID	TransDate	Balance
1	Hua Li-taxi<Purchase department-taxi<Taxi expenses	-101.33	1	87	2021-3-29	-101.33
2	Jun Wang-taxi<Sales department-taxi<Taxi expenses	-129.34	1	91	2021-3-29	-230.67
3	Yi Liu-taxi<Sales department-taxi<Taxi expenses	-1132.56	1	93	2021-3-30	-1363.23

Two-level on a **medium** card

Purchase department-taxi (X5010101) << Administrative expenses (X501)

ID	MultiName	Amount	Unit	GeID	TransDate	Balance
1	Hua Li-taxi<Purchase department-taxi<Taxi expenses	-101.33	1	87	2021-3-29	-101.33

Three-level on a **small** card

Hua Li-taxi (X501010101) <<< Administrative expenses (X501)

ID	MultiName	Amount	Unit	GeID	TransDate	Balance
1	Hua Li-taxi<Purchase department-taxi<Taxi expenses	-101.33	1	87	2021-3-29	-101.33

Three-level on a **small** card

Dan Zhu-taxi (X501010102) <<< Administrative expenses (X501)

ID	MultiName	Amount	Unit	GeID	TransDate	Balance

Two-level on a **medium** card

Sales department-taxi (X5010102) << Administrative expenses (X501)

ID	MultiName	Amount	Unit	GeID	TransDate	Balance
1	Jun Wang-taxi<Sales department-taxi<Taxi expenses	-129.34	1	91	2021-3-29	-129.34
2	Yi Liu-taxi<Sales department-taxi<Taxi expenses	-1132.56	1	93	2021-3-30	-1261.90

Three-level on a **small** card

Xiao Zhou-taxi (X501010201) <<< Administrative expenses (X501)

ID	MultiName	Amount	Unit	GeID	TransDate	Balance

Three-level on a **small** card

Yi Liu-taxi (X501010202) <<< Administrative expenses (X501)

ID	MultiName	Amount	Unit	GeID	TransDate	Balance
1	Yi Liu-taxi<Sales department-taxi<Taxi expenses	-1132.56	1	93	2021-3-30	-1132.56

Three-level on a **small** card

Jun Wang-taxi (X501010203) <<< Administrative expenses (X501)

ID	MultiName	Amount	Unit	GeID	TransDate	Balance
1	Jun Wang-taxi<Sales department-taxi<Taxi expenses	-129.34	1	91	2021-3-29	-129.34

Two-level on a **medium** card

Office department-taxi (X5010103) << Administrative expenses (X501)

ID	MultiName	Amount	Unit	GeID	TransDate	Balance

Three-level on a **small** card

Mike Newsome-taxi (X501010301) <<< Administrative expenses (X501)

ID	MultiName	Amount	Unit	GeID	TransDate	Balance

One-level on a **large** card

Other expenses (X50102) < Parent account: Administrative expenses (X501)

ID	MultiName	Amount	Unit	GeID	TransDate	Balance
1	Mike Newsome-other<Office department-other<Other expenses	-153.72	1	86	2021-3-28	-153.72
2	Hua Li-other<Purchase department-other<Other expenses	-70.30	1	89	2021-3-29	-224.02
3	Xiao Zhou-other<Sales department-other<Other expenses	-52.17	1	90	2021-3-29	-276.19
4	Zhendao Yuan-other<Sales department-other<Other expenses	-111.93	1	92	2021-3-29	388.12

5	Yi Liu-other<Sales department-other<Other expenses	-78.35	1	93	2021-3-30	-466.47
6	Ping Wang-other<Office department-other<Other expenses	-201.99	1	94	2021-3-30	-668.46

Two-level on a **medium** card

Office department-open company (X5010201) << Administrative expenses (X501)

ID	MultiName	Amount	Unit	GeID	TransDate	Balance

Three-level on a **small** card

Ping Wang-open company (X501020101) <<< Administrative expenses (X501)

ID	MultiName	Amount	Unit	GeID	TransDate	Balance

Two-level on a **medium** card

Purchase department-other (X5010202) << Administrative expenses (X501)

ID	MultiName	Amount	Unit	GeID	TransDate	Balance
1	Hua Li-other<Purchase department-other<Other expenses	-70.30	1	89	2021-3-29	-70.30

Three-level on a **small** card

Hua Li-other (X501020201) <<< Administrative expenses (X501)

ID	MultiName	Amount	Unit	GeID	TransDate	Balance
1	Hua Li-other<Purchase department-other<Other expenses	-70.30	1	89	2021-3-29	-70.30

Three-level on a **small** card

Dan Zhu-other (X501020202) <<< Administrative expenses (X501)

ID	MultiName	Amount	Unit	GeID	TransDate	Balance

Two-level on a **medium** card

Sales department-other (X5010203) << Administrative expenses (X501)

ID	MultiName	Amount	Unit	GeID	TransDate	Balance
1	Xiao Zhou-other<Sales department-other<Other expenses	-52.17	1	90	2021-3-29	-52.17
2	Zhendao Yuan-other<Sales department-other<Other expenses	-111.93	1	92	2021-3-29	-164.10
3	Yi Liu-other<Sales department-other<Other expenses	-78.35	1	93	2021-3-30	-242.45

Three-level on a **small** card

Xiao Zhou-other (X501020301) <<< Administrative expenses (X501)

ID	MultiName	Amount	Unit	GeID	TransDate	Balance
1	Xiao Zhou-other<Sales department-other<Other expenses	-52.17	1	90	2021-3-29	-52.17

Three-level on a **small** card

Jun Wang-other (X501020302) <<< Administrative expenses (X501)

ID	MultiName	Amount	Unit	GeID	TransDate	Balance

Three-level on a **small** card

Zhendao Yuan-other (X501020303) <<< Administrative expenses (X501)

ID	MultiName	Amount	Unit	GeID	TransDate	Balance
1	Zhendao Yuan-other<Sales department-other<Other expenses	-111.93	1	92	2021-3-29	-111.93

Three-level on a **small** card

Yi Liu-other (X501020304) <<< Administrative expenses (X501)

ID	MultiName	Amount	Unit	GeID	TransDate	Balance
1	Yi Liu-other<Sales department-other<Other expenses	-78.35	1	93	2021-3-30	-78.35

Two-level on a **medium** card

Office department-other (X5010204) << Administrative expenses (X501)

ID	MultiName	Amount	Unit	GeID	TransDate	Balance
1	Ping Wang-other<Office department-other<Other expenses	-201.99	1	94	2021-3-30	-201.99

Three-level on a **small** card

Mike Newsome-other (X501020401) <<< Administrative expenses (X501)

ID	MultiName	Amount	Unit	GeID	TransDate	Balance

Three-level on a **small** card

Ping Wang-other (X501020402) <<< Administrative expenses (X501)

ID	MultiName	Amount	Unit	GeID	TransDate	Balance
1	Ping Wang-other<Office department-other<Other expenses	-201.99	1	94	2021-3-30	-201.99

One-level on a **large** card

Mobile expenses (X50103) < Parent account: Administrative expenses (X501)

ID	MultiName	Amount	Unit	GeID	TransDate	Balance

Two-level on a **medium** card

Purchase department-mobile (X5010301) << Administrative expenses (X501)

ID	MultiName	Amount	Unit	GeID	TransDate	Balance

Three-level on a **small** card

Dan Zhu-mobile (X501030101) <<< Administrative expenses (X501)

ID	MultiName	Amount	Unit	GeID	TransDate	Balance

One-level on a **large** card

Office supplies expenses (X50104) < Parent account: Administrative expenses (X501)

ID	MultiName	Amount	Unit	GeID	TransDate	Balance
1	Office supplies expenses	-101.28	1	96	2021-3-31	-101.28

One-level on a **large** card

Utility expenses (X50105) < Parent account: Administrative expenses (X501)

ID	MultiName	Amount	Unit	GeID	TransDate	Balance
1	Utility expenses	-323.14	1	100	2021-3-31	-323.14

Table B-35 Parent accounts: Cost of sales on a drawer

Cost of sales (X502)

ID	MultiName	TransDate	Amount	Balance	GeID	SubFirst	SubSecond	SubThird
1	N	2021-3-4	-85200	-85200	79			

Table B-36 Parent accounts: Salary expenses on a drawer

Salary expenses (X503)

ID	MultiName	TransDate	Amount	Balance	GeID	SubFirst	SubSecond	SubThird
1	N	2021-3-31	-23790	-23790	97			

Table B-37 Parent accounts: Amortization expenses on a drawer

Amortization expenses (X504)

ID	MultiName	TransDate	Amount	Balance	GeID	SubFirst	SubSecond	SubThird
1	Truck1-amortization	2021-3-31	-750	-750	98	Truck1-amortization		
2	Computer1-amortization<Computer-amortization	2021-3-31	-61.11	-811.11	99	Computer-amortization	Computer1-amortization	
3	Computer server1-amortization<Computer-amortization	2021-3-31	-75.00	-886.11	99	Computer-amortization	Computer server1-amortization	

	4	PCS system1-amortization< Computer-amortization	2021-3-31	-65.67	-952.78	99	Computer-amortization	POS system1-amortization	

One-level on a **large** card

Truck1-amortization (X50401) < Parent account: Amortization expenses (X504)

ID	MultiName	Amount	Unit	GeID	TransDate	Balance
1	Truck1-amortization	-750	1	98	2021-3-31	-750

One-level on a **large** card

Computer-amortization (X50402) < Parent account: Amortization expenses (X504)

ID	MultiName	Amount	Unit	GeID	TransDate	Balance
1	Computer1-amortization<Computer-amortization	-66.67	1	99	2021-3-31	-66.67
2	Computer server1-amortization<Computer-amortization	-75.00	1	99	2021-3-31	-141.67
3	POS system1-amortization< Computer-amortization	-61.11	1	99	2021-3-31	-202.78

Two-level on a **medium** card

Computer1-amortization (X5040201) << Amortization expenses (X504)

ID	MultiName	Amount	Unit	GeID	TransDate	Balance
1	Computer1-amortization<Computer-amortization	-66.67	1	99	2021-3-31	-66.67

Two-level on a **medium** card

Computer server1-amortization (X5040202) << Amortization expenses (X504)

ID	MultiName	Amount	Unit	GeID	TransDate	Balance
1	Computer server1-amortization<Computer-amortization	-75	1	99	2021-3-31	-75

Two-level on a **medium** card

POS system1-amortization (X5040203) << Amortization expenses (X504)

ID	MultiName	Amount	Unit	GeID	TransDate	Balance
1	POS system1-amortization< Computer-amortization	-61.11	1	99	2021-3-31	-61.11

Table B-38 Parent accounts: Office rent expenses on a drawer

Office rent expenses (X505)

ID	MultiName	TransDate	Amount	Balance	GeID	SubFirst	SubSecond	SubThird
1	N	2021-3-31	-1500	-1500	101			

Table B-39 Parent accounts: Interest expenses on a drawer

Interest expenses (X506)

ID	MultiName	TransDate	Amount	Balance	GeID	SubFirst	SubSecond	SubThird
1	N	2021-3-31	-3333.33	-3333.33	102			

Table B-40 Parent accounts: Tax expenses on a drawer

Tax expenses (X507)

ID	MultiName	TransDate	Amount	Balance	GeID	SubFirst	SubSecond	SubThird
1	N	2021-3-31	-11270.33	-11270.33	105			

REFERENCES

[JIE] Guoping Jie, *A Mathematical Accounting Model and its MathAccounting Software* First Edition. Guoping Jie Press. Ontario, 2016.

[JIE] Guoping Jie, *A Mathematical Accounting Model and its MathAccounting Software* Second Edition. Guoping Jie Press. Ontario, 2017.

[JIE] Guoping Jie, *Digital Currency Embedded In Identities of All Society Members I* First Edition. Guoping Jie Press. Ontario, 2017.

[JIE] Guoping Jie, *Digital Currency Embedded In Identities of All Society Members II* First Edition. Guoping Jie Press. Ontario, 2017.

[JIE] Guoping Jie, *Internet of Things Built Up By Digital Inventory* First Edition. Guoping Jie Press. Ontario, 2018.

[WK] Jerry J. Weygandt, Donald E.Kieso, Pau D.Kimmel, Barbara Trenholm, and Valerie A. Kinnear, *Accounting Principles Part 1* 4th Canadian ed. John Wiley & Sons Canada, Ltd. Ontario, 2007.

[WK] Jerry J. Weygandt, Donald E.Kieso, Pau D.Kimmel, Barbara Trenholm, and Valerie A. Kinnear, *Accounting Principle Part 2s* 4th Canadian ed. John Wiley & Sons Canada, Ltd. Ontario, 2007.

[WK] Jerry J. Weygandt, Donald E.Kieso, Pau D.Kimmel, Barbara Trenholm, and Valerie A. Kinnear, *Accounting Principles Part 3* 4th Canadian ed. John Wiley & Sons Canada, Ltd. Ontario, 2007.

[KW] Donald E. Kieso, Jerry J. Weygandt, Terry D. Warfield, Nicola M. Young, and Irene M. Wiecek, *Intermediate Accounting Volume 1* 8th Canadian ed. John Wiley & Sons Canada, Ltd. Ontario, 2007.

[KW] Donald E. Kieso, Jerry J. Weygandt, Terry D. Warfield, Nicola M. Young, and Irene M. Wiecek, *Intermediate Accounting Volume 2* 8th Canadian ed. John Wiley & Sons Canada, Ltd. Ontario, 2007.

www.ingramcontent.com/pod-product-compliance
Lightning Source LLC
Chambersburg PA
CBHW081458200326
41518CB00015B/2303